Martin Levy

Ban the Bomb!
Michael Randle and Direct Action against Nuclear War

With a foreword by Paul Rogers

GU00535744

Martin Levy

BAN THE BOMB!

Michael Randle and Direct Action against Nuclear War

With a foreword by Paul Rogers

Bibliografische Information der Deutschen Nationalbibliothek

Die Deutsche Nationalbibliothek verzeichnet diese Publikation in der Deutschen Nationalbibliografie; detaillierte bibliografische Daten sind im Internet über http://dnb.d-nb.de abrufbar.

Bibliographic information published by the Deutsche Nationalbibliothek

Die Deutsche Nationalbibliothek lists this publication in the Deutsche Nationalbibliografie; detailed bibliographic data are available in the Internet at http://dnb.d-nb.de.

Cover graphic: Enamel lapel badge produced by the artist and pacifist Eric Austen. Designed by Gerald Holtom for the first Aldermaston March, Easter 1958, the peace symbol appeared on banners, 'lollipops' and badges. Photograph by Gea Jones. CC BY-SA 4.0.

ISBN-13: 978-3-8382-1489-4

© *ibidem*-Verlag, Stuttgart 2021

Printed in the EU

Contents

Contents

Foreword

This book is a delight on many levels. First, Martin Levy gives us a history of a remarkable man in a thoroughly absorbing way. Through many discussions with Michael, as well as some with Anne, he takes us through a life well lived, with many illustrations that help to give us an idea of where Michael came from and what helped make him. Through a series of interviews stretching over many months, we build a picture not just of Michael but of the history of nonviolent action in Britain over seven decades. It is a thoroughly unusual approach to biography, but it works a treat.

Then there is Michael himself, peace-campaigner, activist, scholar and much more, ready to go to prison for his beliefs yet gentle and patient in his determination to do the right thing. Most of his life's work has been in Britain, but the span of his contacts is global and through the interviews we come in contact with many of the leading campaigners and thinkers on nonviolence over all of those decades. That alone gives us a unique perspective on an informal yet resolute belief system that is always there and comes to the fore in unexpected ways, whether in peace campaigning, civil rights movements, the collapse of the Soviet system, or in other contexts.

There are also interludes when the unexpected suddenly intrudes, not least the astonishing and successful attempt to spring the spy George Blake from Wormwood Scrubs Prison and to keep him hidden at various locations in London. The hair-raising story of how Blake's cover was almost blown by Michael's encounter with a friend's wife outside a tube station in London is remarkable enough, but to add to this we have the trial of Michael and Pat Pottle, a co-conspirator, at the Old Bailey many years later. Their acquittal was unexpected and so the powers-that-be inevitably termed it the action of a 'perverse jury', but it would still make a marvellous film.

There is also Michael the scholar, not just his core role in the Alternative Defence Commission's pioneering work on non-nuclear defence back in the 1980s, but his own work on nonviolence and civilian resistance and his wider contributions to the Bradford School of Peace Studies.

I have been fortunate to have known Michael for forty years and have been lucky to work with him on several occasions. In his own quiet way, and with no fuss, he persists in his optimism against the odds and serves as a remarkable inspiration to many. This book is a fitting tribute to a remarkable person.

Paul Rogers, June 2020.

Introduction

> The Judge asked if there was any justification for breaking the law?
> 'An individual has to make a decision where millions of lives are concerned.'
> 'Does that mean you and other members of the Committee of 100?'
> 'Every individual must decide ... . Every individual has to decide between
> the law and his own morality.'
>
> Mr Justice Havers 'in dialogue' with Michael Randle.[1]

Anyone who has ever read a book about civil rights or taken part in an illegal demonstration will recognise the above distinction between law and personal morality, state power and the promptings of the individual conscience. It was some such distinction that inspired the Biblical Daniel to defy a decree of the Babylonian King Darius, and which led to the execution of Socrates for impiety and demoralising the young people of Athens in 399 BCE.

The issue that confronted the jury in Court No.1 of the Old Bailey during February 1962 was the morality of bombing civilians with nuclear weapons. The state in the person of its chief witness, Air Commodore Graham Magill, said that should circumstances so demand it, it was moral. Michael Randle and his co-defendants, to their credit, took the contrary view.

The proximate cause that brought Michael to the Old Bailey trial was a blockade and mass trespass of the NATO air base at RAF Wethersfield, in Essex, a little over three months earlier. On trial were Michael and his five co-defendants: Terry Chandler, Ian Dixon, Pat Pottle, Trevor Hatton and Helen Allegranza, all senior officers in the Committee of 100, an organisation set up to campaign by non-violent means for nuclear disarmament.

They were charged on two counts under section one of the Official Secrets Act of 1911: first, conspiring together to commit a breach of the Act by entering the air base for a 'purpose prejudicial

---

1   "On Trial: A Twelve Page Report with Comments, Disallowed Evidence and Profiles. ... A Peace News Special Supplement," *Peace News* [February 1962]: 8.

to the safety or interests of the State' and second, conspiring to 'incite others to do likewise.' [2]

As for the distant causes which led to the prosecution, I'll say a bit more about those later on.

Here it is enough to state that Michael and his co-defendants were anything but political or legal innocents. They knew their rights. No wonder they got up the nose of the haughty and contemptuous chief prosecuting council, the Attorney-General, Sir Reginald Manningham-Buller.

'Now Randle', Sir Reginald began on one occasion at about halfway through the trial. 'I am *Mr* Randle,' Michael shot back. [3] He simply could not be intimidated.

I first met Michael during the late summer of 2017. Though 'met' probably isn't the right word as I didn't meet him, I met his archive.

Back then I had a part-time job assisting the special collections librarian at Bradford University, where one of my responsibilities was to retrieve the documents that researchers had ordered from the storerooms.

One day someone asked to see Michael's archive and, following my usual custom, I looked into it myself and was intrigued. It was packed with remarkable documents on anti-nuclear protest and letters from such notables as Bertrand Russell, Albert Schweitzer and Noam Chomsky.

A few weeks after that, I was sitting in the staffroom and I had an idea: 'Why don't I interview Michael?' I knew by then that he had been interviewed before, but maybe I could get the whole story, not just the bits that people already knew or thought they knew about.

The next day I sent him an email. Was he up for it? He was.

---

2   Thomas Grant, *Jeremy Hutchinson's Case Histories* (London: John Murray, 2015), 246.

3   "On Trial," 8. My italics.

Michael lives a few miles outside of Bradford, in Shipley, in a turning off the Bingley Road as you proceed towards Cottingley; and I remember thinking as I got off the bus, this is a neighbourhood where I would like to live.

It is suburban with a bit of bling. There are cafes and lots of charity shops and the great, hulking mass of the Victorian Salts Mill not more than a few minutes' walk away.

Michael's a smallish man in his mid-eighties, his head is full of white hair and yet he's surprisingly good on his feet. I liked him as soon as I set eyes on him.

Usually, you can tell a lot about someone from their living room. Michael's is comfortable and unpretentious. There are paintings and family photographs on the walls, two large sofas, a rectangular wooden coffee table, an ancient television in one of the far corners and a well-stocked bookcase near the door, containing volumes by Yeats, Chesterton, Keats and some of the better-known 'sixties poets.

After I'd set the voice recorder up and we'd chatted for about forty minutes, he asked me if I wanted coffee. It was then that Anne appeared. Anne is Michael's wife. She's younger than Michael by ten years or so.

She's also, I soon discovered, the practical one. Michael sees things as they should be, Anne sees them mostly as they are. They could be antagonists, but instead they complement each other.

I could have improvised the interviews, flown by the seat of my pants. But there's more to a proper interview than turning up at the right time and asking a few questions. You need to prepare yourself with a bit of reading, prove to the interviewee that, though you may not be an expert, you do at least know what you're talking about.

Fortunately, from the point of view of preparation, I could not have been better placed. Not only did I have Michael's archive back in Special Collections, but I had a number of other relevant archives too, not to mention the university library itself, which is stocked with all sorts of important-looking books on anti-nuclear protest and social movements more generally.

People who work in special collections departments often talk about the archives 'speaking' to each other, which sounds poetic if not downright fey—the proximity to all that paper must rot the brain. But, in an important sense, it's true. They do speak to each other, even though the order in which they are arranged on the shelves sometimes suggests otherwise.

Michael's archive speaks most to the Hugh Brock Papers and to the archives of the Direct Action Committee Against Nuclear War, the Committee of 100 (collected by Derry Hannam) and *Peace News*.

These five archives therefore provided much of the information behind the questions I asked him.

And then it also speaks to books, pamphlets, magazines and newspapers, including the newspaper that gave rise to the *Peace News* archive in the first place—which, luckily, the university has a full set of. Indeed, it is one of the jewels of the University library's Commonweal Collection.

As for *Peace News*, how many people on the left read it nowadays? Hundreds? Thousands? I know that Michael does. I know that because he is still an occasional contributor.

When Michael joined *Peace News* as a sales organiser in the late 1950s, it was about to enter its golden age. Under the editorship of Hugh Brock, a generation of new and younger activist-writers and writer-activists made their mark: Chris Farley, Alan Lovell, Albert Hunt, Pat Arrowsmith, April Carter, John Arden, Michael himself and many others.

Most of them were anarchists. They brought with them powerful ideas, some of which originated in the New Left, writing about film, theatre, art, music and literature with sharper eyes and ears.

But, most importantly, they brought new thinking on non-violent direct action, specifically in relation to nuclear weapons, turning the paper into what can fairly be described as the most interesting and exciting radical newspaper of the 1960s.

Indeed, it was *Peace News* that drew Michael to non-violent direct action in the first place.

In 1952, just a few weeks after he'd registered as a conscientious objector, he read an account of a sit-down outside the War Office (now the Ministry of Defence) by a tiny group called Operation Gandhi.

The article appeared on the front page on 18 January under the headline 'Pacifists told Police and War Office: "We are coming to Squat"'.

I know they are the exact words, because I'm sitting in the library and holding the paper now.

The article fills about a third of the space and is illustrated with a photograph of two policemen, plus two other men and two women: Geoffrey Plummer, Harry Mister, Dorothy Wheeler and Kathleen Rawlins. Both of the women are smiling.

It describes what inspired the sit-down: opposition to NATO and the facts that Britain was rearming and being 'converted into one of the chief atomic bomb bases of the world'; and explains what happened to the demonstrators when they refused the police request to depart: their arrest and removal to Bow Street Police Court, where they were charged with obstruction.

If it is true that a single newspaper article can change a life, then reading this article changed Michael's. Not that he would put it that way — Michael isn't melodramatic. But, quite simply, it launched him on a lifetime of non-violent anti-nuclear activism.

But why Operation Gandhi? In other words, why the name? What did Gandhi have to do with nuclear weapons, anyway? The answer to the third question is not a lot. But he had a method of non-violent resistance that the little group adopted, as did Michael in his turn.

The method was called Satyagraha or Truth Force — 'satya' in Gujarati meaning 'truth' and 'agraha' meaning 'force' or 'firmness'; and it was a complete method of non-violent resistance, emphasising courage, discipline, self-sacrifice, love and, as the headline makes clear, openness and fair-dealing with opponents.

That makes it sound vague, quasi-religious, and not particularly exciting. In some senses it was vague. Unexciting it was not. In any case, it was the method that inspired them, first to the War Office sit-down, then shortly afterwards to other demonstrations, first at a little known atomic research establishment at Aldermaston, in the Berkshire countryside, then a few months later at a NATO missile base, near Chippenham in Suffolk.

Operation Gandhi then was the organisation that put non-violent anti-nuclear protest on the map, and which drew Michael into non-violent anti-nuclear activism into the first place. But it was the Direct Action Committee (DAC) which followed it, that turned Michael into a national figure.

Operation Gandhi was small-scale. The number of activists never amounted to more than thirty. It hardly bothered anyone, whereas the Direct Action Committee Against Nuclear War (to use its full name) was larger, better organised, more focused, and determined from the outset to be a major thorn in the government's nuclear weapons programme.

Michael was its second chairman, taking over from Hugh Brock during the summer of 1958.

Its purpose? It's there in the title: *direct action* against nuclear war.

In practical terms this meant that it had less patience than Operation Gandhi with moral exhortation. Not that it didn't try it. It did. On numerous occasions. But nuclear weapons were a national emergency. It wanted the unilateral nuclear disarmament of Britain and it wanted it now. Thus, it was much more willing to raise the ante as far as civil disobedience was concerned, while nonetheless remaining firmly within the tradition of satyagraha.

But first, it organised the first Aldermaston march. Or rather Hugh Brock and Pat Arrowsmith organised it, with help from Michael and Labourites Frank Allaun, MP, and Walter Wolfgang.

You'll read more about Pat Arrowsmith in the interviews that follow this introduction. Next to Hugh Brock and April Carter, she was probably Michael's closest DAC colleague.

As for the march, it took place over Easter 1958 and was a huge success. Nothing was able to stop it. Neither the anti-direct action leadership of the Campaign for Nuclear Disarmament (CND). Nor the Communist Party of Great Britain, which tried to co-opt it. Nor the once-famous McWhirter twins with their Mercedes car and megaphone, who called the marchers communist dupes. Not even the weather, which was atrocious.

Thousands of people walked at least part of the route: London via Hounslow and Reading to Aldermaston.

Thereafter, delegates from the marchers carried a resolution to the British, American and Russian governments calling upon them to desist from testing, manufacturing or storing nuclear weapons. All, however, remained unmoved — though the Russian embassy, scenting a propaganda coup, did at least agree to meet and parley with the delegates, amongst whom was Michael.

Indeed, it was this frustration with the government's inaction which partly explains the DAC's next major success in terms of media impact: a series of attempts to obstruct the building of one of NATO's new nuclear missile bases at RAF North Pickenham, near Swaffham, Norfolk, during December 1958 — just as it partly explains the formation of the anti-nuclear organisation that Michael was next involved in: the much bigger, more combative, more politically diffuse and thus inevitably much less Gandhian Committee of 100.

Again, something had to be done. If one method of countering the Nuclear Behemoth didn't work, then the demonstrators would try another one.

But let Michael describe the Committee of 100, of which he was secretary. Here I only want to say that it tested his and the other leaders' resolution to the utmost and that it did indeed, as the beginning of this introduction suggests, lead to increasingly draconian government action.

For his part in organising the blockade and mass trespass of RAF Wethersfield, Michael received a prison sentence of eighteen months, of which he served twelve. At the time, this was the longest sentence imposed by a British court for opposition to nuclear weapons.

That, in a very small nutshell, is the story of the direct action phase of Michael's anti-nuclear activism. But, of course, he wasn't—isn't—just against nuclear weapons. Hating nuclear weapons is the easy bit. He also had a positive vision of what a nuclear disarmed Britain and indeed a nuclear disarmed world might look like.

It's important for me to say something about this as well. For Michael has been an activist on many fronts, not least in association with War Resisters' International, of which he has been a council and an executive member.

Underpinning his position on nuclear weapons was a particular view of politics: deeply respectful of human rights, democratic, but not party-political. But, on the contrary, profoundly convinced of the power of civil disobedience to keep our democracies 'honest' and to hold the dictatorships to account for their many offences.

Here too, Gandhi was—and again is—a central influence. Another was the Dutch anarcho-syndicalist Bart de Ligt, whose book *The Conquest of Violence*, he first read in the edition with an introduction by Aldous Huxley.

As for the other notable organisations and important events that Michael has been involved in: the so-called 'springing' of his former prison mate, the Russian spy George Blake, from Wormwood Scrubs; a further long stretch in prison for 'invading' the Greek Embassy in London; a campaign to support Czechoslovakian independence in the face of a real, Russian, invasion; another major trial at the Old Bailey, this time for helping Blake escape—those too, I'll leave him to describe himself. Needless to say, as even this short list suggests, his life post the 1962 highpoint of his anti-nuclear activism has been anything but short of incident or complications.

Instead I want to say something about the other Michael, the man who Paul Rogers in his foreword to this book calls 'Michael the scholar'. For this is the Michael that I met.

It is the Michael of our interviews, the amusing and unfailingly gracious host, the former rugby player (for Brighton Town, if you're interested), the man who loves literature and music, who laughs a lot and who isn't afraid of showing his emotions.

I've already mentioned how I prepared the questions. This is how the interviews worked.

Following that first morning in 2017, I'd usually arrive for our interviews at about 10 o'clock. We'd then spend two hours or so, working through a portion of my questions.

Sometimes I'd focus my questions on a particular person or organisation, say Ralph Schoenman or Operation Gandhi, but more usually I'd concentrate on a period, perhaps of two to three years, and we'd work through that, week by week or month by month, depending on how busy Michael's schedule had been—and sometimes he had been very busy.

That said, if Michael wanted to take the conversation in a different direction or something interesting cropped up that I hadn't thought about, all to the good. We'd talk about that and then return to the prepared questions afterwards.

Sometimes Anne would join us, sometimes not. Anne's memories are often different to Michael's. Michael is best at public events: the demonstrations, the marches, the big speeches. Anne at the domestic angle. Then she's also good at filling in details. So, if, as occasionally happened, Michael forgot a name, she could usually be relied upon to supply it.

After copying up an interview, I would take it to the library, surround myself with pamphlets, newspapers and books, and go through the factual statements one by one. It wasn't often that I found anything that could be construed as an error. I would then forward the same interview to Michael, in case he wanted to make any changes of detail or emphasis.

In all, I must have done about twenty-five interviews. However, in the interests of readability, I've reorganised them and reduced them to eleven. These are the essential Michael.

Finally, a further word about politics.

Naturally, I didn't agree with everything Michael said during our interviews. He's on the libertarian left. So am I, but I'm grouchy with it. He's a consummate team player. I don't travel well in groups. Michael is also more understanding of identity politics than I am. He sees the benefits. I see intolerance and division.

But on the fundamental issues of non-violent direct action and the intolerable nature of nuclear weapons, I believe that he has absolutely made the right call.

If this book is your first acquaintance with Michael Randle, you can count yourself lucky and unlucky. Lucky because you have much to look forward to. Unlucky because you didn't discover him earlier.

1. Family and Schooling

Let's begin at the beginning. When and where were you born?

I was born on the 21st December 1933 at a nursing home near Worcester Park in Surrey.

Had your parents been in the area long?

I think for a couple of years. My mother came over from Dublin in the mid-twenties and married my dad in 1931.

Did you have any brothers or sisters?

There was only one brother before I was born. But the family kept growing and by 1949, when my youngest sister, Joan, arrived, there were nine of us children in all, three boys and six girls.

What did your father do for a living at the time of your birth?

He ran a children's clothing factory, Hitchen, Smith & Co., Ltd., in Old Street, London. The firm was originally based in Nottingham specialising in lace wear. Nottingham was where his father's family hailed from, though he himself was born and brought up in Folkestone and London. His father took over the firm sometime in the 1920s after it ran into financial difficulties and moved it to London.

Did your father employ many people?

It wasn't a big factory, but there must have been thirty or forty people. I occasionally did some work there when I was on holiday from school.

So, the company stayed in business for some time …

Oh, yes. Later on, in the 1950s, my brother Arthur took it over after graduating in accountancy from the London Polytechnic and doing National Service in the army.

Tell me about your mother.

My mother, Ellen, came from what was pretty much a working-class family, with roots in County Carlow and Kildare. Her father, Patrick Treacy, was from Bagenalstown in County Carlow and set up as a builder in Dublin employing a few people; her mother, Esther Treacy, née Dowd, was from Prosperous in County Kildare. My mother worked in a local shop before coming over to England and entering service.

How did your parents meet?

They met at a New Year's Eve party. I think at a Conservative Club. But neither of them was active in the party and I don't think that my mother was ever a member. I'm not sure about my father.

I know that you were brought up as a Catholic. Were both your parents Catholics?

My father was brought up in the Church of England and it was only after meeting my mother that he decided to change. But it was very much a gradual thing. My mother told me that he asked her so many questions while they were courting about the Catholic faith that she finally asked him, 'Well, are you thinking of becoming a Catholic, Arthur?' And he replied, 'No, no. I'm just interested in finding out a bit more.' This was at a period when there was a revival of interest in that whole Cardinal Newman wing of Catholicism. But then he did convert to Catholicism.

Fig 1:   Michael's parents at their wedding in April 1931. Photographer
unknown. Private Collection.

So, I would imagine you attended mass as a youngster.

You bet. Mass and Benediction [laughs]. It was coming from both sides at that point!

Bearing in mind your father's business interests, you obviously had quite a posh upbringing. Did that include servants?

We always had at least one maid, who was nearly always Irish and usually someone my mother got through contacts in Ireland. I remember one young woman called Moira, whom we all liked and got along well with. Then I also remember an Englishwoman called Rose, who came and helped as well.

Would you say that your parents were happily married?

On the whole, yes. The only cause of serious tension between them stemmed from the fact that during the late 'forties dad changed back to the C of E. Why was that? He had become critical of the whole Catholic ethos and the clericalism. Then there was another reason: he got the idea that there was something going on between my mother and an Irish priest, who used to visit. But *that* I'm sure was nonsense.

Were you a sociable child?

Well, I had my school friends and other children. The first school I went to was St. Cecilia's in North Cheam and one of my best friends there was a boy named Jimmy Seymour, whose parents ran a greengrocer's shop not far from where we lived in Cheam village. But then the war came and my family moved around a bit. In fact, initially, all of us except probably my dad moved to Merthyr Tydfil, in Wales, to a house which belonged to a Cheam couple. Then, when the Blitz started, my brother, Arthur, my sister, Margaret, and I were sent to Ireland, to a Catholic boarding school, St Dominic's College, in Cabra, West Dublin.

Did you miss your parents?

Of course, but probably no more than any other child in that situation. In any case, during the school holidays I stayed with my mother's parents and my aunt, Nan, who had a house in Inchicore on the west side of Dublin, and who all made sure that I was very well looked after. And I wasn't on my own. Although Margaret stayed with cousins during the holidays, I always had my older brother, Arthur, for company. Then, during the latter part of the war, another sister, Terry, arrived, who, incidentally, was very intelligent and quick witted. Then, there was a cousin on my mother's side, a Catholic priest, Uncle Tom, who used to come and play rebel songs on the piano like 'Kevin Barry' and 'Kelly, the Boy from Killane'. So, yes, I did miss them. But not quite as badly as I could have done.

Fig 2:   Michael's maternal grandmother, Esther Treacy, and his Aunt Nan, with child. Early 1940s. Photographer unknown. Private Collection.

Did you return to England during the war?

No, but my parents used to come over at least once a year, bringing with them a growing number of younger siblings to meet me.

Let's rewind a bit back to St. Cecilia's, to 1939. People knew that war was coming. Do you remember gas drill, for instance?

I do remember having a gas mask and learning how to put it on and the smell of rubber that came from it. I don't remember organised drill, but at school when there was an air raid warning, we'd put them on and go down to the main shelter in the playground and have our lessons there. I have a vivid memory of the smell of concrete. We used to have little hand-held blackboards to write things on.

Slates?

That's right. The first time I ever got smacked at school was when I annoyed the teacher by slapping the thing on my knee [laughs]. But at that point the war for me was just an adventure. I had no understanding of the danger. We used to pray for peace, but I remember thinking, I don't want this thing to end too soon; it's too exciting. Not that I wanted to be a soldier. But the air raid warnings and the shelters were thrilling. At home I slept under the stairs, which was supposed to be the safest place. Then at some point we also had an air raid shelter in the garden.

What was your parents' attitude to the war?

Well, my father was against it, not on political grounds as far as I know, but on moral grounds. Early on he registered as a conscientious objector, but his application was rejected. However, because he was in a vital industry, the clothing industry, he was exempted from military service, anyway.

Can you tell me something about the experience of being at St. Dominic's?

For starters, it was run by Dominican nuns. Three of us went there: Arthur, Margaret and me, while Terry went to a local day-school in Inchicore. I remember our excitement at the prospect of being at a school where you slept in. We thought that was terrific.

But when we got there it was very strict and oddly puritanical.

Fig 3:   Michael (on the right) with his older brother, Arthur, on Killiney Hill,
County Wicklow. Early 1940s. Photograph by Arthur Randle senior.
Private Collection.

How so?

Well, I remember one kid who was very young, probably just three or four. One day he got up in the dormitory. His pyjama bottoms fell down, and he was beaten with the thick leather strap that was used for administering punishment. Then I remember other examples of the nuns' severity. In the school grounds there was an institute for the deaf and dumb, some of whose inmates worked as servants at the school. One day, one of them came in to clean out the fireplace in the classroom, and the nun in charge got upset because the boys smiled and nodded to her. Heaven knows what she thought that they'd done, but she reported the matter to Sister Mary Imelda Joseph, and, my God, there were absolute ructions over it. She beat the boys' hands with a leather strap. In fact, the only boy amongst us who did not get beaten was my brother, Arthur. He stuck to his guns and said, 'I don't see what we've done wrong.' I suppose that Sister Mary Imelda Joseph must have respected that.

Incidentally, we learned quite a few signs from the servants, one of which was, 'I'm going to sneak on you.' We thought of them as fellow sufferers!

Did the war impinge much on your life at the college?

Not really, but I do remember very clearly the occasion when the Germans bombed the North Strand district of Dublin, whether by accident or as a warning I don't know. I was asleep in bed at the time and had a nightmare that bombs were falling from the sky and exploding behind me as I tried to run away. Then I woke up and realised that they were real explosions. One of the nuns dashed in and we recited the prayer we always said last thing at night, 'Jesus, Mary and Joseph. I give you my heart and my soul. Jesus, Mary and Joseph assist me now and in my last agony. Jesus, Mary and Joseph may I breathe out my soul in peace with you. Amen.'

Something to cheer you up then.

Yes, I suppose so [laughs]. Afterwards, we were all bundled into a sort of basement in the girls' part of the college, where the resident priest led us in reciting The Rosary.

Did you experience any bullying from other children at the convent, coming as you did from a mixed Anglo-Irish background?

Well, there was certainly quite a bit of hostility towards Britain, but, no, I wouldn't say that I was bullied. Possibly I was helped in that respect by the fact that my mother was Irish and that the priest who came to examine the pupils' knowledge of catechism and Catholic teaching was none other than my mother's cousin, Uncle Tom, from Ballsbridge! However, things in one period did get tense. That was when Churchill demanded the use of the Irish ports, in accordance with a clause in the 1922 Anglo-Irish Agreement guaranteeing the British access to them in an emergency. Such an action would have compromised Irish neutrality and possibly brought the country into the war, so De Valera refused. So, there was a bit of a scare as to whether Churchill's demand was going to lead to hostilities with Britain. I remember a boy called George Harris and some of his mates sitting in a huddle and saying that if it did come to war that they would kill me and all the other English boys.

You must have felt quite threatened.

Not really. Actually, I think it just made me feel more English!

Any republicans on your mother's side?

Yes, indeed. A first cousin of my grandfather, Seán (or 'Johnny') Tracey, from Ballsbridge, took part in the 1916 uprising and was among those interned for a period in an army camp in North Wales after the uprising was suppressed. One family story was that when the insurgents were defending the General Post Office against the British attempt to recapture it, Johnny swapped positions with another man because one of them, I can't remember which, was left-handed. The man he swapped places with was killed in the fighting. However, I didn't discover all that until some years after returning to England. It would have stood me in good stead had I known about it while at school in Cabra.

My mother also recounted to me the story of how her father had hidden some sensitive republican documents at the back of a framed picture in the front room. Soon afterwards the house was raided by the British army, which had been tipped off by one of the neighbours that known rebels had been seen visiting it. My mother told of how she struggled not to look at the picture while the raid was going on. I made a video recording of my mother in 1998 talking about her life, and she gives a vivid account of her experience as a child of 10 of the 1916 uprising, and of afterwards hearing the shots from Kilmainham Gaol as the leaders of the uprising were executed. The man, who'd brought the documents, by the way, was Peadar Doyle. He later became the Lord Mayor of Dublin.

Then there was another republican connection with the family in that my mother's sister, Peg, was engaged to, and eventually married, a Peter Sorahan, who took part in the guerrilla war during the 1918-1921 period and, afterwards, fought on the Republican side in the tragic civil war that followed it. 'Uncle Peter' was eventually taken prisoner during the civil war and served time in Kilmainham Gaol. He and Peg went to live in New York, after his release, though they returned in the 1960s to live with Nan in her home in Inchicore.

I learnt more about all this bit by bit, but certainly knew the essential facts by the time I was myself sentenced to 18 months in prison in 1962. By then the family had moved to a farm in Fletching, a small village near Uckfield, East Sussex. I don't know what it's like now, but then it was a very conservative village. One of the adjoining farms was owned by a retired colonel, and you'd see men and women in redcoats riding to hounds. In other words, it was all very English and traditional. Anyway, the colonel's wife spoke to my mother on one occasion and said, 'Don't you feel ashamed that your son is in prison?' 'No!', my mother replied. 'Where I grew up, we were proud of people who went to prison for their convictions.'

Following the war, Michael, did you return to England immediately?

No, not immediately. My father's great ambition at this time was to have a farm — he was already a keen allotment holder —, and we spent some time looking at farms in Ireland. There was talk then of the whole family moving there. But that didn't work out. We returned to England in August 1945, just a couple of days before VJ Day. I remember we went up to London and watched the King and Queen come out onto the balcony of Buckingham Palace and wave.

Did you move back to your old house?

No, my father had bought a much larger house by then and we lived in that. Again, in Cheam, but halfway up the hill on a road called Burdon Lane, leading to Banstead Heath.

Was your mother happy remaining in England?

I think so. She had two brothers, Bill and Michael and an adopted brother, John. Michael at some time in the 1930s had gone to live in Australia and lost touch with the family. But Bill and John moved to England. We all loved Uncle Bill because he was great fun to be with and had a quick and mischievous sense of humour. He was, in the words of the popular song, one of 'McAlpine's fusiliers', which is to say, a labourer working for the firm, MacAlpine & Sons, which built many of Britain's roads and airfields in the 1940s and 1950s. Bill was also a keen Labour supporter and had a big influence on my political thinking as a youngster.

Fig 4:   'Uncle Bill' with Michael's maternal grandmother, Esther. Photographer unknown. Private Collection.

After St. Dominic's you attended Douai School in Woolhampton, Berkshire, which says to me a couple of things: firstly, that the family had

had a 'good war', at least in financial terms; and secondly, that your
parents had high personal and social ambitions for you. Can you tell me a
little bit about that experience?

After St. Dominic's, Douai was very relaxed. The first thing
that struck me, oddly enough, was to do with bath-time. The
individual bathtubs were partitioned off from one another by
wooden cubicles, where perhaps half a dozen boys or so took baths
at the same time. The priest in charge on this occasion, Father
Alphonsus Tierney — or Alf as we called him amongst ourselves — ,
said, 'If you're not out in five minutes, you'll get the stick.' And one
boy said, 'Where?' And the priest said, 'On your bottoms.' And I
thought, Oh my God [laughs]. You can use a word like that. It was
a much freer atmosphere.

The person who had the biggest influence on me at Douai was
a lay teacher, Oliver Welch, a very good historian and teacher. He
and the headmaster, Father Ignatius Rice, were part of a Catholic
intellectual circle, which included G.K. Chesterton and Ronald
Knox. He injected a lot of common sense into our understanding of
religion and politics. On one occasion we were studying the
medieval popes' habit of excommunicating their political and
religious rivals, when one boy put a question which, I think, was
troubling many in the class. What effect, he asked, did the
excommunication have on the individual concerned? Welch looked
puzzled for a moment, then, realising what the boy was driving at,
replied 'You mean on the future of his immortal soul? Oh, none
whatsoever!'

Another history teacher whom I liked a lot was a very genial
monk called Father Dunstan. He was very partial to betting on the
horses!

I once asked another priest, the man in charge of the junior
school, Father Norbert Bill, if people who had been Catholic but lost
their faith would be destined to go to hell. It was an important
question for me as it wasn't long since my father had ceased to be a
Catholic. 'We always have to trust in the mercy of Almighty God,'
he replied. 'But it is a grim outlook!'

By the way, one of Welch's books was about Mirabeau and the French Revolution. But the history lessons I remember best were about the English Revolution. That said, by the time that I was about fourteen or fifteen, I was most absorbed in Irish history. I even had an argument in class with Father Ignatius Rice on the subject. He put forward an English point of view about the Ulster settlement. I think his line was that the north of Ireland was underpopulated, so it was reasonable for Scots and English people to settle there. I put forward an Irish republican position. But then, later that day, when I was walking in one of the cloisters, he tapped me on the shoulder and said, 'Some day you should talk to Mr Welch about Ireland. He's just been destroying all my theories.' This conversation took place at about the same time as I was in the habit of teasing some of the boys with the Irish nationalist ballads, some of which I'd learned from Uncle Tom. You could probably say that I had become a bit of a rebel! I remember upsetting one boy by reciting the opening lines of one very anti-British ballad, which I'd come across in an Irish songbook. It began:

> God's curse be on you, England,
> God strike your London Town,
> And cursed be every Irishman
> Alive or yet to live,
> Who'll e'er forget the death they died
> Who'll ever dare forgive.

Were there any other subjects that you enjoyed besides history?

English. I've always read a lot. But at that stage it became a bit of a passion. One Christmas, while we were still living in Ireland, I was given a copy of Sir Walter Scott's *Ivanhoe* as a present and I absolutely loved it. Then I read Scott's other books, none of which, by the way, lived up to that first one. Another writer who was very popular with the boys at Douai was G.A. Henty, despite his being an old-school imperialist. I remember, in particular, his novel *St*

George for England about the war in France during the reign of Edward III. It celebrated the English victories at Crécy and Poitiers.

What about activities outside of school? Were you taken to the pictures, for instance?

Oh, better than that. Once a week during the winter and spring terms we had our own film shows. These were another one of Father Dunstan's responsibilities. He used to operate the projector. It was great when it worked, not so great when it broke down which was fairly regularly Then, occasionally, some American airmen from the nearby Aldermaston air base would drop by with some of their films, which, bearing in mind my later activities, seems a bit ironic. At Cabra we'd also had film shows, but much less frequently. I remember my sister, Margaret, telling me about one film which included a scene in which a woman was undressing. The nun in charge put a card in front of the lens so the pupils wouldn't see it.

Before we leave your schooling, what exams did you take? I think children took the School Certificate in those days.

That's right. At Douai, I took the School Certificate when I was sixteen and just scraped through. I got a distinction in English and did well too in history. Then I also passed the French exam.

Actually, I was keen to stay on at school for another year or two, partly because I wanted to play regularly in the rugby first team. But my father did not think that was sufficient reason to spend more on school fees!

So, what then? You found a job?

My dad apprenticed me, as it were, to a City firm called Sharp, Perrin and Company, which carried on a wholesale business in clothing and which dealt with dad's factory. It was situated bang opposite the Old Bailey. I worked there in a couple of departments, the idea being that they'd train me to take over my father's business. But I hated it there; I got increasingly fed up and only lasted about a year. However, to avoid a confrontation I didn't tell my dad. I just gave in my notice and left. Then I took on another job as an orderly in a children's hospital in the Banstead Heath area.

Every morning I would go through this pantomime of leaving the house for the London train at the usual time, but walk instead to the hospital. But then, eventually, he found out. Talk about the shit hitting the fan. My God!

Then, when that one finished, I applied for a job at *Tribune* and then for another one with a local newspaper. But I was very naive. In the latter case, I didn't even sign the letter. I remember receiving this very snotty reply, something along the lines of thank you for your unsigned letter, but we're sorry to tell you that there's no vacancy here [laughs].

But, anyway, I suppose that what I really wanted to be was a writer. I used to go home in the evenings and write a bit. I even published an article in a magazine for young people. But then other things took over.

2. The Birth of a Satyagrahi

Michael, you mentioned in our last conversation that like many young people you wanted to be a writer. Any favourite authors after Sir Walter Scott and Henty?

Aldous Huxley. I read several of his books and really liked them.

Why?

Well, for starters I liked Huxley's style. Then, he put forward a quite radical view of politics and life which I found sympathetic.

Did any particular books appeal to you? One title that I have in mind is Ape and Essence, *his post-nuclear apocalypse novel of 1948.*

I don't remember reading that. I did, however, read *Brave New World*, but some time later. No, the Huxley book that I read then and which stuck with me wasn't a novel at all, but an anthology of readings from the mystics. It was called *The Perennial Philosophy*. I was profoundly influenced by it.

On the subject of religion, were you still a Catholic at this point? I take it that you'd been confirmed.

I've mentioned already my father's return to Anglicanism. Well, as time went by I too became very critical, not just of the clericalism, but also of the hierarchical side of Catholicism. In part I came to these opinions myself, but then I was also hugely influenced by a very good friend of my father's, a Dr Errington Kerr, who came from somewhere in the West Indies and practiced as a GP in North Cheam. Dr Kerr had also had a Catholic upbringing, but he had become a convinced atheist. I remember him saying that though he was still attracted to the ritual and to the music, he didn't believe in God. And I think that that was more or less where I ended up. Even today, I'm moved by plainchant and other choral religious music. So, I suppose, at that level only, once a Catholic always a Catholic!

Anyway, yes, I was confirmed, and at that time and for some time after leaving school I remained a Catholic.

What made you decide to be a conscientious objector?

There were a number of things. But certainly talking to Dr Kerr was one of them. Kerr was a conscientious objector himself. He was also a vegetarian.

What about your father's influence? Wasn't that also important?

Yes indeed. In fact, it was my father who encouraged me to talk to Dr Kerr in the first place. And then my mother too played a role. I particularly remember having a conversation with her about the use of flamethrowers that set your enemy on fire. She said, 'You can't possibly agree to that.' But it was Dr Kerr who was the main influence.

Did your parents join the Peace Pledge Union (PPU) or any of the other pacifist organisations?

No, I don't think either of them ever did that. Neither of them were really joiners. But on the matter of conscientious objection my father certainly had strong views as he had registered as a conscientious objector himself. I would say that my mother was anti-war on moral and humanitarian grounds.

I used to think that your pacifism stemmed from your feelings about the bomb.

Well, yes, that was a central consideration. In fact, in the first draft of my statement applying for recognition as a conscientious objector I did not take a totally pacifist position but argued that nuclear weapons were indiscriminate and contravened just war principles. But, really, I think it was discussing the matter with Dr

Kerr that was the tipping point on the issue. When the A-bombs were dropped on Hiroshima and Nagasaki I was in Ireland and I was hardly aware of what had occurred. On my return to England I did speak about it to one of my aunts, my father's sister, Margery, who told me how it had destroyed a whole city. But only later on did I think, 'Oh, my God'. And then, of course, I had another reason to think a lot more deeply about pacifism and conscientious objection. The Cold War had begun and there was a lot of talk of war with Russia.

Let's go back a bit now. Surely there must have been some discussion of conscription at school?

No, I can't say there was. We knew, of course, that at a certain age you were expected to go into the army or into one of the other services for eighteen months or two years or whatever it was. But, really, I was very naive. In fact, one of the other boys told me he didn't think it was possible to be a conscientious objector in peacetime.

You discussed political and moral issues more generally though?

Of course, we were Catholics after all. Morals were a very important part of the curriculum. I remember when the 1950 elections came up—this is about politics now—, I took part in a school debate with a boy called Pat Chambers, who went on to work for *The Daily Telegraph*. He spoke from the top table and I spoke from the floor, but both of us for the Labour Party. As was the custom, there was a vote both before and after the debate and the only boy to vote with us at the beginning changed his vote at the end! Then I remember one master saying to me, 'You, Michael, could argue the hind legs off a donkey', because I was always getting into these long discussions. Another teacher, a priest, Father Dean, 'Dixie Dean', used to call me Karl Marx, so you could say that I had quite a reputation.

Do you have any regrets now that you didn't join up? After all, it wasn't all bull and the real possibility of fighting in Korea or somewhere in the empire. I've spoken to others of your generation who have described their National Service as amongst the best years of their lives, not least for exposing them to people from different backgrounds.

Not in the least. Arthur did his National Service though. He was deferred whilst studying at the London Polytechnic, and then joined the army. I remember receiving a very friendly letter from him in which he said that he was finding the life that I'd rejected very interesting and how amused he was at all the nonsense of shouting sergeant majors and so on and at how the tears would well up in the young lads' eyes. But, of course, he'd been to public school, so he'd been well prepared! If I remember rightly, he reached the rank of sergeant himself.

You did join the PPU didn't you? Was that before or after you registered as an objector?

I don't know for certain, but I think that it was probably a little earlier. I registered, I think, sometime late in 1951. Yes, I think it would have been before that.

What about the Central Board for Conscientious Objectors, Fenner Brockway's outfit? Did you receive any advice from that?

Yes, I did. I wrote to them and I received some indications of the sorts of questions that objectors were asked. In fact, maybe it was through them that I learned about the Peace Pledge Union in the first place.

You've said elsewhere that much of your application to the tribunal was 'pure Huxley', not meaning the novels, of course, but his various writings on pacifism.

Yes. I was very much influenced by one of Huxley's essays, in particular. Actually, it was more of a pamphlet than an essay. *What are you going to do about it? The Case for Constructive Peace.* In fact, I still have a copy of it somewhere. And then there was another book that I think I read about that time, Richard Gregg's *The Power of Non-Violence.* That book, by the way, was very influential not just on my generation but also on the generation before mine. Then I read it again, a bit later as well, at about the same time as I got involved in direct action.

I should say that I did a sneaky compare-and-contrast sort of thing between the Huxley text and your application for C.O. status before talking to you today, and it really is, as you've described it, 'pure Huxley'. You've taken entire sentences and hardly bothered to re-write them. Which makes me think that the tribunal was … . How can I put this? A bit remiss? I would have thought they would have been more tuned in to what young people were reading.

I'd forgotten just how much influence he had upon me.

For instance, in the application you raise some of the common objections to pacifism, and then you dismiss them using Huxley's arguments. I also have a further observation: the nuclear issue is hardly mentioned. There's a line, but that's about it. It doesn't seem to have been much on your mind, which isn't the impression I get from some of your later writings.

That's interesting. You know, when I did the first draft of the application, I didn't take a completely pacifist point of view. As I said earlier, I said then that nuclear weapons were indiscriminate and that it was on those grounds that I wasn't prepared to be part of the military. But then I read Huxley and was influenced by Dr Kerr, so I went down the completely pacifist route. And then I also discovered Gandhi, though without learning much about the whole history of what he had been doing. I had, I think, a rather simplified view of how Gandhi had operated. But yes, your observation is interesting, the fact that I hadn't emphasised the nuclear issue.

One, I think, very valid point you make, again it's very Huxleyan, is about the connection between ends and means. You use the example of the Russian Revolution.

Well, Catholic teaching insists that the ends do not justify the means. I concluded from that that killing even for a just cause was wrong. Huxley I think goes further and concludes that the means determine the ends. For instance, if you use lethal violence to achieve a revolution the result will be a violent and unjust society. As another writer on non-violence and revolution, Bart de Ligt, puts it, 'The more violence, the less revolution.'

By the way, on the subject of communism were you drawn to any of its variants?

Certainly not to any of the authoritarian forms. The idea of equality did appeal to me. But the top-down, Stalinist, style of leadership? No, I've always hated that.

Would that have had anything to do with reading Orwell, say, his Nineteen Eighty-Four, *for instance?*

It may have done. I did read *Nineteen Eighty-Four* and *Animal Farm*, but I can't remember at what age exactly. *Nineteen Eighty-Four* had a big influence on me when I did read it, but that may have been a bit later, probably sometime in the late fifties.

What about one of the other very influential anti-communist books of the period, The God that Failed, *with the striking essays by Koestler and others?*

Yes, that had a profound impact upon me. I forget which of the essays it was. It may have been the one by Gide or Spender. But it contained an account of one of the great leader's speeches. Apparently, everyone had to clap. And they were frightened of what could happen to them if they were among the first to stop clapping. And then there was another thing that stayed with me from that book—this one may have been in the essay by Koestler. Anyway, it described a meeting somewhere where people were discussing policy, and an English communist said, 'We can't say that. It would be a lie.' And they all burst out in cynical laughter, as if to say, what's the problem with that?

Following your application for C.O. status you were interviewed at Fulham, in March 1952. You appeared before a certain Sir G.P. Hargreaves. and one or two others, including the Reverend Professor Edwin O. James. They sound like a pretty formidable bunch.

I don't remember feeling particularly nervous. I was so definite about it all. But I do remember that they asked me about my qualifications, and it came out that I had a distinction in School Certificate English. One of them said, 'So that's what this is about!', meaning that's what had fed into my lengthy statement as to why I was a conscientious objector. My mother gave evidence in support of me. She told them how I'd lain awake night after night, thinking about it all. And that probably had an effect as well. Anyway, my application was accepted.

Now, Michael, by this time the family had moved out of Cheam to a much larger house in Reigate. Tell me a bit about that if you would.

The house we moved to was called Little Gatton and, you're right, it was in Reigate, which was about ten miles further south, not far from the Surrey Hills and Betchworth. It was quite an interesting building. This wasn't because it was an old historic building; I think it was built in the thirties. It was interesting because of the people who'd lived there: first, the author Sax Rohmer, creator of the wicked Dr Fu Manchu, and then Sir Malcolm Campbell, the famous racing driver. My father bought it from Sir Malcolm's estate—Sir Malcolm, I believe had died there. That said, I didn't give two hoots about that aspect. From my point of view, it was simply a nice house. One of the reasons why my father was attracted to it was that there was a small farm attached to it. You see, the farming bug hadn't left him.

And what about you? Were you interested in farming too?

Oh, yes. I really took to it. I started making compost heaps and so on. I remember we had three cows, which I hand-milked. I can still do that by the way. So, come the nuclear holocaust I might well be self-sufficient [laughs].

How was the farm run? On idealistic lines?

Not in the least as far as my father was concerned; it simply tied in with his lifelong interest in the land and in growing things. After all, he was still a businessman. Indeed, when he bought a 200-acre farm in Sussex in 1953, like a lot of farmers at that period he grubbed up most of the hedgerows to make what he called his prairies. I'm pleased to say my brother, John, put them back in again.

I might also add that he was quite keen for me to take over the farm. So, I suppose that had it not been for *Peace News* and the whole direct action thing, that's where I would have ended up, as a farmer I mean!

I suppose you still discussed politics with your father.

Yes, I did. We particularly discussed war and peace issues. He was still a decided pacifist, which was a bit of a contradiction in a way with his conservatism. But then, as I said before, he was a pacifist on moral grounds. Of course, at Douai I'd been taught the just war approach to international relations. But he'd have none of that: all wars were wrong and that was simply the end of the matter. Then I suppose that like most of us he'd been brought up to believe that lying was a sin and that warfare involved spying, and therefore deception and lying. He used to ask me, 'How can you justify all of that?' In fact, he hated every form of violence.

You never saw him lose his temper then?

Oh, Jesus. Of course, I did. On one occasion when we were still living in Burdon Lane he ripped up all the flowers in the front garden because he thought that one of the priests was having an affair with my mother, which was the last thing that would have happened. And then I remember another occasion: he got himself into such a rage that my mum actually left and spent the night with one of our Irish friends in the area.

But I don't want to end on a negative note regarding my relationship with my dad. I was hugely influenced by him, not only on the issue of peace and conscientious objection, but on a range of issues and interests. It was from him that I imbibed a love of classical music, and of J.S. Bach in particular. Dad was an excellent pianist and spent many hours at a time playing and practicing Bach's preludes and fugues. He said that it was his ambition to be able to play all forty-eight of them before he died. Well, he didn't quite manage that. But he had quite a few of them under his belt by the end, though in later years when his health was failing, he wasn't able to play as much.

He also had an extensive library, with quite a few first editions, some signed by the authors. They included books by G.K. Chesterton, James Stephens and Henry Williamson amongst others. Then he had many slim, limited edition books of poetry, printed on English hand-made paper with a single poem and illustration in each. Mostly they too were signed. I suppose they must be worth something now, but I wouldn't part with them.

Finally, he was also a great walker. When I was a teenager, I used to go on long walks with him of up to twenty miles in the Surrey countryside. We would discuss all sorts of topics.

Let's talk about Operation Gandhi now, the first non-violent direct action group with which you were associated. Am I right in saying that the group emerged out of the PPU's decision in 1949 to set up a commission with the brief of looking into the relevance of Gandhi's ideas to Britain?

That's right. The Commission met for a couple of years. Then a number of people, including Hugh Brock and Kathleen Rawlins, both Quakers, decided it was time to put some of the ideas into action. Hugh was then deputy editor of *Peace News*, becoming its editor in 1955.

Gandhi's ideas being what?

Well, it's not easy to describe them succinctly. At least it wasn't then! But, in essence, Gandhi argued that war and violence were not inevitable; that there was an alternative method of struggle, of non-cooperation and non-violent direct action, which he called satyagraha, or truth force.

How much did you know about Gandhi at that point?

I certainly hadn't any in-depth knowledge. But then, I suppose, neither did some of the others in Operation Gandhi. What I did have, however, was the enthusiasm of a convert, so I read as much about him as I could and talked to those who knew more about him than I did. I've already mentioned Richard Gregg's book *The Power of Non-Violence*. Well, I read a lot about Gandhi in that and also in a book by Bart de Ligt called *The Conquest of Violence*, which has a short preface by Huxley. In fact, if you were to ask me which books influenced the members of Operation Gandhi the most, then I'd have to say that it was probably those two. Those two and another book, Krishnalal Shridharani's *War without Violence*, were usually in the background to our discussions.

Incidentally, while we're on the subject of Gandhi, I remember one day at school being in the refectory with a boy who we nicknamed Gandhi because of his light brown skin, and the priest who was in charge saying, 'Oh, Gandhi's just been killed.' Not surprisingly, we were both a bit shocked because he was such a well-known figure, even though we knew little about him.

There's a phrase which Gregg uses in his book when discussing non-violent direct action: moral jiu-jitsu. Can you say something about that?

The idea in jiu-jitsu is that you use the force that your opponent is directing against you to throw them off balance by not reacting as they expect. In other words, he was saying that if someone attacks you, they'll expect a certain sort of violent response, and if you don't give them that then it will psychologically and morally throw them.

After all, most people when they attack someone expect physical resistance. But the satyagrahi, to use Gandhi's terminology, doesn't respond with that. He or she *accepts* the blows. Not because they can't fight back. But because they choose not to. That's a different sort of resistance altogether.

Near the front of his book, Gregg quotes a newspaper account of an incident during Gandhi's campaign against the salt tax. The police beat up hundreds of unresisting demonstrators. But, finally, it was the police who backed down. Can you think of any times from your own experience when the technique of moral jui-jitsu worked for you like that?

I don't think that I was ever quite in that situation. But certainly, the way that we responded to the use of force at demonstrations was very much part and parcel of that general philosophy. Probably, many policemen in those days would have expected someone they were arresting in the context of a political demonstration to offer some form of physical resistance; whereas the essence of our approach was *not* to do that, so we offered them resistance of a different kind. We didn't threaten or abuse them, and that made some kind of rapport possible.

I get the sense that Gregg's is a very practical book?

Oh yes. We took it and other literature on non-violence as a guide to how we should react and to how we should campaign. We went to it for inspiration and for examples. The very interesting thing to me now is that Gregg was looking at the whole psychology of non-violent resistance. But then Gene Sharp came along and changed the terminology from *moral* to *political* jui-jitsu, so it wasn't just the individual reaction; it was how it would affect the politics if you didn't comply, but you didn't violently resist. And that was a very interesting shift.

Tell me more about that.

Okay, I'll give you an example. In India, it wasn't that the opponent was necessarily converted, though of course some people may have been. The real difficulty for the colonial power was enforcing laws when there was mass non-compliance. You had a large population who were simply defying the laws, that is the ones they considered unjust or unreasonable. And what did the authorities do about it? They couldn't put millions of people in jail [laughs]. If a small number of people had used force, okay they could have dealt with that. But in India the resistance was widespread. I think that Richard Gregg, although he uses the term moral jui-jitsu, was also pointing to the political difficulties of dealing with that kind of resistance.

I was so taken with the idea of non-violent resistance and the power of it, that I even began to think of it as something that you could use on almost every occasion. Once, following a meeting in Redhill, I took a shortcut home, and saw this big man, swaying from side to side, coming directly towards me. Then he came right up to me and grabbed my wrist. And I thought to myself, what the hell am I going to do about this? I could have resisted violently or at least struggled to free myself from his grasp as, I suppose, most people in that situation would have done. But, instead, I didn't make any attempt to escape his grasp, but simply stood there and spoke to him very calmly and very rationally, telling him where I had been and where I was going. And as I did so, I felt his grip loosening. Then he let go of me. It turned out that he owned a house nearby which had just been burgled and that he thought that I was the burglar! I remember afterwards thinking to myself: this is non-violent resistance work. But, of course, it had taken place in a particular context.

What about the other book you mentioned: Bart de Ligt's The Conquest of Violence?

Like Gregg's book, that was also from the 1930s. He too was very much in the Gandhian tradition but at the same time he also looked towards other methods of struggle, notably those employed by the anarcho-syndicalists. He gave examples not only of Gandhi's methods, but also of those of many others, including Abdul Ghaffar Khan. He may even have mentioned Shelley and William Morris; I'm not sure. He certainly has a few pages on Ruskin and Tolstoy. But, all that said, I didn't see the books as having a very different approach, but as sort of backing one another up. De Ligt does make some criticisms of Gandhi. Of course, he was writing at a time when India hadn't yet got its independence. But de Ligt was long dead by then; he died in September1939.

There's a line in the book which I find particularly compelling. In fact, you've already quoted part of it: 'The more there is of real revolution, the less there is of violence: the more of violence, the less of revolution.'

That's right. Yes, that did influence us profoundly.

The book also has this huge appendix called 'Plan of Campaign against all War and all Preparation for War'. Can you tell me what you remember of that?

What I remember is that we discussed it and, though we never did so, we planned to reprint it as a pamphlet because it showed the politics and many of the facets of the kinds of resistance that we were interested in and promoting. It gave lots of examples showing how you could work at both the individual and at the collective level. It was very influential.

Before we get onto Hugh Brock and the policies and the activities of Operation Gandhi, do you remember much about the other people involved in the organisation? Hilda von Klenze, for instance?

Yes. She was very much involved. She may have come over before the war. She had quite a distinct German accent. Later on, she married Stuart Morris, the head of the PPU. So, from Hilda von Klenze she became Hilda Morris.

Then I remember a disabled lady called Mazella Newman, who was closer to communism than the majority of us. In fact, if you got her onto the subject of the Soviet Union, she used to become quite defensive. I don't think that she was a member of the party though; it was probably more a matter of sympathy. She also worshiped Gandhi and the other leaders of the liberation movement in India, to the extent that she used to get quite emotional whenever any Indian people came to see us or Gandhi was mentioned. The other thing I remember about her was that she was a regular at *Peace News* on Wednesday evenings when the paper was packed to go out for arrival at people's houses on Friday. That was her big thing, in fact. She was a very nice woman.

What about Kathleen Rawlins? Any recollections of her? I mention her particularly because Brock in one article I've seen describes her as an 'ideological' influence on Operation Gandhi.

That's true. She was a major contributor to our discussions. I don't think that she published a great deal. But she was someone we looked to for her knowledge of Gandhi and of Gandhi's methods. She was very close to Hugh and Eileen Brock and a very significant presence.

A Quaker? I suppose that some of these ladies were. There was certainly a preponderance of women. Another one I might mention is Doris Wheeler.

Yes, several of the meetings were held at her house. The daughter of Tom Wardle, who was another prominent member of Operation Gandhi, was in touch with me about her recently. Tom, by the way, was a clergyman, who had worked in South Africa with Gandhi's son, Manilal Gandhi, and so was able to give personal examples of his involvement in the campaigns there. I remember having discussions with him during our demonstrations. He was an impressive man who founded something called the Congress of England, which looked at the constructive side of Gandhi's teaching. Then he also wrote quite a lot for *Peace News*. Anyway, his daughter sent me some photos that were taken in Doris Wheeler's house. Her name is Shanti, which means Peace in Hindi. Tom and his wife brought Shanti, who was then a baby, to one of our meetings.

Another person I remember from the discussions was Rufus de Pinto, an artist, always a bit scruffy and unkempt, but a big walker and a very interesting man. A few years after the Mildenhall demo, he died while walking on the hills somewhere. Hugh Brock wrote an excellent obituary of him in *Peace News*.

Can you tell me something about Hugh now? Some of the meetings, I believe, took place at his house, in Lordship Road, Stoke Newington.

That's right. Hugh's house was at number 79 and that was where we held most of our meetings. I'd come up at weekends from Reigate or wherever it was on the train and we'd sit and drink tea — it was all very English — and talk about Gandhi and his ideas, ideas that would lead to the possibility of arrest and imprisonment, so in that sense moving us away from that totally respectable middle-class environment that many of us, I suppose, had grown up in. Usually, Hugh would take the lead. All in all, he was a very genuine, thoughtful man, a Quaker and very self-effacing, though his contribution to the peace movement was huge. He had a background in publishing and was assistant editor of *Peace News,* before taking over from J. Allen Skinner as editor in 1955. His house, incidentally, was also the headquarters of the Direct Action Committee for a while. Hugh was married to Eileen and they had a daughter named Carolyn and a son, Jeremy. In fact, I have a picture of our Porton Down demonstration with Jeremy in it as a teenager. We all got on well. Hugh and Eileen were lovely people. When I came back to England, after a year in Ghana, towards the end of 1960, Hugh and Eileen put me up; I had a room with them. That, I should add, was a very busy time. It was the start of the Committee of 100 and we were building up to our first demonstration.

Was it via Peace News *that you first heard about Operation Gandhi?*

Indeed, it was. Which would have been in January 1952, so a couple of months or so after I'd registered as a conscientious objector and then a couple of months again before I went before the tribunal. *Peace News* carried an account of Operation Gandhi's first demonstration, which took the form of a sit-down protest in front of the War Office. Anyway, after that I subscribed to the newspaper and became a distributor. I used to be sent several copies from Blackstock Road in London and go from house to house in Reigate selling them, knocking on doors, trying to interest people in the issues. I didn't get many takers, but I remember one man who invited me in. He was really supportive, but that was probably because he was in the Communist Party. Then there was another man who was also welcoming and sympathetic, who turned out to be a Quaker. So, he was probably already a subscriber. Of course, my whole approach was so random [laughs]. I must have been crazy.

Of course, many older people at this time would have associated Peace News *with appeasement and the failures of the 1930s. Did that issue ever come up?*

I don't think it did, at least I don't remember people associating me with appeasement. The truth is that probably most people just weren't interested either way.

Getting back to Brock again, when, later on, he wrote up the Operation Gandhi story for Peace News *he noted that although the War Office sit-down was hardly a success, it did have three enormous benefits. Not only did it bring David Hoggett and Roger Rawlinson into the organisation – I think Hoggett was some sort of 'observer' on the occasion –, but it brought you into it as well. About you, he was particularly flattering. He quotes a letter you wrote to him in May 1952, which, quote, 'shows something of the mettle of the man who nearly ten years later was to organise the sit-down outside the Ministry of Defence for the Committee of 100 of which he is now the secretary.' Basically, Brock was having second thoughts about one of Operation Gandhi's projects, and you were urging him not to lose courage.*

I'll have to look that one up [laughs].

Would you agree that part of your appeal to Brock would have been your relative youth and the fact that like other young people you were full of new ideas and energies?

That seems likely. People like Kathleen Rawlins were a bit older. Other young people who were also conscientious objectors were coming into the movement. You've mentioned David Hoggett, but there was also David Graham and Ian Dixon. Later on, those two went off to India together and met up with Vinoba Bhave of the Bhoodan Movement, though they were not all that impressed by him. They were also among the people who volunteered to go with Harold Steele to the site of the first British H-Bomb tests in the Pacific.

When I looked through the minutes of Operation Gandhi I was struck by the extensive planning that went into your actions. On every occasion you and other committee members spent hours poring over bus timetables and maps, organising food deliveries and so on. And then another thing that struck me: you were very candid with the authorities.

Well, that was part of the Gandhi tradition, at least as far as we understood it. You acted quite openly, so you informed the police of what you were planning to do. But, then of course, we also wanted the publicity. If you didn't tell the police and the press what you were going to do, then they possibly wouldn't have turned up. And that went on through the Direct Action Committee and even, to some extent, through the Committee of 100 period. If you were having a sit-down or you were planning a demonstration, you let the authorities know about it.

And you'd engage the police in conversation. You'd ask them what they were doing and why they were doing it. That must have been pretty difficult, I imagine. Policemen can be pretty bloody-minded. Did it work?

I think it did. It certainly meant that our relations in general with the police at that point were quite good, even when they were arresting us. We didn't express any hostility towards the police. The attitude then was very much you do what you do and we do what we do. And if you happen to arrest us, well, that's the law.

As for the planning, after a while I really learned to enjoy it. I was always very thorough, partly because I felt responsible for people and partly, I suppose, because it was an opportunity to do something that I was good at. However, during most of the early period the lion's share was done centrally, from London by Hugh or one of the other people, though I do remember organising a demonstration in Reigate or Redhill. I guess I did that one because I was local!

Looking back now at the platform of Operation Gandhi, at least to the very early months, there isn't the emphasis on the nuclear issue that I would have expected. Take one of the early leaflets, the platform is this: the withdrawal of American forces; the withdrawal of Britain from NATO; the disbanding of Britain's armed forces; and the stopping of the manufacture of atom bombs in Britain. So, you weren't then calling for unilateral disarmament.

It was implied; it was implied in the whole disarmament programme. But, yes, I'm quite interested to be reminded of these early emphases. Maybe under J. Allen Skinner and Hugh Brock the word 'unilateralism' didn't figure much, but it was implicit. The Whitehall War Office demo may have been against the military in general. But think of the places that we went to after that. Mildenhall was not just any big military base; it was also strongly suspected of carrying nuclear weapons. Then we also went to Aldermaston, to Porton Down and to Harwell. These were all places related to weapons of mass destruction.

By the way, was Aldermaston the first action you took part in? That would have been the one in April 1952.

Yes, I think it was. Following the picket, we held an open-air meeting in Aldermaston village, at which Stuart Morris, a big figure in the PPU, was one of the speakers. We set up a stand in the village and preached to a few people, though really the main audience for our demonstration was a herd of cows in the adjoining field. They took fright as we walked past and stampeded into another field [laughs].

Fig 5:   Stuart Morris addressing the public meeting organised by Operation
          Gandhi in Aldermaston village on 19 April 1952. The man on Morris'
          right is Francis Deutsch. The woman holding the banner with the
          words, 'His hope for the future' is Doris Wheeler. University of
          Bradford, Special Collections, Cwl HBP 1/5.

Why didn't you go to the second demonstration?

You mean the one at Mildenhall? I didn't go to that for the
simple reason that my dad blew his top over it. I was still working
for him on the farm, and he said, 'No, you can't have the time off.'
The fact was, I suppose, he saw the Operation Gandhi type of
activity as provocative. I think he actually said, 'It's waving a red
rag at a bull.' And then the idea of one of his sons going out and
courting arrest or being fined and imprisoned was way outside his
comfort zone.

*You mentioned in our first interview that Aldermaston wasn't very far
from Douai. Did any members of the school come along? There must have
been some curiosity about what you were doing.*

No, I don't think so. But Pat Chambers, the person I mentioned
earlier, did write something jokey for the school magazine

mentioning that, 'Michael Randle was last seen on his way to Aldermaston.'

Later on, you changed Operation Gandhi's name to the Non-Violent Resistance Group (NVRG). Why was that?

I think that partly came out of discussions with some of our Indian friends, who were unhappy about linking Gandhi's name to something that sounded so military. They were certainly a bit uneasy. But, yes, we didn't stay with the Operation Gandhi name for very long. By early 1953 we'd changed it.

Moving forwards to the middle fifties now, do you remember some of the other people involved in the NVRG and its type of activism, say Norman Iles, Olwen Battersby, Jack Salkind, Lady Clare Annesley, Irene Jacoby or Dorothy Morton? You've already mentioned Tom Wardle.

Lady Clare Annesley was a dedicated pacifist and someone else who used to help out at *Peace News* on a Wednesday evening. She had been a suffragette. I think that she stayed with us into the Direct Action Committee period as well. She certainly stayed with the peace movement anyway.

Then I remember Irene Jacoby as well. She was a very forceful and outspoken woman. Much later, following the NVRG period, we met again, in 1967, at a conference in Sweden to do with the Vietnam war. We even had a couple of people from the National Liberation Front, the NFL, at that one.

Dorothy Morton, I think, was a Quaker. She and a young woman, Connie Jones, lay down on the road in front of the gates of the American air base at RAF Mildenhall in Suffolk, in June 1952. A week or so earlier, Hugh and myself had gone up and done a reccy of the base. Both Connie and Dorothy were brave, principled and gutsy women.

Did the national papers report this and the other demonstrations?

Yes, but not in a big way. They certainly didn't make the headlines. *Reynolds News* would usually carry something. And then there would often be reports in the local newspapers.

During the summer of 1953, I think it was, you left Little Gatton for another house, this time in Fletching, near Uckfield. Was this also to do with your father's farming interests?

Yes, he wanted to move on to a proper farm, so he bought Church Farm, at Fletching, in Sussex, a mixed diary and arable farm of 200 acres.

This is about the time when you started your 'Farmer's Log Book' articles for Peace News. *They really come out of the blue. At least there's nothing in* Peace News *like them.*

Yes, Hugh encouraged me to do that. After all, if I hadn't been taken up with the whole peace issue I could happily have stayed at the farm. I really enjoyed working there, and Hugh's offer gave me the opportunity to write about my experiences.

But then by the end of the year, you left the farm for a house in Limpsfield, near Oxted. Do you remember why you moved? Reading between the lines, I wonder if you'd had fallen out with your father?

No, I didn't leave as a result of falling out with dad. It was rather the other way around. We fell out to some extent *because* I decided to leave the farm. By that point I simply felt happier growing vegetables than working with animals, and here we're back to Dr Kerr and vegetarianism again. My dad was certainly angry and upset when I decided to leave, and actually I was upset too to see how much distress my decision was causing him. I remember writing a letter to my mother saying this.

In Limpsfield I took lodgings with a woman and worked at a nearby market garden for a short period, then came home at

Christmas. My dad was so keen to get me back that he said that I could plough up a field and do what I liked with it and not have anything to do with the animals. I agreed to that and came back to the farm for a time. But that arrangement didn't really work because I was still part of the farm team, and the idea of cultivating and growing stuff separate from the others just wasn't practical. Anyway, I still had my peace work to think about. In fact, it was about that time that I became involved with the Pacifist Youth Action Group.

Oh, tell me about that?

This was a group I joined with other young conscientious objectors, including David Graham and Ian Dixon, both of whom I've already mentioned, and Chris Farley. I don't know whether it was formally affiliated to the PPU, but it was certainly in line with their policies. We used to have regular pickets outside the prisons where they were holding conscientious objectors, and I travelled by train to London on one or two occasions to join in. And then some of these same people were involved in speaking at Speaker's Corner at Hyde Park. There was a young woman too, Carol Taylor from Manchester, who died I think recently. She became Carol Fitz-Gibbon and a very well-known educationalist. She was a brilliant speaker. A small woman and very feisty. She would get a big crowd. There was one occasion: a heckler there was really getting us down, saying things like, 'Warfare? It's just cannibalism.' And she said, 'It's not cannibalism. Because they don't eat the bodies!'

Talking of oratory, were there any other speakers who particularly impressed you at this time? The Methodist churchman Donald Soper, for instance?

Soper had the reputation of being an outstanding orator. He spoke regularly at Tower Hill as well as at Speakers' Corner, though I don't think he ever spoke from our platform and I didn't myself hear him speak in public. He appeared frequently on the radio programme, 'Question Time'. He also joined the Direct Action Committee. Most of us then were virtually unknown and he was one of the 'names'. He even came and sat down with us at Aldermaston at the end of the first Aldermaston march, in 1958, though we weren't causing an obstruction and so didn't risk arrest.

Can you tell me something about the background of the people you've mentioned in the Pacifist Youth Action Group? For some reason, I imagine that most of them were a bit Oxbridge.

Well, certainly neither Ian Dixon nor David Graham were Oxbridge. Ian was born and brought up here in Yorkshire, in Hipperholme I think. I don't know what Chris Farley's background was. He may have been public school; I don't know.

3. The Direct Action Committee and the first Aldermaston March

Michael, let's begin today by talking about the Suez Crisis of Autumn 1956. Can you say something about its impact upon you?

It was a real shock when the bombing started, and the more facts that came out the more disgraceful it seemed. It was so obviously a war of aggression, an act of imperialist folly. It emerged that there had been collusion between Israel, France and Britain before the war started. There was a division within my family about it. My brother Arthur, who was in the army at the time, took a very pro-British line as did my father initially. I remember going to Haywards Heath railway station to pick my brother up and having a fierce argument over Suez on the drive home. Then, later on, I overheard my dad and Arthur joking about how they'd seen some tanks being loaded up. I was absolutely livid. Then a cousin of my father, an Anglican clergyman, 'Uncle Howard', who lived up Manchester way, also took their side when he was visiting us. Anyway, when I was preparing to go up to London to demonstrate with the Pacifist Youth Action Group and some other organisations, Howard, who was a decent man actually, said, 'Oh, well. Anthony Eden has always been a man of peace', and I was incensed. I shouted, 'No. He's a warmonger!' I went up to London on a couple of occasions to join with others in distributing a leaflet that Donald Soper had written calling for civil disobedience to halt the Anglo-French-Israeli aggression. But, to my shame, I missed the big demonstration in Trafalgar Square, the one addressed by Aneurin Bevan for the trivial reason that I was committed to playing in a rugby match with the Old Dowegians. I didn't realise that Nye's speech was going to be the big one, the key event. I also sent a telegram from our local post office calling upon Eden to resign and to desist from this act of aggression. I mean, it was appalling what they were actually prepared to do.

Which would you say was worse? The aggression or the subterfuge?

Well, it was the military aggression that cost lives, including the lives of civilians, but the subterfuge that facilitated the aggression. We weren't fully aware of the subterfuge until later. Michael Foot wrote a book about it called *Guilty Men, 1957,* which was based on a lot of research. I saw Suez as very much a recrudescence of imperialism.

What were your feelings about Nasser?

Well, it's hard to think back and be sure, but my feeling as far as I remember was that the canal was in his country, so why shouldn't he nationalise it?

What about your father's view? I wonder if, like many people at the time, he compared Nasser to Hitler?

No, I don't think that he went that far. From his point of view, it was more a matter of the canal being British property. But the odd thing is that when *Peace News* published some very graphic photographs of the effects of the bombing, he switched completely and said that the bombing was a war crime. He was emotionally affected.

And then following Suez you had the uprising in Hungary.

Yes, exactly. And, of course, again there were protests. Like many towns and villages, our village held an event to raise money for Hungarian refugees. In fact, I was the one who took the initiative in getting a committee together to work on the issue. The irony is that some of the people who supported the Suez aggression opposed the Soviet intervention in Hungary [laughs].

So, then you decided to take your own action?

That's right. In consultation with Hugh Brock and Gene Sharp and some of the other people at *Peace News* I decided to get a group together to walk from Austria to the Hungarian border in order to express our support for the non-violent resistance to the Russian invasion. The newspaper headlines in this country were all about the violent resistance: the Molotov cocktails, the bombs, the bullets and so on. But there was a women's march in Hungary and quite a lot of other non-violent forms of protest.

Am I right in thinking that Hungary had a tradition of non-violent protest?

Absolutely. There was a man called Ferenc Deák. I'll have to check out the details, but yes, Hungary had had a sort of autonomous status within the Austro-Hungarian Empire, and there was an attempt by Austria during the nineteenth century to close that down or to incorporate it. The protests lasted ten or twelve years, and they did get some concessions eventually. You can read about them in the writings of people like Richard Gregg and Aldous Huxley. Arthur Griffith, the founder of Sinn Féin, also wrote a book about it called *The Resurrection of Hungary: A Parallel for Ireland,* which urged Sinn Féin, which was initially a non-violent party, to follow the example of Hungary. Eventually, of course, the more violent wing took over or became more prominent, but that's another story.

So, you got a group together.

Well, I got one or two people interested. But, in the end, I went on my own. I felt I *had* to go; I was so passionate about the issue. Gene Sharp, who had recently come to England to take over from Hugh Brock as assistant editor of *Peace News,* helped me put a leaflet together. Then some of the people in the Non-Violent Resistance Group helped out in other ways. Dorothy Glaister was particularly good in that respect. She had had quite a lot of experience of the weather conditions in Central Europe and she gave me advice about clothing and so on.

You left London when? In December?

That's right. Just before Christmas. I stayed overnight with Terence Chivers, who worked for *Peace News*. Then I took the train to Vienna, where I spent some time with a Hungarian who was a supporter of *Peace News*. He knew a bit about the situation.

Francis Rona?

Yes, Francis Rona. And then I also got help from a woman, another Quaker. She got the leaflet translated into German and printed by a sympathetic publisher. Then someone else printed it in Hungarian. So, I had it in English, German and Hungarian. But not in Russian, which was a big gap in a way [laughs] because I was appealing to Russian troops not to fire on unarmed demonstrators.

Anyway, as soon as I got to Vienna I told the police precisely what I was planning to do and made a poster to wear which said in English, German and Hungarian, 'Freedom — Not through war but through non-violent means!' 'Freiheit — Nicht durch Krieg, sondern durch gewaltlase (sic) Mittel!' I remember I had some quite detailed negotiations with the police. I told them that when I got to the border I wanted to fast and hold a vigil. They didn't want me to distribute the leaflets in the towns, but they said that I could go through the villages and into the countryside. You see, the situation in Austria was still very sensitive at that point, because of Austria's role in the Second World War and because it had a policy of strict neutrality. They certainly didn't want a foreigner like me rocking the boat with Moscow!

On the second day, it snowed heavily. There's a picture of me in *Peace News* with flat cap and poster, and I have others which show the landscape covered in snow. When I got to the border the communication from Vienna still hadn't arrived, so the border police stopped me and rang through to Vienna. Then some other police officers came from Vienna and drove me back to police headquarters there. I explained what I'd been doing and that it had all been cleared with the relevant authorities. But they couldn't find the person I'd spoken to, so there was a lot of confusion. The police got in touch with someone at the British Embassy, who was totally unsympathetic to my position. When he came into the police headquarters to speak to me, he said 'Oh, so you're the person who has caused all the trouble.'

Eventually I agreed to leave Austria within, I think, three days.

Fig 6:   Michael on his walk to the Hungarian border. University of Bradford, Special Collections, Cwl PN 11/19.

What about Francis Rona? Was he any help at that point?

Not at all. In fact, like most of the Quakers he'd introduced me to in Vienna he hadn't been keen on the project in the first place. Their view was that I should have been at home protesting at what the British had done in Egypt. But I said, 'I've already done that.'

Indeed, when I got back to Vienna, he was quite unsympathetic. He compared my agreeing to the police demands to a former Austrian President who had stumbled and fallen while climbing a stairway.

Well, I felt that I'd made my protest despite his opposition. Yet here he was telling me I should not have agreed to leave Austria.

I've read in one of the archives at Bradford University that Kathleen Rawlins was also against the project. She thought that you were putting yourself at unnecessary risk and for, potentially, very small gain.

I can't remember the details of what she said. She was always very friendly and sympathetic. But I think she did feel that it was risky, and that though she had a lot of admiration for my enthusiasm the action I was proposing was foolhardy.

You could have been shot!

Oh, yes [laughs]. Which would have been just the sort of incident that the Austrians certainly didn't want!

That said, and this may seem a strange question, I wonder if at some level that's what you did want, that you would have welcomed martyrdom?

I certainly felt the need to bear witness, if that's what you mean. I was so impressed by what I understood as Gandhi's methods. Having read Richard Gregg and Bart de Ligt and others, I had become totally convinced of the efficacy of non-violent resistance. And, yes, that did involve sacrifice.

Did you fast in Austria?

Not to the extent that I wanted to. I needed all my energy to do that walk. After all, it was about fifty miles in the depths of winter. It was bitterly cold. I certainly fasted during the Suez crisis. But that was just an individual gesture.

Why? As an act of penitence for British imperialism?

I suppose it was that, yes.

Let's talk now about the next major organisation with which you were involved: The Direct Action Committee or the DAC. I think that emerged out of Harold Steele's attempt to reach the British H-Bomb test site at Christmas Island in 1957.

Yes. As you say, it was very much an outgrowth of Harold Steele's attempt to sail to Christmas Island. About fifty people volunteered to go with him, including Reginald Reynolds, Ian Dixon, David Graham and Pat Arrowsmith. Harold Steele went to Japan first and got a boat which he intended to sail into the test area, but the tests took place before he arrived. Anyway, in March 1957, Hugh Brock called a meeting to offer him support. Now, I didn't attend that meeting for the same disgraceful reason that I missed Aneurin Bevan's famous speech on Suez [laughs]: I was committed to playing rugby.

There's a pattern forming here.

After that, it gets a bit confusing. The group formed to support Harold Steele called itself the Emergency Committee for Direct Action Against Nuclear War. The one that was set up after Harold Steele came back was called the Group or Committee for Direct Action Against Nuclear War, which after the first Aldermaston march, changed its name to the Direct Action Committee Against Nuclear War or DAC for short. I was a member of the sub-group which organised the first Aldermaston march. The other members of that group were Hugh Brock, Walter Wolfgang and Frank Allaun, with Pat Arrowsmith as organiser secretary. The four of us used to meet once a week in a room in the House of Commons to plan the actual march.

Frank Allaun was a Labour MP.

That's right. He was MP for Salford East.

A Bevanite?

I'm not sure if he would have identified himself as a Bevanite, though he certainly wasn't from the Gaitskellite wing of the party. We still had hopes then that Bevan would lead an anti-nuclear campaign. But then he made that famous speech at the 1957 Brighton conference, the one about sending a future Labour Foreign Secretary 'naked into the conference chamber.' He wasn't actually unsympathetic to the aspirations of the people who were calling for unconditional unilateral nuclear disarmament. He was saying that this wasn't the way to go about it. Nuclear disarmament, he argued, could only be achieved through international agreements.

I remember that Brighton Conference very well. I met up with Gene Sharp there. The whole thing was a big disappointment. It was held at about the same time as J.B. Priestley wrote his famous article on the H-Bomb for the *New Statesman*, the one that led to the founding of the Campaign for Nuclear Disarmament (CND). *Tribune* too was banging on about nuclear disarmament. So, there was all this fermentation. But, yes, the conference was a big disappointment.

Would you say that it was about that time that you lost your faith in party political politics as a way of dealing with the nuclear issue?

Well, even before that I had been influenced by anarcho-pacifist ideas, so I don't think that it was just that. I certainly didn't want to reject the support of parliamentarians like Frank Allaun, for example. But I saw the way forward as something much more revolutionary. Revolution by non-violent means; that was the idea.

In some of your Peace News *articles of 1956 you talk about employing the anarcho-syndicalist tactic of the general strike. On reflection, how realistic do you think that was?*

It wasn't realistic at all. I was reading all these ideas about the forms that non-violent resistance could take, and that was one of the possibilities. But, of course, there was no chance that the trade unions at that point would back a general strike for nuclear disarmament.

However, Frank Cousins came out very strongly against the bomb. One of our Direct Action Committee leaflets cited the occasion in May 1920 when dockers refused to load British weapons onto a ship, *The Jolly George*, bound for Poland to be used by Russian White armies against the Bolsheviks.

Just to be clear: there was the Labour Party and there were the unions and you had hopes from elements in both of them?

Yes, but I think that we were looking more to the grassroots. But, having said that, we were also divided amongst ourselves. I think that Hugh had his feet more firmly on the ground than some of us. On the one hand, he had this great millennial vision of a Britain without weapons. But, on the other, he was a very practical man, with a realistic grasp of the steps you had to take to move towards that. He was a Labour County Councillor, after all! So, he was meeting MPs like Frank Allaun and being very persuasive. But I don't think that he expected a non-violent revolution during his lifetime.

Was it at the November meeting of the DAC that the first Aldermaston march was suggested?

Yes. Two people suggested it: Laurence Brown and Hugh himself. Laurence lived in the Aldermaston area and was the person who alerted Hugh Brock to the activities going on at Aldermaston back in 1952, which led to the first protest at the base by Operation Gandhi. Then when the Direct Action Committee Against Nuclear War was formed after Harold Steele's return from Japan, Hugh and Laurence proposed a two- or three-day march from London to Aldermaston. I remember Terence Chivers saying to me, 'Oh, it's Hugh going on about Aldermaston again', suggesting I suppose that he was reliving something in the past. But this was something different, a march as against a day trip by coach and a protest lasting at most two or three hours. But the atmosphere in the country too was very different. Why? Because you'd had Hungary, with communists and communist sympathisers, people like Edward Thompson, saying that what the Russians had been doing was imperialism under another name. And you'd had Suez, and all the demonstrations against that. And then also journals like the *Universities and Left Review* and, up in this part of the world *The New Reasoner* had come out. So, the context had changed utterly.

So, the idea of a march caught on very quickly?

The reaction was absolutely staggering and somewhat daunting. We quickly came to realise what a huge venture it was going to be. But, fortunately, we had an excellent Chief Marshall in Michael Howard who played a vital role in the practical organisation of the march.   Also, a number of voluntary organisations stepped in to help. For instance, the Quakers agreed to open up their meeting houses for people to stay in en route. Then the London Cooperative Society said that they'd provide some catering.

How did the people at the CND take to it? I've read somewhere that the bigwigs didn't approve of direct action of any kind.

That's right. Its executive was even divided about the Aldermaston march. Some were doubtful about the wisdom of taking the issue of nuclear disarmament onto the streets. It took all Hugh Brock's skill to persuade Canon Collins to address the marchers in Trafalgar Square at the start of the march. J.B. Priestley was against it. Richard Taylor, in one of his books on the anti-nuclear movement, focuses on some of the letters that passed between members of the committee of the CND on this very topic. People like Priestley saw the campaign, at least initially, as a pressure group campaign, a bit like the anti-hanging campaign. They really weren't prepared for people going out onto the streets.

Did you meet Priestley at this time?

There was one occasion when some of us from the DAC met a number of people from the CND executive, but I don't think Priestley was among them. I know that Kingsley Martin was there. But there was this definite rivalry between the two organisations. CND didn't want to be upstaged by us. When, later that year, we announced another march from two different places to London, they jumped in and said that they would organise a march as well on the same day. We were furious about that, but finally agreed to cancel our proposed march, so CND would have a clear run. There was a real tussle for publicity, to be recognised as the number one organisation.

When you invited A.J.P. Taylor to sponsor the DAC, he refused, on the grounds that he was in the CND already. And you got similar responses from Rose Macaulay, Herbert Read, Jakob Bronowski and Joseph Rotblat. You even sent an invitation to Canon Collins of all people. Was that just to wind him up?

Possibly. He was a big character.

A very vain man?

Yes, he definitely was that. But there was no doubting his commitment to nuclear disarmament and to supporting the anti-movement in South Africa through the organisation Christian Action, which he founded.

Can you tell me something about the origin of the so-called peace symbol? A lot of people think that, again like the march itself, it owes it origin to CND. But that isn't the case, is it?

Well, as I've said, there was this huge build up to the first Aldermaston march and people and organisations were volunteering to help. Now, I don't know whether Hugh Brock already knew the artist Gerald Holtom or whether Gerald just got in touch, saying that he had an idea for publicising the march. But, at any rate, sometime either in February or early in March 1958 Gerald came up to the office of the Direct Action Committee, in Blackstock Road, in the same building as *Peace News*, and produced these sketches. I was a bit unsure at first, But Hugh was definite. 'Yes, we'll use that.' So, we agreed to adopt Gerald's design as our symbol. Gerald explained that it was based on semaphore; ship to shore signals, that sort of thing. The 'N' for 'Nuclear' was signalled with the arms down like this [forms an inverted V-shape] and the 'D' for 'Disarmament' with one of the arms straight up and down, and he put a circle round it. He also had other ideas about the meaning of the symbol, though I don't know whether they preceded or followed it. One idea connected it to a painting by Goya, where a man is about to be shot. His arms are like this [holds them again, in an upright V-shape this time]. I've got a copy of a letter, which Gerald wrote to Hugh Brock in the early sixties, in which he says, 'If it wasn't for you, Pat Arrowsmith and Michael, this symbol would never had been produced.'

Harry Mister, who was working at *Peace News* at the time and who had been on that first Operation Gandhi sit-down outside the War Office in 1952, looked at the first leaflets carrying the symbol and said, 'What an earth were you, Hugh and Pat thinking about when you adopted that symbol? It doesn't mean a thing and it will never catch on!' However, to be fair to him, he always wore a badge with the symbol for the rest of his life. Of course, if the march had been a complete flop he would have been absolutely right. People wouldn't have taken a second look at it.

Fig 7:   One of Gerald Holtom's sketches for the first Aldermaston march, showing how the peace symbol could be used. University of Bradford, Special Collections, Cwl ND.

What did the people in the Peace Pledge Union think of it? Were they concerned that the symbol placed too much emphasis on 'nuclear' pacifism? I'm thinking now of Sybil Morrison and Stuart Morris.

Sybil Morrison's position was that nuclear weapons were an extension of the whole military system, and that you had to take a stand against that system rather than against one particular aspect of it. So, yes, the PPU were definitely sceptical. Hilda Morris, who had been with the Non-Violent Resistance Group and who was also with the Direct Action Committee in its early days resigned from the DAC for that very reason. She said that it wasn't logical to call just for nuclear disarmament.

The symbol didn't just appear on banners; you also put them on 'lollipops' and badges. Who came up with the badge idea?

That I think was Eric Austen's. I believe he had a kiln where he could produce them.

You said that the first Aldermaston march started in London. Can you describe it now? It must have been an amazing experience.

There was a great send-off in Trafalgar Square with a crowd of some seven or eight thousand people. There was a sort of carnival atmosphere, with various bands and lots of jazz. I remember Kenny Ball and his Jazzmen and George Melly. I think that all the members of the DAC were there; certainly Hugh and Eileen, Irene Jacoby, Ian Dixon, David Graham, Kathleen Rawlins and Pat Arrowsmith. You could say it was a bit middle class. There were lots of students, but also mothers with pushchairs. The march began on Good Friday with about seven or eight thousand of us, which narrowed down a bit to, I think, about four hundred at one point, but then it picked up again to about the original number at the end. The weather on the first day was fine, but on the second or third day it poured with rain and sleet in what was described as the worst Easter weather for forty years. But I think even our critics in the right-wing newspapers were impressed as the marchers kept going, including the mothers with their pushchairs. We stayed in all sorts of places, but mainly church halls or Quaker meeting houses. It was wonderful the way they opened their doors to us. We'd lie on the floors in our sleeping bags. We really couldn't have done it without them. And, as I've said, the Co-op provided a van, which really did feed the five thousand!

But the part that I remember best took place near the end. We passed the base in complete silence. This may have been Hugh's idea, but, in any case, it was an impressive and moving moment. I remember my future brother-in-law, Alan Lovell, saying how magnificent it was.

But then afterwards there was some sort of incident involving the once-famous McWhirter twins, who some readers will recognise as the founders of The Guinness Book of Records.

That's right. I didn't see the incident at all; few people on the march did. But it took place at the entrance to Falcon Inn Fields, which is right opposite the base and where we had our rally. Apparently, the twins drove up in a black Daimler car and started broadcasting propaganda and there was a bit of a scuffle when somebody jumped up and pulled out the wires. Possibly some people rocked the car from side to side. But that was about all it amounted to. But the headlines in one of the papers on the following day, I think probably *The Daily Telegraph,* went something like, 'Aldermaston March Ends in Violence'. That was nonsense. In fact, I wrote a letter to the paper saying as much.

Even before the march we'd handed out this briefing leaflet, which Gene Sharp had played a large part in drafting, warning people against responding violently. If they were attacked or arrested, they were simply to go limp. In other words, they were not to cooperate, but they were not to violently resist either. None of us would ever have authorised an attack on a car or anything like that.

What the brothers said – and here's the quotation – was, 'You're playing Khrushchev's game. The Kremlin is making use of you.'

Yes. It was certainly something provocative.

But then they did hit a very sensitive spot. How did you defend yourself from accusations that you were, at some level at least, in league with the Soviets?

Well, of course, some communists were sincerely involved in anti-war activities. The Stockholm Appeal of 1950, for instance, was backed by Moscow and by the World Peace Council. And there were other activities which were also communist backed. But we wanted to make clear we were against all nuclear weapons on principle.

That said, it's also fair to say that you got it in the neck from the other side as well. For example, John Brunner wrote an article for his publication Noise Level, *in which he accused you of acting like a gauleiter, a Nazi.*

Before the march, John Brunner's group got in touch with Pat Arrowsmith and said that they wanted to go ahead of the march and sing anti-war songs. Okay. So, Gene Sharp had a look at what they were proposing and decided that they were a bit too one-sided, too anti-American. Anyway, I was the person delegated to negotiate with the group, who were either communists or sympathetic to the communist viewpoint. Eventually they agreed to only sing the songs that we said would be okay, so that we'd have a balance. But then on the march itself they didn't stick to that. I had the unenviable task of walking with this group and telling them to stick to the agreement. So that was my gauleiter role ... . Karl Dallas, who was one of Brunner's group never forgot it. Right until he died, he would always have a dig at me over it, though we did later work together. But they did think that I had gone over the top. John Brunner, it's worth adding, later joined the Committee of 100. I had some quite reasonable dealings with him then. He was very committed and headed Hampstead CND. So, all of us made our peace after a fashion. But on that first march we were determined that it would not be written off as a Khrushchev or communist initiative.

But this was a line that needed negotiating and re-negotiating. I say this because during April 1958 you were in Paris speaking at a conference organised by the Mouvement de la Paix, which was the French arm of the World Peace Council, which was itself taking instructions from Moscow.

Within the DAC, we had serious discussions about whether or not I should go to that. Both Hugh Brock and Gene Sharp were involved in the decision. On the one hand, it was a chance to publicise the Aldermaston march. But, yes, there were risks on the other hand. In the end, we agreed on some of the things I should say. We wanted to make it clear that our position was not a communist one. There was a certain frostiness on the part of the organisers I remember. I'd written something which they translated and then I added something in my halting French, which stated that we were against all nuclear bombs, not just those of the capitalists.

Finally, before we leave the first Aldermaston march, am I right in saying that both Michael Foot and Bayard Rustin spoke from the plinth in Trafalgar Square?

That's right. I didn't speak; I really wasn't in the forefront in that way. But Canon Collins spoke and Michael Foot gave this tremendous speech with a loud rhetorical climax that sent the pigeons flying. And, yes, Bayard Rustin, who went on to be a very important figure in the civil rights movement in the United States, spoke as well. A sort of voluntary group of filmmakers, from a film institute in London, made a film of the march. You can see him in that. The film was edited by Lindsay Anderson and the voiceover is by Richard Burton.

Can you say a little more about Rustin? I'd be surprised if he's a figure that many people in the UK are familiar with.

One of the things that Hugh Brock would do when people who'd been involved in radical action in other countries came through London was to organise meetings with them at *Peace News.* That gave us the opportunity to hold discussions with them and to swap ideas. And one day, Bayard Rustin came through; it may have been as simple as that. Anyway, Bayard was a very strong, powerful figure. I remember on one of these occasions, he spoke about the actions that he and his associates had taken against racism in the States. One of the big questions that used to come up a lot in those days was whether it was right in a democracy to use civil disobedience. I'd written something in one of the DAC's newsletters, giving a justification for it. But on this occasion, I just threw it out as a question for Bayard. But he came down on me like a ton of bricks, but adding when I tried to explain my position, 'I know, we're all taking off the top of our heads.' He was thoughtful and very firm.

4. Peace News and Ghana

Michael, we're still in 1958 at this point. Was it about this time that you moved to London?

No, I moved to London after my Hungarian venture, so sometime in late 1957. That was to Avenell Road, which is just outside what was then the Arsenal stadium. I had come to London to work for *Peace News*, with nowhere to go. I knew the *Peace News* offices were in Blackstock Road, of course, so I took the tube to Finsbury Road underground station and looked at various adverts for digs in a shop window and found one for a room in Avenell Road. It had a gas stove and a sink. The shared bathroom was on the next floor. It was 30 bob a week, which seemed reasonable, so I took it. I suppose it was a lodging house really. I lived on boiled eggs and cabbage, plus a few other vegetarian delicacies. You could buy a tin of something that looked very like meat. It wasn't Sausalatas, but it was something like that, something burger-shaped. Then I used to go to Indian and Chinese restaurants for the veggie curries. There was a good Indian restaurant in Finsbury Park.

I should imagine your needs were few.

I think they were really, yes.

So, you had a salary from Peace News. *Were you paid by the DAC as well?*

Initially I worked voluntarily for the DAC. Then when I moved around the corner from *Peace News* to the DAC offices, in Seven Sisters Road, I worked full-time for the committee. I had a salary then, but it was minimal. All of us were on minimal wages. April Carter and Pat Arrowsmith were in the office. Later we were joined by Will Warren. But Will mainly worked in the field. We had a big demonstration at North Pickenham and he was there in a caravan, making connections with the local trade unionists and church people and so on. Will was a Quaker and a communist, but not of the Stalinist variety. He certainly never joined the party. He simply believed in the ideals of communism, which I also think are alright actually.

What were your dad's views of what you were doing at this period?

At first, things were very difficult between us. He even wrote to Harry Mister at *Peace News* to try to dissuade him from employing me. I was taking a cut in wages, I was going up to London, I was living in a bed-sit. He just couldn't fathom it. But then we sorted things out after a while. Certainly, he was furious with Macmillan when I got my long prison sentence a few years later, in 1962. He blamed Macmillan personally for my imprisonment and even started voting Liberal. But then bearing in mind that he was a conscientious objector it was odd that he voted Tory in the first place. He also continued to take *The Daily Telegraph*.

Let's talk about Peace News *now. So, you started in 1957.*

Yes, I got an invitation from Harry Mister to fill a vacancy on the sales and promotional side, but I helped out with a lot of things. By then Hugh had taken over from J. Allen Skinner as editor, but Allen still contributed regularly and attended the weekly editorial meetings to discuss what would be in the paper the following week and what line we'd take. So, I got to know him fairly well also.

J. Allen Skinner's name is not as familiar to me as Hugh Brock's. What was his background?

Allen's background was in trade unionism and conscientious objection. He'd been a conscientious objector during the First World War and treated very harshly like a lot of other objectors in that period. He served two years in prison, and though I don't know what caused it, he ended up with a bad leg. Whenever we had a meeting, he always had his leg on a chair. It may have been some form of tuberculosis; it was something very serious anyway. Allen was older than Hugh. He was originally from the Manchester area.

I saw some advertising copy you wrote for Peace News, *which I wish I'd brought with me. I know that you won't think much of it, but it's very impressive. Did the circulation rise as a result of Randleian efforts?*

I doubt it [laughs].

Earlier on, you said that Peace News *was based in Blackstock Road.*

Yes, it was in Blackstock Road, Finsbury Park, a stone's throw from the underground station and just off Seven Sisters Road. So, very convenient from my point of view.

Fig 8:   *Peace News* in Blackstock Road. Note the cramped conditions. The man on the extreme left is Harry Mister. Photographer unknown. University of Bradford, Special Collections, Cwl PN 11/1.

I get the sense that that whole area has a history of radicalism.

You might be right. It certainly seems to go back a long way. Fish & Cook, the stationers, occupied the building at street level. Housmans was on the first storey, and *Peace News* was on the one above. Mr Cook had been a conscientious objector. The shop also had a printing department, which Hugh's brother, Ashley, had taken over and which was later moved to Fonthill Road. Then when the Committee of 100 was set up we had an office above the printing works.

Thinking now about some of the older figures who contributed to Peace News, *do you remember much about Reginald Reynolds?*

Well, I never got to know him properly. He was simply one of the people who contributed articles, though I also remember him writing a number of letters on the subject of direct action. And, yes, I also heard him speak once at the Friends' Meeting House in Reigate. Anyway, he had a famous article in *Peace News* called 'The Map of Mrs. Brown', in which he stressed the importance of better understanding the psychology of 'ordinary' people in relation to nuclear weapons. A number of readers replied to it, including me. And then when he in his turn came to make *his* replies, he mentioned my comments. He was one of those people 'up there', who I never really knew, but who I admired and who influenced my thinking. He also used to do a regular column and write political satirical poems for the *New Statesman*. There was one about the muckraking journalist, Chapman Pincher. Pincher had written about the benefits of nuclear power including the possibility of nuclear-powered cars. Reynolds' poem ended with the lines:

But when some curious visitor from Mars
Inspects this planet's self-inflicted scars,
He will not know this was the price we paid
For you, dear Chapman, and our little cars.

Was Reynolds a Quaker?

Oh, yes. He was very much on the Gandhian wing of the peace movement and quite critical in some ways of traditional pacifist organisations for not being radical enough. He's not someone much spoken about today, but it's possible you've heard of his wife, the writer Ethel Mannin.

Regarding 'The Map of Mrs. Brown', it's interesting the way Reynolds divides the peace movement into three groups, what he calls the 'Pacifist Old Guard', i.e., those determined to carry on as before, people like Sybil Morrison and Stuart Morris; the 'Perfectionists', who want to change the entire world; and a third group, which includes, I suppose, you and your friends in the DAC, people consumed with a sense of urgency and 'a passion for action', but without any real understanding of what they are up against. Is that a fair criticism?

Well, I was very optimistic and probably very naive in many ways. I thought that Gandhi's method of non-violent direct action would get through to people at another level. Then anything could happen.

There was another senior journalist, B.J. Boothroyd.

I met Bernard Boothroyd only when he came into the office to talk to Hugh. He edited Peace News prior to both Hugh and Allen.

Okay, let's leave Peace News for a while and return to the DAC. After the Aldermaston march, you reconstituted and enlarged the committee, notably with the addition of Alan Lovell, who you've briefly mentioned, and Bill Crampton. Do you remember much about Bill Crampton?

Bill was a student at the LSE. I can't remember exactly how active he was, but it was certainly good to have people from that background involved. Alan Lovell by that stage was working for Peace News as well, writing a regular column on film, So, I knew him through that. He brought quite a sophisticated political understanding to what the DAC was doing.

You mean that you and the others weren't sophisticated!

Well, some of us weren't. I mean, I'd never been to university. I'd left school at sixteen. Hugh Brock had never been to university. April Carter went on later to one of the Oxford colleges. Although she was still very young at the time, she had worked for the Foreign Office, so she had, and still has, a wider political grasp of things than most of us. Pat Arrowsmith had definitely been to university.

By the way, what was Pat like in those days? The newsreels of the period give the impression of a very formidable young person.

Generally, I got on well with her, though, of course, as in any organisation, things did get difficult occasionally. She could be very abrupt. For starters, if I was at home and Anne happened to answer the phone to her, she'd say, 'Is Michael there?' in this very posh Cheltenham Ladies College voice. There was never any 'Hello' or 'How are you?' or anything like that. But she had great guts. There were very few people like her.

Would it be fair to say that she wasn't really a committee person?

No, I wouldn't say that. She was, after all, secretary of the Direct Action Committee for a while. Then, when April Carter took over that role, she became field secretary. She would go out to the places where we were demonstrating and talk to people.

Then the other thing that I would say about her is that she had a wide range of interests. She painted and wrote novels and poetry. But, yes, she was also very single-minded and determined.

Have you read her novel of 1965, Jericho? *It's a sort of roman-à-clef based in part upon the DAC's summer picket of 1958 at Aldermaston. I've often wondered if the 'Charles' character is based partly on you.*

Ah, I don't think I've ever read it cover to cover. I must get it out of the library and do that. But, yes, the book certainly is based on our picket at Aldermaston following the first march. And, it's true, that she was quite critical of me at times on a number of counts. We weren't planning to block the base initially. We were just going to sit down at the entrance. But then the idea came up that we would move on and do that as well. But I didn't think that we were quite ready for it, at least I wasn't. Anyway, I think that Pat described me, not necessarily in the novel, but in something else she wrote, as a 'wet blanket'.

That's not the impression I get of you from the novel. Here's a quotation, which I picked out this morning. '[Charles] disapproved of the state or any form of compulsion on principle. Yet he hankered after law and order, and he hated confusion.' Would that be a fair way of describing you at the time?

Yes, it probably would.

Another point that the book makes is that you thought quite a lot about the best way to present yourselves. You had discussions about whether women could wear trousers or not and whether men could grow beards.

There was a discussion of both those issues. We wanted to look respectable. I remember April Carter saying, 'We don't want to put people off by our appearance.' That was basically it. There was another man who had been with the Pacifist Youth Action Group: David Lane. He was critical of the idea that we should all appear middle-class and respectable.

He was a bit of a beatnik?

I think more working class than beatnik. I don't think he dressed that way. At the time of Suez he had been arrested. He used the technique of going limp. He was quoted in one of the newspapers at the time, saying something along the lines of 'This is the Gandhian way.' He died a few years ago.

There's a caricature of Gene Sharp under the name of Alvin Niceman. The character is described as an 'intense, intellectual, young American', domineering and speaking in multi-syllabics and as a teacher of socio-drama.

Well, Gene Sharp did do a lot of role play in his classes for us and for other people. In fact, at about this time he gave a series of public lectures on non-violent techniques, which Hugh helped to organise. One of the points that we in the DAC made about direct action was that it communicated at a level that went beyond argument, that it could reach people in a different way, in much the way that drama does; in fact, that it was a *form* of drama. I remember Alan Lovell arguing that point. Anyway, Gene and Pat Arrowsmith never got on. I remember that very clearly.

There's also a lot of violence in the book. On one occasion the protest camp is attacked by local youths. Then, on another occasion, one of the women is raped and the protestors have a big discussion over whether they should go to the police or not. Were you ever attacked?

Not really. I think that the worst thing that happened to me took place in Newbury or Reading. I was speaking on a platform and a guy came up with a glass of beer and threw it over me.

How much time did you spend at the camp that summer?

I didn't spend a lot of time there, except for the concluding week when we had the sit-down in the forecourt. That was the occasion on which Donald Soper joined us for a day. The rest of us stayed there day and night for a week, so it was quite an effort. Both Pat Arrowsmith and April Carter were there as well as DAC stalwarts like Laurens Otter, a proclaimed anarchist, and Inez Randal, secretary of Reading CND, as well as a member of the DAC.

Immediately after the protest I went to the 1958 Labour conference, in Scarborough. Alan Lovell was there with a number of the *Universities and Left Review* people, handing out leaflets and lobbying. That's where I heckled very effectively, though I'm sorry now that it was against someone so renowned and important as Aneurin Bevan. He was clearly reaching the final peroration of his speech, without having said a word about the bomb. And I just shouted from the floor, 'What about the bomb?' I believe that he was somewhat nonplussed [laughs]. He said, 'I'm making this speech, not you.' People turned around and looked at me, I remember. One of them was Tony Benn, who always looked very young in that period. He turned and looked at this cheeky upstart, who had interrupted the great Nye Bevan.

Fig 9:   Michael, in 1958. Photographer unknown. Private Collection.

By the way, were you still writing in those days?

I tried my hand at short stories. But I don't think that I published anything. You know, when you look at the DAC and the Committee of 100 there was a large number of artists and writers involved: Arnold Wesker, Margaretta D'Arcy and John Arden, Robert Bolt, Shelagh Delaney, Hugh MacDiarmid, and many others.

Let's look at the DAC's activities against the Thor missile base at North Pickenham, in Norfolk, during December 1958. You were arrested, but not straightaway.

Well, with North Pickenham, we didn't just go to the base and demonstrate; we campaigned in the area also, contacting churches, trade unions, and other organisations. The government had decided to build five missile sites for the US Air Force, so we had a great sense of urgency. Someone, I remember, turned up with a draughty caravan and some of the protestors lived in that. Will Warren was there, Pat Arrowsmith and possibly Frances Edwards.

In fact, there were two demonstrations at North Pickenham, one at the beginning of December and one a couple of weeks after that. Pat Arrowsmith and Inez Randal were amongst the people who went inside on the first occasion. Pat carried this long banner which read, 'Direct Action Committee'. At that point, the base was still under construction and defended by nothing stronger than a few rolls of barbed wire, so they threw the banner over that and walked across it. Some of the workers threw mud at them and water was sprayed when Pat and the others tried to obstruct some lorries that were loading up with gravel. But the police didn't do anything. It was extraordinary in a way. We were doing something new. We were taking radical action, but totally non-violently.

Both demonstrations got a lot of publicity, but in the second case it was absolutely extraordinary. On the first occasion, there was no one in our group who was well known, but on the second occasion we had the Reverend Michael Scott, who had campaigned against Apartheid in South Africa and set up the Africa Bureau in London. I remember reading an article about that in *Tribune*. He was on the left and a very important figure. Indeed, if I'm not mistaken there's an issue of *Peace News*, which has some such headline as 'Michael Scott flies in from Africa to join demonstration'. He was that big; we were very lucky to have him.

Didn't you write an article for Peace News *about that first North Pickenham demonstration?*

Yes. I wrote a piece for *Peace News* defending the action. There were many people, even within the DAC, who thought that we were wrong to stop the lorries, that our actions were coercive.

On the second occasion, the police were ready for us. They weren't going to have any more nonsense. The base had increased its defences as well. They'd fixed and strengthened the barbed wire, so we had to go to the main entrance to get in. The police were there. The first time you sat down they dragged you away. Then if you went back, they arrested you. You just went limp, as had been agreed at one of the earlier briefings.

Those of us who were arrested — I think that there were about thirty or forty of us out of about a hundred or so — were taken to a police station where we spent the night.

Christopher Driver's book, The Disarmers, *has an interesting passage about the second action. He says, 'With the first pictures of puffing policemen pulling away limp bodies the British public now took in the fact that 37 otherwise respectable citizens were spending Christmas in jail for being too enthusiastic about peace.' That's a striking observation.*

Obviously, there had been various political demonstrations where the police were involved. But this was different in that there was absolutely no fighting with the police. This was challenging and different.

I suppose the police didn't look good on either occasion. The first time for not doing anything and the second time for apparently doing too much.

No, I wouldn't say that they came out badly on that second occasion. They did their job, carrying us away and arresting us, and we did ours. It was civilised. And certainly from the whole Quaker, pacifist, point of view there was no direct hostility to the police. Indeed, people like Hugh Brock would be quite insistent about that.

After we were arrested, we were taken before the magistrate. That I think was at Swaffham. Anyway, we were given the opportunity of pledging to be of good behaviour and to keep the peace. We refused that, so we were taken to Norwich Prison. That was my first experience of prison. I shared a cell in Norwich with Michael Scott, who as I've said was a big figure, really something of a hero. It was an honour to be sharing a cell with him.

How long did they keep you in Norwich for?

We were in Norwich over the Christmas period. There were so many of us that they didn't have enough workshops in the prison for us to work in, so they set up a workplace in the main hall and had us sewing mailbags there. On one occasion when one of the prison officers came round, telling us what to do, some of the Quakers who were having a meeting said to him, 'Shhh. There's a religious meeting going on here.' And he went off muttering, 'There's a time and a place for everything.' [laughs] However, the thing that really stands out for me about the experience was this: when I was in a cell with Michael Scott, there was another prisoner there as well, a non-political awaiting trial for an alleged criminal offence. Anyway, he got diarrhoea, so we rang the bell for him to be let out to use the toilet on the landing. What used to happen was this: you rang the bell and a little metal flag dropped out into a horizontal position, so the prison officer could see who had rung. But the officer in this case just came over to the cell, put the flag back into its vertical position, and said, 'Use your pot.' The poor man was so embarrassed. It was real diarrhoea and it smelled like

God knows what. Both Michael Scott and I felt very nauseous. Afterwards Michael applied for and got a cell on his own. I think that he had stomach problems also.

After Norwich, what happened then? You were sent to another prison?

We were released on bail to await a trial. Eventually, we were taken in ones and twos to a magistrates' court again and anyone who didn't agree to be of good behaviour was sentenced to two weeks imprisonment. I was sent to Brixton, in South London. Hugh had been there a little bit before me, so he was coming to the end of his sentence when I was beginning mine. It doesn't seem long two weeks, but at the time it felt like a very long time! However, for us, the publicity which, by and large, was sympathetic contributed to the success of the demonstration.

So, you received food parcels, letters of support and so on?

When we were in Norwich Prison we were inundated not only with cards, but with telegrams. I still have one from Alex Comfort, where he quoted from 'Henry V':

And gentlemen in England now a-bed
Shall think themselves accurs'd they were not here,
And hold their manhoods cheap whiles any speaks
That fought with us upon Saint Crispin's day.

People sent in cakes and all sorts. By agreement with the prison authorities they were given to local charities, because there was no way we could eat them all [laughs].

I suppose another indication of the success of the DAC at this period is that you had a meeting with the defence minister, Duncan Sandys. This was in March 1959. Were you part of that?

I think I was. Hugh certainly was. Yes, I'm sure I was. If I'm not mistaken it was all very polite.

That would have been your first meeting with a British government minister?

I think it was. The government was certainly beginning to take us a bit more seriously by then. After all, they'd seen that we could mobilise quite a lot of people.

Were you involved with the Stevenage campaign targeting trade unionists? That began in April 1959.

Yes, But the people who were most involved in that were Pat Arrowsmith, April Carter and Will Warren.

What about Laurens Otter?

Well, there was the DAC and the followers of the DAC, and Laurens was in the latter category. He came to the demonstrations and was certainly involved in the picket at Aldermaston. He was a very independent man. He studied at Trinity College, Dublin, but I don't think that he had an Irish background. He certainly didn't have an Irish accent. It was English and upper-class.

Let's talk now about the Sahara Protest Expedition, aka the Sahara Project. Had you thought about the DAC taking an international role from the beginning?

Yes, we had. We always had an internationalist outlook. Not only was there the connection with Bayard Rustin and Gene Sharp, but, as I've already mentioned, Hugh Brock would make a point of setting up a meeting for us with anyone interesting who came through London.

Bayard at that time was involved with the Committee for Non-Violent Action (CNVA) back in the United States and they gave us a lot of help as did A.J. Muste who used to write a regular column for *Peace News*.

When the issue of French nuclear tests in the Sahara came up, I went over to Paris and met the people from the Fédération

Française contra l'Armament Atomique and tried to involve them with the project. André Trocmé, who was a pastor in France during the German occupation and part of a small non-violent resistance group, was there on that occasion as was Pierre Martin and an American woman whose name escapes me. But Trocmé, who I think was chair of the group, took the view that direct action wouldn't resonate in France. So, he said, they wouldn't go along with it. But then I went with some of the people to a local café to eat and Pierre Martin was there and this American woman, and she said, 'What you've heard from Pastor Trocmé is not the whole story. There are other people in that group who would be much more sympathetic.' Anyway, in the end, Pierre Martin joined the transnational action in Ghana against the French tests, as did a young French woman, Esther Peter, who had worked with Claude Bourdet, and who, years later, became a prominent Green campaigner. But it is true that they did not have the backing of any French anti-nuclear campaign.

But that said, do you think that Trocmé was right to say that the idea of direct action wouldn't resonate?

Well, non-violent direct action *was* controversial. It was so in Britain and would certainly have been so in France too, but that's not the same as saying it would not resonate. As Pierre Martin and the young American woman pointed out in the café afterwards, there were people even at the meeting with Trocmé who took a different view, including obviously Pierre himself as he subsequently joined the protest. We were doing things that were either breaking the law or going outside normal political campaigning. Even within the Direct Action Committee itself there were people who were not in favour of some of our actions. I had a big debate with Allen Skinner on the subject of civil disobedience in a democracy in the pages of *Peace News*.

Beyond what one might call political scruples, do you think there was a nationalist tinge to the French reluctance?

Yes, I think there was. Indeed, the American woman brought up that very point. She said that it was partly because they were French. I think that the French decision to explode their bomb was partly nationalistic. The Brits have it, so we'll have it too. Why not? Not that the French were unique in that respect. After all, there was even a kind of nationalistic sentiment within CND itself. You know, the idea that the Brits with their superior morality would lead the world out of this thing.

Anyway, after that meeting in Paris I hitchhiked down to La Communauté de l'Arche, which was a pacifist community in the South of France founded by Lanza del Vasto. We thought that he would be sympathetic to our plans. He used to carry a big wooden crucifix, which I thought was a bit over-the-top [laughs]. I travelled with one of my old Pacifist Youth Action Group friends, Carol Taylor, who I bumped into at the Gare du Nord. We hitch-hiked together to the Community only to find that Lanza del Vasto was away somewhere. However, we did meet his mother and had a long talk with an activist named Rolland Marin about the Community's work and philosophy.

Didn't you also meet Louis Lecoin at this period?

Yes, but that meeting had more to do with conscientious objection than the nuclear issue. Lecoin had himself been a conscientious objector and a very important one. Later on, he would be largely responsible for getting a law on conscientious objection inscribed in the French constitution. He went on a hunger strike, putting huge pressure on the government to introduce this law for conscientious objection. I'm not sure what year that was. But, in any case, I met him in Paris and was very impressed by him. He had huge determination. He edited an anarcho-pacifist journal called *Liberté*.

Who came up with the idea for the Sahara Project?

It was April Carter. I remember her pouring over maps of the Sahara and explaining what we would have to do to get across it to the test site, which was at Reggane in the Algerian Sahara.

So, April Carter, you, Bayard Rustin and Muste ... . Who else was involved?

Bill Sutherland and Michael Scott were very important. I'd first met Bill back in the Operation Gandhi/NVRG days, when he'd helped us with a campaigning initiative in North London. He was a friend of Bayard Rustin. They went back a long way and had been in prison together for draft refusal. By the time of the Sahara Project, however, Bill had moved to Ghana and married a woman called Efua, a poet and playwright who later became Minister of Culture in Nkrumah's government. Bill, meantime, had become private secretary to Komla Gbedemah, who was Minister of Finance. So, both of them had access to President Kwame Nkrumah.

Why did you base the project in Ghana rather than somewhere else? After all, it was a very long way from the test site.

The main reasons were first that we had a key contact in Ghana, Bill Sutherland, second, the Nkrumah government was strongly opposed to the tests, and third, there was an anti-nuclear campaign already there, the Ghana Council for Nuclear Disarmament. Moreover, Algeria itself was ruled out as a base because it was still under French control and the guerrilla war of independence was in progress. Finally, we were influenced by Nkrumah's own belief in non-violence, to which he gave the title 'Positive Action', and which he modelled on Gandhi's campaign in India.

The Ghana Council for Nuclear Disarmament had government backing but was a voluntary organisation that people could contribute to in support of the project. They helped us with publicity and money for the hire of trucks and other expenses.

Michael, talk me through your attempts to get to Reggane. There were three, weren't there? But first who was Francis Hoyland, the chap who you travelled to Ghana with in the first place?

Francis Hoyland was, and still is, a well-known artist. He was also a Quaker and a member of a well-known Quaker family. I can't say that I knew him well before the Sahara Project, but he was one of 'our people. He'd come out on the demonstrations and we knew him as a reliable and committed person. He and I flew out to Ghana together. I remember how struck he was as an artist by the quality of the sunlight. I also remember that he almost always cut himself when shaving. Bayard for some reason never really got on with him.

You made your first attempt to reach the test site during the early part of December, in 1959.

The first attempt was made by the whole group, which is to say Bayard, Bill, Michael Scott, Esther Peter, Pierre Martin, Francis Hoyland, Ntsu Mokhehle, who was then President of the Basutuland National Congress, a guy from Nigeria named Hilary Arinze, several Ghanaians and myself. After that one failed, on Bayard's suggestion, I think, several of the members split off from the main group and went off to rustle up support in Nigeria, France and Ghana itself.

The second attempt was much smaller. That one involved Michael Scott, Bill and myself again and just four Ghanaians, including Orleans Lindsey and Kwame Frimpong Manso. Orleans was quite an interesting man. He was a science teacher and a musician. In fact, he composed an anti-nuclear song during the protest which he performed on a guitar. The hope was that a smaller team would prove far more flexible.

Fig 10:   The first attempt to reach Reggane. Stand-off with police at Bittou,
           Upper Volta (now Burkina Faso). Photograph by Michael Randle.
           Private Collection.

For the third attempt, which took place about a month later, we hitched a ride on some lorries that were passing through into Upper Volta. But as soon as we got off at Ouagadougou we were met by the same French officer who had stopped our second attempt. He said, 'Ah, it's you again.' Thereafter, the French military drove us to the other side of the country and dropped us over the border into Ghana.

Didn't Muste come along on that first attempt?

Muste wasn't on the team that attempted to cross the border, but he did travel to northern Ghana to coordinate and take part in discussions with several district commissioners about conditions on the Upper Volta side of the border. Having him on board was extremely important. It was an honour to meet him and to be linked up with him. He was such a huge figure in the peace movement in those days and I keenly read his regular column in *Peace News*.

In one of the articles you wrote for Peace News *about the project you describe the warm feelings towards you of ordinary Ghanaians and of how Bayard Rustin was moved to remark that his reception felt 'like a homecoming'.*

I actually have a photograph of Bayard meeting one of the tribal leaders and bowing low to him. He was very excited by the contrast with what he was used to, not only in Europe but back in the United States, where it was unusual to come across black people in positions of power.

Fig 11:   Bayard Rustin greeting a tribal chief. Photograph by Michael Randle. Private Collection.

But weren't the tribal chiefs enemies of Nkrumah?

Well, if they were, we certainly didn't experience any of that tension. In fact, I think that the government was very pleased for us to meet the chiefs. They facilitated our travelling to meet them.

Didn't you bring some films over to show the Ghanaians?

Yes, we did. We showed them in the university in Accra. We showed the Lindsay Anderson film about the first Aldermaston march and another film about the effects of the US Bikini Atoll nuclear tests in the Pacific in 1954 on a group of Japanese fishermen.

Getting back to the cultural complexities of the Sahara Project, there was an issue involving Esther Peter, one of the French members of the team. It was suggested that she was a spy.

Some of the Ghanaians were certainly suspicious of her. They thought that she was too pally with the French military, speaking to them in fluent French and so on. But there was nothing in that whatsoever. After all, she had a good history of working with the French resistance leader, Claude Bourdet. She'd been his secretary, you know. And then, of course, there's her history since. She was involved with War Resisters' International and became a leader of the ecology movement in France. I think she won some prestigious prize for her ecology work. Then, at some point, she married World Citizen No.1, Garry Davis, who wrote the book *My Country is the World,* and she became Esther Peter-Davis.

Incidentally, I also remember being told by A.K. Barden, who worked at the Bureau of African Affairs in Accra, that Nkrumah himself didn't approve of her presence in the Bureau. This followed a visit she made to me there. He wrote me something along the lines of the Osaigyefo, which means the 'Saviour', doesn't approve. This was a title that Nkrumah had taken on himself or been given. Barden, emphasising the point said, 'The Osaigyefo must be obeyed at all times.'

Then, there was also some tension between her and Bayard. But I don't know why.

Between your second and third attempt to get to the test site British Prime Minister Harold Macmillan came to Ghana. I wonder what was behind the timing of that?

That was the occasion of his famous 'Wind of change' speech, which he first delivered in Accra and then repeated in Cape Town the following February. He visited a number of African countries and spoke about the 'wind of change' blowing through Africa. Naturally, I was quite critical of Macmillan for being a conservative and pro-nuclear, and some of my critical comments were quoted in one of the main dailies in Accra.

You also wrote something for Peace News, *taking issue with his statement that the tests in the Sahara would not harm people. Quote: 'I am ashamed as an Englishman that a British Prime Minister, after what he himself describes as a warm welcome by the people of Ghana, should make such an untrue statement.' So, people were damaged by the tests?*

I don't know. But there was certainly fall-out from the tests, in northern Ghana. This was widely reported in the Ghanaian press. My comments came in response to Macmillan's statement before the tests took place that they would not harm people, something he was not in a position to say, especially given the injuries to Japanese fishermen after the US Bikini Atoll tests in 1954.

Following your third attempt to reach the test site, you stayed on in Accra to work at the Bureau of African Affairs and to help set up a training centre for non-violence. Then you also helped with the planning of The Positive Action Conference, which took place in April 1960. Can you tell me a little about those experiences?

Before going back to England, Michael Scott talked to Nkrumah about hosting a conference of liberation movements and Black-African governments to oppose both imperialism and what we in the DAC called 'nuclear imperialism', in other words, the use of African countries as test sites. There was real anger about that, not only in Ghana but in other parts of Africa. So, at Michael's suggestion I stayed on in Ghana to work with A.K. Barden at the Bureau of African Affairs, and the man who was in charge of the Bureau was N.A. Welbeck, a minister in Nkrumah's government. Basically, Barden did the running about, so to speak, but Welbeck was the minister in overall charge. My role was to bring radical leftists from Britain and other countries to Ghana to take part in the conference. So, people like John Rex and others associated with the *New Left Review* and *The New Reasoner*, and Gene Sharp, A.J. Muste, Ralph Abernathy and April Carter.

Among those who came to that conference was Frantz Fanon. In fact, he played quite a prominent role. I remember that Bill Sutherland had a lot of respect for him, for his general political radicalism that is but not for his position on violence.

So, you met Fanon?

Oh, yes. He was very determined and he had tremendous energy. I can still remember him striding through the streets of Accra. I also remember his anger. He was angry because a distinction was made in the seating at the conference between government representatives and the representatives of the liberation movements, and the Algerians were seated among the latter. As far as he was concerned, the Algerian Provisional Government/FLN was the legitimate government of Algeria, as I suppose they really were. He said, 'No. We should be seated with the Moroccans and the Tunisians.' If I'm not mistaken, he also objected in a particular meeting to the presence of Pierre Martin. Why? Because Martin was a pacifist and, as you know, Fanon was very far from that.

Of course, Nkrumah's own idea of 'positive action' was very much influenced by Gandhi. Nkrumah had been at that famous Pan-African conference in Manchester, in 1945, where many members of the African liberationist movement got together. They actually said there that the way forward was through the Gandhian method of non-violent direct action, though they didn't rule out other methods. But, in any case, in Ghana, it became a matter of pride if you'd been jailed for positive action. They used to wear these Gandhi caps with 'PG' on them, 'PG' standing for 'prison graduate'. Michael Scott, I remember, was given one.

Anyway, Nkrumah's government was hostile to the French exploding their bomb in Africa, so they were sympathetic to what the DAC was doing. People used to say, 'Go and explode your bomb in Paris if you're so keen to explode a bomb.'[laughs].

And then wasn't C.L.R. James in Ghana at that time too?

He was certainly in Ghana for a time in 1960, though I can't remember if he actually attended the conference. If you look at *Peace News* you'll see that I wrote an article about him. Like Fanon, he was another powerful figure. I had a meeting with him, which Bill Sutherland helped set up and he gave a talk to a small group of us at the Ringway Hotel where I was staying. Later on, following my involvement with the Committee of 100, I worked with his wife, Selma, in an anti-racist group, which itself led to the formation of the Campaign against Racial Discrimination (CARD). James was a very interesting person as, of course, is Selma

If I recall the article correctly, you didn't agree with his analysis of the political situation in Africa. You said that he put too much emphasis on economic factors.

Well, I must re-read it. But, of course, anarchism was my basic perspective, so I would have thought that, yes.

Wasn't it also the case though that Nkrumah had his own agenda, and that agenda ultimately trumped your own? The big issue for Nkrumah presumably was imperialism: national autonomy, the control of the

country's natural resources and so on. And in that context the nuclear issue was rather small.

Because the bomb was about to be exploded in Africa, it was very important. But in the longer term perhaps not so. But at the time there was a very immediate and passionate concern about the French exploding their bomb in the Sahara. I should add that those of us in the peace/direct action movement were also adamantly opposed to imperialism.

I mentioned earlier that one of the reasons you stayed on in Ghana was to help set up a training centre in non-violent action. Did anything come of that idea?

No. We were offered the use of a school, but nothing ever came of it due to opposition from figures within the Ghanaian government, most of whom were not pacifists. I stayed on in Accra until it became almost certain that nothing was going to happen. That's when I got a letter from Michael Scott, saying, 'Look. There's a new grouping starting in London which is looking to do direct action, but on a much larger scale than the DAC.' And that, of course, became the Committee of 100.

I get the sense from reading some of the things you wrote about your Ghanaian experiences that your views about what was happening there evolved quite quickly. That said, right from the outset you must have been uncomfortable working so closely with a government.

Yes. It was always an issue for us as to how far we should be involved with the government.

A government that from the outset was oppressive.

The Preventative Detention Act in Ghana was introduced in 1958, but the government became more oppressive during the time that I was there. Then there were limitations on the freedom of the press. I wrote an article about the issue in *Peace News*.

You also worked as a journalist during this period for an African publication. I think that it was called Voice of Africa.

Yes. *Voice of Africa* was essentially a pro-government publication. I wrote a few articles for that and helped edit it for a while. This would have been after the Sahara Project had ended. Probably at the same time as I was helping to organise the Accra conference.

Finally, while you were in Ghana did you have any private meetings with Nkrumah?

I had lunch with him on one occasion.

An interesting experience? I would imagine that for most people the prospect would have been daunting.

The meeting was to discuss Michael Scott's idea for a conference about imperialism and nuclear weapons. But, yes, I suppose that the prospect did awe me a bit. In the event, however, it was perfectly relaxed. Of course, eventually, in February 1966, Nkrumah was overthrown whilst on a visit to China. But that was a long time after my departure.

5. The Committee of 100

Michael, you've said that you were in Ghana when the Committee of 100 was first mooted.

That's right. There were two reasons for my return from Ghana. Firstly, the plan to set up a non-violent training school near Accra wasn't going anywhere. Secondly, I got a letter either from April Carter or from Michael Scott telling me that some people were discussing setting up a new committee which would put direct action against nuclear weapons on a much larger scale, and asking me if I would come back and be the secretary of that committee.

Was Alan Lovell on the committee?

Yes. He was one of the prime movers. Of course, he'd also been a key member of the Direct Action Committee.

What was the attitude of the DAC to the idea for the Committee of 100?

Well, though I wasn't party to the early discussions, I think that feelings were mixed. Certainly, my own were when I first heard about it [laughs]. On the one hand, I thought that if it did succeed in putting direct action on a much larger scale that would be all to the good. But, on the other hand, I had no idea how committed the organisers were or even if they had the organisational strength to do it.

I take it for granted that April Carter was in favour of the new committee, but what about Pat Arrowsmith?

Both April and Pat may have had some doubts about the venture. But if so, they weren't such as to prevent them joining it and devoting a great deal of energy into making it a success.

Many people, I assume, viewed the new organisation in terms of a trade-off. Okay, you'd have a larger organisation, with all the potential that would give you in terms of mass demonstrations and public impact, but then there'd be less control from the centre.

Well, it also brought in people who didn't take a pacifist position. Not that everyone in the DAC did either. For instance, Michael Scott never called himself a pacifist. He had been in the RAF during the war. But the DAC was much more orientated to the non-violent Gandhian approach. Pacifism, if you like, was part and parcel of its origins. Whereas many of the people coming into the Committee of 100 did not have that background or that perspective, though they were against nuclear weapons. And that was the meeting point for pacifists and non-pacifists.

So, right from the beginning there was a mix of pacifists and non-pacifists. Michael Scott and Bertrand Russell were at the forefront of the Committee of 100, but the initial driving force was a young American studying in Britain, Ralph Schoenman.

We'll get on to Ralph Schoenman in a moment, but one name that is new to me in relation to the Committee is Wendy Butlin. Can you tell me something about her?

Oh, yes. Great woman. She became involved with the anti-nuclear issue when the DAC were campaigning in the Midlands and she was living in Peterborough. She was working for the council at the time and became Pat Arrowsmith's partner. She was a quieter sort of person than Pat, less forthright, but just as determined. She now lives in Leeds with a different partner.

Presumably, you met Bertrand Russell shortly after returning from Ghana.

I don't think he was at the inaugural meeting of the Committee, which took place at Friends House, in the Euston Road, on October 22, but he did take part in the first Committee of 100 demonstration, which was on the 18th February 1961. In fact, he led it. One of the Sunday papers, probably *The Observer*, published a marvellous picture of him in the fading light, his hair blowing in the wind and a crowd of people behind him.

That photograph was taken close to the Ministry of Defence, wasn't it? You were protesting against the stationing of an American tender (the Proteus) *at the mouth of the Clyde.*

That's right. What happened on that occasion was that we sat down in front of the Ministry of Defence and attempted to nail up our declaration calling for the scrapping of the agreement with the Americans to base the Polaris-carrying submarines in Scotland.

I suppose that that was your 95 theses moment.

Yes, it was based precisely on Martin Luther's action. But someone, I think from the Ministry, rushed up and said, 'You can't hammer nails into the door', and a policeman seized the hammer and took it off me. Not to be defeated, however, we attached our declaration to the door with Sellotape!

Then later — it was probably during the summer — Russell invited me to his house to have a talk with him and I spent a weekend at his place at Penrhyndeudraeth, in North Wales. It was an amazing experience. His wife, Edith, was there as well and I think they were both put out by the fact I was a vegetarian. On one occasion, I was talking to Russell about prime ministers, and I remember him saying that he had known Gladstone. He actually knew the man! And then I said to him, rather naively, 'Who was the first prime minister you met?' And he said, 'The first prime minister I ever met was my grandfather, Lord John Russell.' Jesus! [laughs]. I should have done a bit more research! You see, he really was a very old man. During the First World War, he was already too old to be conscripted. But he did six months in prison for an article he wrote in a conscientious objection journal advocating that the Americans keep out of the war.

Did Ralph Schoenman go with you?

He wasn't there on that occasion. In fact, one of the reasons for the meeting was that Ralph had rowed with other members of the committee, and Russell wanted my take on it. So, I was there to try and hold things together. Ralph, after all, was a very controversial figure. He was very forthright and somewhat suspicious. Was he justified? I don't know, but before the Committee had even been publicly launched someone had inadvertently leaked our intentions to a Tory journalist called John Connell, and then we also had a problem with some of the discussions within the steering group getting into the papers. Ralph was very agitated about the latter, in particular. On one occasion he even got upset about Trevor Hatton, muttering under his breath, 'Who is this Trevor Hatton?' But Trevor Hatton was about the most genuine person you could get. He was a very steady, safe pair of hands.

I wonder to what extent these personal factors weighed with other members of the Committee? Schoenman, after all, wasn't just a suspicious person himself. He inspired suspicion in others.

There were rumours that he was a CIA agent. I don't know to this day where they came from, but I certainly have never given them any credit. The last but one time I heard from him he was working with Dick Gregory, the comedian and civil rights activist.

He could, incidentally, be quite witty. Later on, we all spent a month in Drake Hall open prison and there were quite a few well-known people among us like Christopher Logue, Arnold Wesker and Robert Bolt. On the night before we were due to be released, we got together to decide whether we should make a statement or not, and Arnold Wesker said, 'Well, it's been very much like a public school, with a little less beating and a little less buggery.' And Schoenman looked across at him and said, 'For the absence of both of which you deeply regret.' [laughs]

I also remember another occasion which reveals something about his character. We were billeted in Nissan huts, which, by the way, are much worse than conventional cells because you can't do any studying. They're too open and generally too noisy. Ralph was sitting on his bed when he should have been standing up, and this screw came over to him and said, 'Get off of yer bed!' Well, Ralph bristled and started to talk about his rights. 'I don't care', said the screw. 'Get off yer bed!' Of course, in the end Ralph had to, but he was very bolshie, quite courageously so.

What was the attitude of the CND to the Committee? One would imagine that they'd had enough trouble with the DAC already.

I think that after a while the attitude of people like Canon Collins and others in the CND was that the actions of the DAC were rather symbolic, that they weren't really coercive. This was not their view of the Committee. Because it was much bigger than the DAC they saw it as a rival and a threat and its actions as anti-democratic. In one conversation with me Canon Collins compared CND to the dog and us to the tail and complained that the tail was wagging the dog.

That said, I should add in fairness to Collins, that some months after I and others in the Committee were sent down in February 1962, he sent me a friendly and encouraging letter which I still have. I was very moved by that.

Of course, the big split between us and the CND occurred when Russell resigned from the presidency of CND. That was just after the Committee's inaugural meeting at Friends House in October 1960. He had a fierce row with the Canon over that, mixed in, it's worth adding, with a great deal of personal animosity. Russell had absolutely no time for Canon Collins. There was real hostility between them.

Am I right in thinking that Ralph Schoenman came up with the name of the Committee, with the mention of a hundred names or signatories?

It was him and, I think, Gustav Metzger and possibly one or two others. Naturally, numbers were very important to the

Committee. They wanted to ensure that it wasn't just another small Direct Action Committee-style organisation; the idea of *mass* demonstrations was that important. In fact, it was agreed that the first action would only go ahead once 2000 people had pledged to support it.

That was clever, I mean the idea of insisting on a minimum of 2000 supporters.

It was clever. But it could also have misfired. About ten days before the first demonstration we were still a bit short on the number of pledges we had received. But Ralph had terrific energy. He went around the coffee shops telling people about it. You know, 'We're gonna do it'. That sort of thing. Certainly, if we hadn't got the numbers, we couldn't have gone ahead. We'd made such an issue of it. But, in the end, we got more than 2,000. I think that it was about 5,000.

Can you tell me about your own role in the Committee? As secretary of the Committee what did you actually do?

Well, I spent most of my time just organising, writing letters, answering the phone, those sorts of things. It was a very busy time. I was in the office with Trevor Hatton and, for some of the time, with Wendy Butlin. Then Ian Dixon was also there.

So, the 18th February 1961. That, as you've said, was the date of the first demonstration.

Well, before the demonstration we received a police notice saying that certain streets were not to be used. In effect it was a warning: go there, and you'll be arrested. These streets included the area around the Ministry. You see, we were still keeping up the DAC's tradition of letting the police know about our plans in advance.

Anyway, we met in Trafalgar Square, walked down Whitehall then round the back and squatted in front of the Ministry of

Defence. That was where I didn't manage to nail up those theses you mentioned [laughs]. It wasn't a silent march like the first one to Aldermaston, but it was certainly sober. We sat down and the demonstration stretched right round to Whitehall. Michael Scott was there and the Scottish poet, Hugh MacDiarmid, Lord and Lady Russell, Herbert Read, the MP Anne Kerr, and other notables.

Fig 12:   Part of a flyer advertising the first C100 demonstration. University of Bradford, Special Collections, Cwl MRL/2.

What kind of public response did you get to the demonstration?

It was everything we wanted. In the run-up to the demonstration, the press had been speculating: is this going to be a flop? Can they pull it off? But it was an absolute triumph. And the reaction was, we'd done it! It may also have been carried in the international papers, particularly as Bertrand Russell was involved.

Your next major action was at Holy Loch in March.

That wasn't a Committee action. It was organised by the DAC, of which I was still the chair until it dissolved soon afterwards on the grounds that the Committee of 100 was continuing the work on a larger scale.

But still a great headache to the state. Where do you put these people if you do arrest them?

Well, that was part of Ralph Shoenman's and George Clark's approach: we'll fill the prisons. It was part of the rhetoric at any rate.

By the way, you've just mentioned Anne Kerr. Did the Committee have the support of other Labour MPs?

I can only remember one Labour MP on the Committee. That was Anne Kerr. I think that she was actually arrested on one of the demonstrations. But, yes, we still had the support of our old Labour friends, people like Frank Allaun and Fenner Brockway.

You just mentioned George Clark. What do you remember of him?

George was very involved with the organisation of the Committee. I first met him at the inaugural meeting, back in October 1960. I think he came from a radical left, Labour Party background. He was quite egotistical and tended to rub people up the wrong way. He also made something of a habit of threatening to resign when he didn't get his way. On one occasion Ian Dixon called his bluff and said 'Ok, George, resign.' But he didn't. He was a good organiser and was also prepared to put his liberty and even his health on the line, on one occasion going on a prolonged fast. Later, he set up the Caravan for Peace project. He and others went around the country in a caravan, promoting nuclear disarmament and non-violent action. At some point he married a journalist and author called Mary Gregg, who was also involved in the campaign. However, George and Ralph never got on.

In terms of your own politics, a couple of weeks after the first Committee of 100 demonstration you published an article in Peace News *called, 'Is it Revolution we're after?' In that you say, 'Mass disobedience means revolution'. That sounds like extreme incitement.*

Well, that was my feeling. So much had to change. You couldn't just knock off one element and expect everything to be alright. Violence was built into the whole structure of the state system. I was still very much on the anarchist wing, after all. I remember the response of Allen Skinner to it. He said he found the article stimulating but that there was a big hole in it. However, he didn't spell out to me what and I wish now that I had pressed him on that.

Would it be fair to say that you and your fellow anarchists were living in a bubble, egging each other on, becoming unreal about the situation?

I think that we hadn't thought through exactly how this would all work, the notion of a *levée en masse* as it were. We were influenced by anarchist ideas about self-organisation. I remember having a discussion with April Carter on the subject: how do you actually see this working out? She had her feet more on the ground than I did.

Do you remember anything about the April 1961 Aldermaston march?

I certainly didn't speak in Trafalgar Square on that occasion or at the start of any of the marches. But it was a huge march that year. That was the occasion when Ralph Schoenman led a breakaway contingent to the US embassy. That did nothing to sweeten relations with the CND leadership.

What were Schoenman's politics, by the way?

He wasn't a pacifist. He was radical leftist. He wasn't a philosophical anarchist, but he did tend in that direction, which is to say towards the idea that I've just mentioned, the idea of the *levée en masse,* getting thousands of people to object to the whole system. I don't know if he ever expounded a total position.

The second major Committee demonstration was in late April, and again in London.

That's right, 29th April 1961. That was the one where we planned to hold a public assembly outside Parliament when the MPs were sitting, and that was illegal. The action began with a public meeting in Trafalgar Square, followed by a walk down Whitehall to Parliament Square. We had declared in advance that if the police blocked our passage down Whitehall we would sit down in the road. The police funnelled us to one side of the road and then prevented us from going any further. We then sat down. According to one account, 999 people were arrested. Quite a contrast with the February demonstration when no one was arrested. I think that if the police had not arrested us the demonstration might have been written off as a bit of a flop because the numbers involved had about halved. So, the authorities really saved it for us [laughs]. The charges were trivial; they were obstruction. Demonstrators were taken up before a magistrate on the same day and he or she imposed a fine. And if you didn't pay the fine—as I didn't—you were sentenced to a day in prison, which meant that you were held in the police cells until the court rose.

Wasn't this about the time that you first met your future wife, Anne?

It was. Anne was friends with Helen Allegranza, who was the Committee of 100's Welfare Officer … . Well, I'll let her tell you about what happened afterwards.

Was Russell involved in this demonstration?

No, he wasn't.

Let's talk about Peace News *again. During this period, it was going through a metamorphosis. Some of the older, PPU, hands were pushed to one side and a livelier, more culturally literate group took over.*

Yes, a new radical wing was in charge, which included people like Chris Farley and Alan Lovell. Alan as I've said was writing about film and very much from the anarchist perspective. That said, Hugh Brock was still there, and he was on the radical wing as well.

Sybil Morrison felt particularly ill-used.

Sybil's column was shunted onto the back page. At the time I was delivering *Peace News* as part of my job and one of the places I delivered it to was the Peace Pledge Union. On one occasion, Sybil was there, and she was definitely not amused. She said, 'So, I'm on the back page now, am I? I suppose the next thing is that I'll disappear altogether.'

It got a bit worse than that. She accused Chris Farley of deliberate rudeness and claimed in one extraordinary letter to Brock that you as a group were spying upon her.

Oh, I didn't see that.

In the letter, she deplored – and this is a nice phrase – 'certain journalistic attitudes' that had crept into the paper. What do you think she meant by that?

I think that we were a bit too brash. But there was still some continuity, in spite of our New Leftish preoccupations. Hugh Brock and Allen Skinner were still around.

```
.... Peace News
.... Treatment of her article, date ......
.... Treatment of her article (general)
.... Peace News
.... The Editor (Hugh Brock)
.... The ex-Editor (Hugh Brock)
.... Not publishing her letter about pacifism, date .....
.... The rudeness of Alan/Chris/......
.... Ignoring THE PLEDGE
.... Peace News
.... Editorial policy
.... Not reporting her speech at ........ ("Say No to War")
.... A proposed Dick Sheppard anniversary number
.... "The Campaign for Nuc...." (muffled scream)
.... An important news story (someone signed the pledge)
.... Lack of attention to her complaint of ........(date), no.....

She will be:

.... Raising the matter at ...... committee/Board/AGM on ......
       at which she will be totally disarming
.... Calling an emergency conference/committee
.... Resigning (again)
.... Writing/phoning again today
```

Fig.13.   Part of a Chris Farley skit on Sybil Morrison's habit of complaining about her treatment at *Peace News*. 'She [Sybil] will be: ... Raising the matter at ...'. University of Bradford, Special Collections, Cwl HBP 5/2.

In May 1961, Michael, you published another important article in Peace News, *'Principles, Strategy and Tactics at the Holy Loch'. I mention this article because you describe the action at Holy Loch as 'probably the most significant piece of direct action and civil disobedience' since Swaffham, i.e. North Pickenham, in December 1958. It was the occasion when 50 or so demonstrators tried to board the 'Polaris depot-ship',* Proteus.

Yes. That one did have a very considerable impact. It was preceded by a march from London during which we were in touch with churches, trade unions, Quaker meetings and so on along the way. Not that I was on the whole march. I think I went up by train later on and stopped with a trade union activist in Glasgow. They were a very lively group there. I didn't take part in the attempt to board the ship, but Terry Chandler did. He was one of a number of people who tried to get to the ship by kayak.

This was the swansong for the DAC?

It proved that. Again, we had a very responsible position. When it looked as if the Committee of 100 was having a really big impact, that our job was being done, but on a larger scale, we decided that there was simply no point in having two separate committees. In any case, most of the people who were on the DAC were on the Committee, some of them on the steering group.

That said, there were a few diehards, people who didn't want to see the DAC disbanded. One was Mary Ringsleben. Do you remember her?

Very well. She was from Leeds and a very good friend of Wendy Butlin. She was a very strong CND and Direct Action Committee supporter. And then later she joined the Committee of 100. She died a couple of years ago.

By the way, did you have much in the way of a social life at this time? I have the sense that your anti-nuclear activities swallowed up your other interests.

I certainly didn't have much social life [laughs]. If I did go to the pictures it would be with Anne and my fellow campaigners. I remember seeing Bergman's *Wild Strawberries*. We used to go the Academy Cinema in the West End, where they showed films like that. I used to take note of what Alan suggested. If he said that a film was a good one, then I would make a point of seeing it. In fact, my cultural horizons were widening in all sorts of ways at this period — not just thanks to Alan and *Peace News*, but also to the *New Statesman*, which I was still reading. I was particularly interested in what some of the younger playwrights were doing, people like John Arden and Arnold Wesker. And then in some of the more interesting things coming from the Continent. For example, I remember seeing the Brecht play, *The Good Woman of Setzuan*, at Stratford East.

What about music? Were your main interests still classical?

Not entirely. Alan Lovell got me into jazz and the blues, pointing me in the direction of George Melly, who I also knew from DAC days and the Committee of 100.

Do you remember what sort of books you were reading at the time?

Well, following the April demonstration and I was in the police cell for the day, I know exactly what I was reading. It was *Brighter than a Thousand Suns* by Robert Jungk. Another book I read at about that time was *Doctor Zhivago*. I remember mentioning it to Bertrand Russell, who said that he found it 'overlong'. And then I was also reading poetry.

Did you take part in the late August demonstration at the Russian embassy?

I don't think I took part. But I was one of the people who organised it. We were protesting against the resumption of Soviet nuclear tests. Anne was arrested and fined for her part in it.

Now, during September 1961, with another major demonstration on the horizon, you, Russell, George Clark, Schoenman and a number of other leading figures in the Committee were imprisoned for refusing to be bound over to 'keep the peace'.

That's right. In the lead up to September we called for an even larger demonstration in Trafalgar Square, followed again by a public assembly in Parliament Square. Well, this time the authorities banned the meeting in Trafalgar Square. And here again they made a tactical mistake because gatherings in Trafalgar Square were a long-established tradition. About a week before the event could take place about forty or so members of the committee, including Russell, his wife Edith, Arnold Wesker, Christopher Logue, Alex Comfort, Robert Bolt, Ralph Schoenman, George Clark and myself were summoned. We all appeared before the magistrate. There's a nice picture of us walking towards Bow Street Magistrates' Court. We were ordered to be bound over to keep the peace. Our response was that we were the ones trying to keep the peace.

If you didn't agree to be bound over, you were sentenced to a month's imprisonment or in some cases to two. Russell and I also think his wife, Edith, were initially sentenced to two months. But the lawyers had a word with the magistrate: 'You do realise, don't you, that Lord Russell is aged ninety and on an all-liquid diet? Do you really want him to die in prison?' That put the wind up the magistrate who reduced the sentences on both Russells to a week. At their respective prisons, Brixton and Holloway, they were taken straight to the hospital wing for the duration. I was given a month, as were most of the others.

So, there was a good crowd of us. We were held in Brixton Prison overnight and then taken by coach to Drake Hall open prison, in Staffordshire. That wasn't a bad experience because there were enough of us to form a fairly homogenous community. However, there was one screw in particular who was very hostile. We would all have to line up in the morning—it was all very military in style. 'Attention! Turn left! Quick march! One, two. One, two. One, two.' And one of the ways of rebelling was to refuse to march, though, curiously, one or two people seemed rather keen on it and doing it properly, among them the anarchist Alex Comfort!

Robert Bolt, the playwright, had actually resigned from the Committee before being summoned. But as an act of solidarity he stuck with us and accepted the sentence. But the film producer Sam Spiegel, who was working with Bolt on *Lawrence of Arabia* drove up from London and demanded he signed the binding over order to secure his release. Reluctantly, he did so as did Alex Comfort. We all had that option. You only had to sign a paper promising to be of good behaviour, because, of course, what they were trying to do was to stop us from organising any more demonstrations. Anyway, Alex signed himself out on the grounds that he had to get back to this illegal transmitter he had assembled which broadcast anti-nuclear propaganda when the main television transmitter went off. It was a great idea. But I'm not sure how big an audience it ever got.

Something else that stands out in my memory took place during one of the evenings when we could do more or less what we liked. There was a space where we could all meet, which may have been part of the refectory. Anyway, Christopher Logue gave a poetry reading, in which he included a dramatic rendering of Yeat's poem 'Easter 1916', with its refrain, 'A terrible beauty is born.'

I suppose the jailing of Bertrand Russell must have had a huge impact in publicity terms.

Oh, it did. The impact of that was huge as was the jailing of Labour MP, Anne Kerr. It was headline news.

Before going to Bow Street, had you arranged with other members of the Committee of 100 to take over your roles?

Oh, yes, absolutely. We had a shadow committee in waiting that worked very well. Pat Pottle took over my role.

Pat Pottle is a new name in this context. Had he been involved with the Committee for long?

I think so. He wasn't involved at all in the Direct Action Committee. He probably knew Ralph Schoenman and came in from that direction. I liked him right from the start, but I don't think I really got to know him until we were in Wormwood Scrubs together.

Okay, so you missed the 17th of September, 'Battle of Britain Day' demonstration.

Yes, I missed it, of course. But I did catch it on the prison television. I remember the occasion. Albert Schweitzer's picture came up as the first item on the news because he had sent a message of support to Bertrand Russell. Schweitzer was a sort of saintly figure due to his work in Central Africa. I still have a letter that he wrote to the Committee. It's in German, and someone has done a translation into English on the other side. Incidentally when the press and television were no longer around the police were very rough. About 1,300 people were arrested.

Christopher Farley and one or two others described the demonstration as the Committee's highpoint, but others took a contrary view. Nicolas Walter, for example, writing in Peace News, *said that it was disorganised; there was 'no sense of direction, no one knew what to do.' This was because you and other central figures were in prison, presumably.*

Well, all we knew was that we were inside and that the demonstration had gone ahead. In the open prison we didn't get a sense of things falling apart. For us, it was a triumph that it went ahead in spite of all the warnings and the banning of the meeting in Trafalgar Square.

I think I'm right in saying that it was at about this time that pressure built up to decentralise the Committee, to give more autonomy to people in the regions.

My feeling, and it was a feeling consistent with my anarchism generally, was that if the Cambridge Committee of 100 and the Sussex Committee of 100 and the Welsh Committee of 100 and so on wanted to go their own way that was all to the good.

Well, the theory may have been good, but what about its practical impact? Didn't the Committee lose some of its momentum?

Yes, I suppose it did. But, anyway. following the September demonstration, which, from our point of view, had been such a success, there was a move to take these large numbers of people to the bases and to have some practical effect there, by blocking their operation. We called for 50,000 people to go to the bases. This was where having divided up and having different committees was less successful because it diffused our forces. Now, whether it would have been much different if we'd all gone to the same base, I don't know. I believe a total of around 7,000 demonstrated that day, a substantial number but well short of the numbers we had called for. Moreover, the demonstrations didn't have the same impact as they would have had if that number of people staged a sit-down in one place. On the other hand, in the larger localities, like Glasgow and Cardiff, the demonstrations probably did still have a major impact. But, on subsequent actions, the numbers declined. Some people in the movement argued that to keep the numbers up you needed to keep the protests in the city centres, others argued it made more sense to blockade a base than to stop people from going about their normal business.

So, on the 9th of December, demonstrations were held at a number of bases, but most importantly at RAF Wethersfield?

Yes, we're now at Wethersfield. But prior to Wethersfield the police raided the Committee office and everyone who was there had their names taken. The police took papers, anything they thought relevant to our plans: minutes, jottings, a part of someone's diary. They even took a list of people who had attended my sister Terry's twenty-first birthday party! I was lodging with Hugh Brock at the time, and they raided Hugh's house. Then the Attorney-General warned that if the Wethersfield demonstration went ahead anyone who took part in it would risk prosecution under the Official Secrets Act. That was a draconian threat. You could be given 14 years or even more if they convicted you of conspiracy to breach the act. In that case the sentence could be of indefinite length.

On the 8th of December I held a press conference. While it was still going on, the news broke that Ian Dixon, Trevor Hatton, Helen Allegranza had been arrested for conspiracy to breach the Official Secrets Act, and that there were warrants out for the arrest of Pat Pottle and myself. There'd already been a story that day in the papers stating that the Official Secrets Act would be invoked, and

I'd responded that this was either a bluff or a very serious threat to civil liberties.

You were in a pub near Fleet Street, weren't you?

That's right. I was in The Feathers in Tudor Street. The journalists were all taking notes, and they immediately all ran out to file the story. I came out and Chief Inspector Stratton was there. He put his hand on my shoulder and said, 'You know me, Mike.' [laughs] I knew him right back from the days of the Direct Action Committee, so he was a very familiar figure. He used to keep an eye on all of us. Pat Pottle, when he heard there was a warrant out for his arrest, went on the run. He played cat and mouse with the police for a while, but then he decided that our defiant response was the correct one, and effectively handed himself in.

He'd seen what you were made of.

Well, he never doubted that. But he saw that we were having an impact by standing by our opinions and by saying that if the issue went to trial we'd defend ourselves.

There's a photograph of you on the phone at the pub. You look rather chipper.

Well, I knew what was coming and it was part of the whole Gandhian tradition that you were to go to prison for your beliefs.

So, then what happened? You were taken again to Bow Street?

That's right. They took us to Bow Street magistrates' court, charged us, and then released us on police bail.

But then, of course, Wethersfield and the other demonstrations still went ahead. Would you say that they were a success? George Clark, in a very interesting pamphlet called Second Wind, *describes the planning that went into the demonstrations as deficient. 'The preparations [for*

Wethersfield] were slight, and there was a minimum of consultation with supporters.' And then Nicolas Walter and Peter Cadogan also put in a pennyworth. For starters, says Cadogan, the machinations concerning the cancellation of the coaches taking people to Wethersfield should have been foreseen. In other words, that you'd become out of touch and elitist.

Well, as for the cancelled coaches that really couldn't have been helped. We'd booked a particular coach firm, but a day or two before the demonstrations the authorities persuaded another firm to raise an objection. The grounds were that they had the franchise for that route and as people were to be charged a small fee, this amounted to a breach of it. The firm we had booked then abruptly cancelled. Fortunately, British Rail stepped in and agreed to put on a special train, and a few people turned up in cars. So, everyone who turned up to catch the bus was able to get to Wethersfield. I can be quite definite about that because I stayed at the pick-up point until everyone had gone.

Fig 14:   Wethersfield and Ruislip: Legal Briefing. Front cover. C100 supporters were typically well prepped in respect of their rights if arrested. University of Bradford, Special Collections, Cwl MRL/2.

Before we finish today, I'll just quote a remark of Nicolas Walter. He said, 'In September they arrested the wrong people, but in December they arrested the right people. Before Wethersfield the initiative was in our hands, after Wethersfield it was in theirs.' Do you think that's a fair comment?

I think that Wethersfield and the other demonstrations weren't successful in the way we had hoped. That is certainly the case. But neither were they disastrous.

Do you remember much of the demonstration?

Oh, yes. I can still remember the helicopter whirring overhead. But discretion being the better part of valour, I decided not to take part in the actual blockade. I spoke to Alan Lovell about it before taking my decision. It wouldn't have looked good. Ian Dixon did take part and was arrested and imprisoned during the lead-up to the trial. But I decided not to put my liberty on the line between the demonstration and the upcoming trial. I thought that it was reasonable not to take part.

Finally, just to put the situation in a larger context, Michael, this was also the time of the Eichmann trial in Jerusalem. Eichmann, of course, claimed that he was just following orders, that he never hurt anyone directly himself. I wonder if the trial played into your responses to Britain's possession of nuclear weapons in any way?

Peace News covered the Eichmann case extensively. We saw ourselves as following the dictum that you don't just obey orders, that you have a responsibility to follow your conscience.

6. Marriage, The 'Official Secrets' Trial and Prison

[On this and on other, later, occasions Michael's wife, Anne, was present for at least part of the interview].
Before discussing the trial, Michael, and your subsequent imprisonment, I'd like to begin by talking to Anne.

Anne, I believe that you were working as a volunteer in the Welfare Section of the Committee of 100 when you first met Michael?

That's right, I was simply doing some voluntary typing for Helen Allegranza. Helen was the Welfare Secretary of the Committee. But I had no idea what those guys were about at all. Helen's husband, Stan, owned a London cab, and he moved me and a friend, who was a niece of Helen, when we were doing a flit from one flat to another, and I said, 'Is there anything I can do for you two in return?' And then Helen sparked up and said, 'Well, you can type, can't you?' I guess she must have known that I worked at an ad agency. So, I went to the Committee's office to type up envelopes for a mail shot. That was all I did [laughs].

So, you knew nothing about the Committee before that moment?

All I knew was that Carol, my flatmate, was a relative of Helen's and that her father was a policeman in Bridlington, who had said to Carol, 'Steer clear of Helen. She's trouble.' So, Carol didn't get involved in anything. She didn't type anyway, so I ended up going along and doing this favour for Helen. Then I went along a few more times.

Then at the end of the first day Michael appeared, having spent a day in the cells at Bow Street for the non-payment of a fine. I was vaguely shocked by the fact that he'd been locked up all day. Anyway, I thought, what kind of a man is this?

What was his appearance like in those days?

He was pretty scruffy in a middle-class sort of way. You know, Jesus sandals and a tweed jacket. But he was wearing a tie. There's a picture of him with Vanessa Redgrave, that's how I remember him. He's wearing a brown tweed jacket.

He was eight years older than me. I was twenty, so he was definitely in the older man category and, anyway, I had my eye on another guy in the Committee office, a Cambridge undergraduate called Nick Johnson, and he had his eye on me!

The ad agency I worked for, by the way, was Young and Rubicam. No one remembers this now, but they put out the first advertisement on ITV for Murray Mints. They were very American. They certainly wouldn't have approved of me volunteering for the Committee of 100! It was through the ad agency that I'd first met Carol.

Do you agree that you were the keener one, Michael?

Michael: Oh, I was definitely the keener one.

Anne: I had to be persuaded. That particular weekend, I was staying over with Helen Allegranza. It was Hiroshima Day, August 6, by which time I'd got very interested in what she was doing. After the demo it was pouring with rain and I was soaked through. I went back to Helen's flat, off Oxford Circus, and it was there that Michael phoned to ask me out. I said, 'No', thinking I'm not going out with that scruffy old man! The fact that he'd been locked up bothered me too. But Helen, who I think had a bit of a crush on Michael herself, and also I think revered him to some extent, sort of told me off. She told me a bit about Michael. Then when he asked me again, I said, 'Yes'. But that was nearly the end of it as well. He shamed me in a public place [laughs]. We went to the Odeon, Leicester Square, to see a film and the Pathé News came on, which was part of the programme in those days, and it was about a German Panzer regiment training in Wales. Michael shouted,

'Shame!' I was so shocked. I'd never been with anyone who would do that sort of thing. I was wriggling in my seat, thinking I've got a whole evening of this. And then they played the bloody national anthem. Everybody stood up. They used to play it before the main film, because if they played it at the end of the programme everybody rushed out. So, I stood up. But who didn't stand up? The man next to me. I just thought, who is this person?

It was a man of iron principle!

But that didn't mean a thing to me at that age. I just stood there wondering how I could escape from the situation. I still haven't found out [laughs].

But you went out again, of course.

Well, after that I got seduced in a sense by his mother. He described his family and for some reason I got the idea that they had a farm in Ireland. But the truth was that she was Irish and that they had a farm in England. Anyway, I liked the sound of all that, and thought, oh well, maybe. In fact, shortly after that Michael saw me home to Clapham Common. He missed the last bus, so he had to stay the night, and we stayed up all night talking.

Looking back at Michael's schedule during this period, I'm surprised that he had the time for a relationship.

It was difficult. He was always off at meetings or something like that. And, yes, that did cause some friction. I even went on a demonstration outside the Russian embassy because he was at a meeting. I was so cross. I thought, I'll show him. I sat down and got arrested—the only time I have been. I remember thinking to myself: I've done it. I was arrested with Ewen MacColl, the Scottish folk singer. That was quite reassuring because [whispers], I was very scared. I was bailed and a month later I thought I'm not going to pay the fine. But I did pay it because I got a letter saying that I would be arrested and taken to court if I didn't. Five pounds it was, nearly a week's wages. Anyway, by then, I'd begun to think of Michael as very special.

And then you got to know Michael's friends in the movement. You've mentioned Helen.

Yes, and the likes of which I'd never met before. You see, I came from suburban Bedfordshire. I wasn't in that sort of world at all. But it was leave him or join them really. And then I began to like the people that were involved, especially when they were quite well-known people [laughs]. That was attractive.

Any impressions of Hugh Brock?

Oh, he was a lovely man. He was very tall and a real gentleman. In fact, both Hugh and his wife Eileen were always very welcoming to me. I remember when Michael was imprisoned for a month and I went to their house to pick up some things for him and Eileen opened a wardrobe on the landing that was full of Michael's socks, and she joked how nice they smelled! They were really very fond of him.

Let's talk about other things now. In late December 1961 to early January 1962, Michael, you attended a conference in Beirut to establish a World Peace Brigade.

Yes, that's right. This was something that had been in the air for a while, based on Gandhi's Shanti Sena or Peace Army. The idea was that instead of having an armed international army of some kind you could build up a non-violent peace force. War Resisters' International came in behind it very strongly. A.J. Muste and Bayard Rustin were at the conference and among the prime movers of the idea in the States. I travelled back from Beirut with Bayard and we got on very well. I remember that one of my old friends from Ghana days, E.C. Quaye, Chairman of the Accra Municipal Council was there. When I went over for the Sahara Project, he was one of the people who had greeted me when I landed at the airport near Accra. Later on, after I had left Ghana, there had been an attempt on Nkrumah's life, and Quaye was one of the people who was arrested in connection with it. Some of them I think were sentenced to death. I remember writing to Nkrumah noting what a positive role Quaye had played in the Sahara Project and pleading that he should not be executed. Anyway, he did come to Beirut but found it incredibly cold and left early. Bayard said, 'Well, in terms of his usefulness, I don't think it's going to make much difference.'

One other thing: I remember travelling over on the plane with an extraordinary man called Ernest Bader, who ran an engineering company which had a strong element of workers participation. We had to stop off in Prague, this at the time when I was on bail under the Official Secrets Act! I thought then that maybe I should send a postcard to Inspector Stratton. I didn't actually do it. But it really would have put the wind up them [laughs].

Am I right in thinking that most of the delegates at the conference were Westerners?

Yes, that's right. There were some Indians and very few Africans. There were two very prominent Indians there, Ramachandran and another man called Devi Presad, both of whom had been involved in Gandhi's campaigns. Devi went on to become the general secretary of War Resisters' International. I'm still in touch with his sons and grandsons. There was also a French priest, who was very well known for his work amongst the poor, Abbé Pierre.

Would you say that from your point of view the conference was largely an extension of the work you'd done in Ghana?

Yes. But it added a more international flavour to it. I think it arose in part out of those international expeditions; another one was the peace walk from San Francisco to Moscow, which was organised by the Committee for Non-Violent Action (CNVA).

Bayard was involved in that too, and April Carter dropped her other commitments to organise the European phase of it.

I'll bowl some of the names of other people at the conference at you: Albert Bigelow ...

Oh, yes. Albert Bigelow sailed his ship the *Golden Rule* into the United States' nuclear testing zone in the Marshall Islands in 1958, so shortly after Harold Steele's attempt to sail to Christmas Island.

Arlo Tatum.

Arlo Tatum was the secretary of War Resisters' International. He was very enthusiastic about the World Peace Brigade idea. In fact, at one point, he said, maybe we should put the WRI to one side for a while and focus instead on the brigade; let that be the focus of our energies.

And then there was another chap, who may not have attended the conference, but who did attend some of the preliminary meetings, Richard Hauser.

He was married to Yehudi Menuhin's sister, Hephzibah. I didn't really know him, but, indirectly, I got a very negative report from Ted Roszak, the American who was to take over the editorship of *Peace News* in 1964. I don't know the details of the dealings Roszak had with Hauser, but he really didn't like him at all. By the way, Roszak was a great guy, a very interesting character. Ted, Alan Lovell, Marion Glean and myself set up this anti-racist group, which eventually led to the formation of the Campaign against Racial Discrimination formed (CARD).

Now, you married on the 9th of February 1962. I'm surprised that you had the time to fit the wedding in. Can you remind me, was it a church wedding?

Michael: It was; it was a Church of England wedding. Not that I believed in the religious part of it. But I think that Anne's mum would have been upset had we chosen a registry office.

Anne: And yours. Things were very different in those days. Nowadays you can get married in someone's back garden. But we went to the local church.

Anne, am I right in thinking that your dad was dead by that point?

My biological father was killed near Arnhem in 1944. He was a paratrooper and part of that 'bridge too far' episode. So, 'dad' was my mother's second husband. My mother remarried when I was about eight.

The best man at your marriage was a man you've mentioned a couple of times already: Trevor Hatton. What can you tell me about Trevor?

Michael: Trevor had been in the Friends Ambulance Unit (FAU) as an alternative to National Service. The FAU was an Ambulance Service run by the Quakers. He was treasurer of the Committee of 100 and an accountant. I didn't know very much about him before he came on the Committee of 100, but he was very steady and very respectable. He was one of the six Committee people sentenced under the Official Secrets Act in February 1962. I shared a cell with him for a while. He had quite a wry sense of humour.

Anne: He was a humanist, a bit like a Quaker and a very quiet and unassuming man. He died young.

Michael: Yes, very suddenly.

I read somewhere that you took your honeymoon in a bubble car. Is that right?

Michael: Yes, it belonged to my sister, Terry, who I was very close to.

I didn't think that you could get two people in a bubble car.

Anne: Oh, yes. And you could get a baby on the back shelf as well. A couple of years later, we borrowed it again and travelled in it with our first son, Seán [laughs]. We hadn't made any plans to go away, but Terry lent us the car for the weekend, so that we could go on honeymoon before the trial. We headed for the New Forest.

Michael: Yes, we stopped off at Henley and Salisbury.

Being February, it must have been freezing!

Anne: Yes, it was beautifully planned [laughs]. We stopped off in Henley at a hotel by the river. The staff were very snotty when we arrived, possibly because we were a bit scruffy. But then when the next morning pictures of the wedding were on every front page, their attitude changed. Even though we were not their cup of tea, I suppose they were impressed by the publicity. The lady on the front desk was certainly a lot nicer. But Michael himself was often preoccupied with other matters. Even on our honeymoon he had to go off and ring Ralph Schoenman, who I hated with a vengeance. We were in Winchester by then and I was bloody annoyed [laughs]. There was just something about the man. I'd never met anyone like him. And I couldn't understand why he was so powerful.

Michael: He had a lot of energy and drive and nerve. He thought nothing of going to see Bertrand Russell and Jean-Paul Sartre, telling them things like, 'You've got to support this. It's a life and death issue.'

Anne, you didn't have a soft spot for Schoenman then, but what about your future brother-in-law, Alan Lovell?

Anne: Oh, gosh. I liked Alan a lot. He was a softly spoken, very gentle person. Later, we shared a house: me, Michael, Michael's sister, Terry, and Alan. Terry was at University in Leeds at the time, so she'd usually only come down at the weekend. Alan was alone in the house a lot and we'd share meals and so on. He was really into cooking; he taught me a lot. Lots of things were new to me at the time [laughs].

In personality, he was a bit like Michael perhaps?

Anne: Yes. I think that's why Terry married him! Alan was Michael's best friend at the time. Michael's mum used to say that Terry, who was very close to Michael, would have to marry someone like him. Nowadays, Terry looks after Alan as well as her later partner, Mick. By the way, Terry was the first women to get a first in sociology at Leeds. Now, she's an emeritus professor of gender studies. She was also a pioneer feminist. She's a really incredible person.

Did Terry draw you into feminism?

Anne: Initially, I was in awe of her. I didn't have a political background at all. Whenever she came home from Leeds, she and Michael would be having intellectual discussions, whereas I always seemed to be pregnant, so I would just be standing there at the stove, boiling nappies, etc. and feeling rather stupid. However, I wouldn't say that I felt excluded as such; but I did lack the knowledge to take part in their conversations. I was also tired a lot of the time. It was only later on when I too had done something with my career that I felt really able to engage with her. And then something funny happened that further levelled us a bit. One day, Terry revealed that she was watching *Coronation Street*, but for sociological reasons. And I thought, God, that's amazing. Because I like *Coronation Street* too. She's human, after all! And then I went on to discover that there were many things that she was unsure about. Things evened out in the end.

Of course, for a lot of the time during those years you were effectively a single parent.

Anne: Well, yes. And for much of the time I just felt swamped. Seán, our first son, was born halfway through Michael's first major prison sentence. We were always struggling for money. It was a daily struggle to keep things going. We moved into the house with Terry and Alan when he came out, in February 1963; that was how that came about.

Okay, you've had your honeymoon, so we've come to the 12th of February 1962, the beginning of the Old Bailey trial. I must say that both of you look quite carefree in the photographs taken of you on your way to the trial. But, surely Michael, you must have been very anxious?

Michael: Possibly I was a bit, but we had the support of the Committee and that whole commitment to Gandhi and the non-violent struggle and an acceptance that prison was part of that.

Just to be clear, who was standing trial? You and who else?

Michael: There were six of us: Terry Chandler, Trevor Hatton, Ian Dixon, Pat Pottle, Helen Allegranza and myself. In other words, the entire paid staff. A few days before they arrested us, the Attorney-General made a speech in the Commons warning that anyone who took part in the demonstrations would be liable to be arrested and charged under the Official Secrets Act. We didn't back down, so I guess they wanted to make an example of us.

And the charges were?

We were charged on two counts under the act: firstly, conspiring to enter Wethersfield air base 'for a purpose prejudicial to the safety and interests of the state'; secondly, conspiracy to incite others to do likewise.

Tell me about your defence council, Jeremy Hutchinson?

Michael: He was spot on, an absolutely first-class barrister. The way things worked in those days was that you went to a solicitor and he or she put you in touch with a barrister, and Jeremy I suppose was the obvious candidate. Of course, we had several meetings with him before the trial. Originally, my name was first on the list and I was going to defend myself, but then Jeremy said, 'Look, I'm prepared to do it, but I don't want someone going before I put the legal case for the defence.' So, he persuaded me that I should be one of the people defended by him, and Pat Pottle would be the one who defended himself. I think that Pat was a bit disappointed because he wanted us both to do it. A few years ago, Thomas Grant wrote a very good book about ours and other cases.

Anne: We went to the book launch and met Jeremy. I have a picture on my phone. He was coming up to a hundred, so he was a very old man, but he gave the most amazing speech; it was crystal clear and you could hear every word of it. Our granddaughter was with us and she was stunned by his clarity. I went up to him afterwards and got him to sign our copy of the book.

Michael: Yes, he signed the book and wrote, 'What a client!'

Why was Jeremy Hutchinson such an important figure? What had he done before?

Anne: He'd represented Penguin in the *Lady Chatterley's Lover* case.

Michael: And, of course, the other big thing he'd done was the Blake case, just a few months earlier.

Meaning what?

Michael: Oh, that he'd defended George Blake on the charge of spying.

Now, for you and the others this was primarily a 'political' trial. You were being tried for your beliefs, first and foremost that you had a moral 'duty' to act against nuclear weapons. But the prosecution didn't accept that argument, did they?

As far as they were concerned, we were simply law-breakers. They took the view that the reasons for our actions were totally beside the point.

I think I'm right in saying that you had a bit of beef with Sir Reginald Manningham-Buller, the Attorney-General.

Michael: Yes. Even before the trial could begin, he'd made it clear that he was not best pleased with us. A lot of our supporters had made their way into a large hall adjacent to the court room. Some carried banners bearing the words 'Hutchinson v. Manningham-Buller', as if the trial was some sort of football match! Others handed out a pamphlet supporting us. And then there was also a lot of, what I suppose could be called, righteous mucking about and chanting. In fact, I distinctly remember him saying that the pamphlet could be construed as an attempt to influence the outcome.

Why? Because the jurors might have read it?

That was certainly part of it.

Had any?

No, I don't think so. But anyway, when he first got to quiz me he kept on suggesting that I wasn't being completely straight in the answers I was giving him. Then when the cross-examination continued the next day, he said, 'Now then Randle ...'. And I said, 'Call me Mr. Why is everybody else Mr?' And the headline in the *Evening Standard* that day was 'Call me Mr.' This clearly had some effect because afterwards he did indeed address me as Mr. Randle. I'm still quite proud of that.

Much of the drama of the case centred round Jeremy Hutchinson's and then Pat Pottle's cross-examinations of the prosecution's chief witness, Air Commodore Magill, the Air Ministry's Director of Operations.

That's right. If we could have nailed him down we would have been very satisfied. But the judge made it difficult. The crux of our case, of course, was that we were the defenders of the national interest and not the Air Ministry. How could it be in the interests of the state to destroy the state? In our view, that was precisely what the government risked doing. But, anyway, Pat was brilliant at skirting round the judge's restrictions. He'd ask a loaded question. The judge would jump in. 'No, you can't ask that.' Then he'd ask another one. And so it continued. Then he did this great thing. He asked the Air Commodore if he'd actually press the button knowing that it would lead to the annihilation of millions? And the commodore replied, 'If circumstances demanded it, I would.' We thought that was an incredible admission. To think that somebody would do that!

Pat called some interesting witnesses, I believe.

He did. Not only did he call Sir Robert Watson-Watt, the inventor of radar, but he also called Vanessa Redgrave, our old friend Gene Sharp, and a number of other distinguished people, including a former archbishop and a cluster of Nobel laureates and Bertrand Russell.

I get the point of the other witnesses, but why Vanessa Redgrave?

We chose Vanessa to show that if we were guilty so was everyone else who took part in the demonstration at Wethersfield.

If we conspired, she conspired. Not that her testimony made any difference to the judge. He may even have ruled it out as inadmissible.

I suppose, bearing in mind the judge's attitude a guilty verdict was inevitable. But it must still have come as a shock.

Michael: Well, the judge's summing up was so one-sided the jury didn't really have a choice, though the foreman did ask for leniency. We were all given eighteen months except Helen who, on the rather spurious grounds that she had played a less active role than the rest of us, was given twelve. It was then that she did a very brave thing. Instead of just accepting the judge's comments, she said she was as responsible as the rest of us.

Anne: When the judge gave sentence, Pat's mother shouted, 'He's only twenty-three!' But then she didn't have much time for Manningham-Buller either. I was with her when she went for him with an umbrella in a corridor at one of the courts. I had to restrain her. Pat's name for him, by the way, was Bullying-Manner [laughs].

By the way, how long did the trial last?

Michael: Just over a week, from the 12th to the 20th of February. We stayed in a flat in Hampstead, lent to us by Lady Jane Buxton. She had been on the Direct Action Committee. She was a supporter of the Committee of 100 as well and had spent 6 months in prison over a DAC demonstration. She and another woman, Margaret Turner, co-wrote a book called *Gate Fever*, which described some of their experiences in Holloway. Anyway, when we arrived at the flat there was a friendly note and a bottle of champagne waiting for us.

Anne: She was lovely. That, by the way, was actually the first time we'd lived together. It was also the first time that I'd ever cooked for Michael. Whenever we'd gone to his mum's she'd always given us Heinz tomato soup, so I thought I'd do that and follow it with macaroni cheese. Bear in mind that though I'd lived in a bedsit, I hadn't really cooked. Anyway, I heated the soup. Michael sat down, had a mouthful and then said it wasn't hot enough. I returned it to the pan. But I was mortified that the very first thing I'd offered him had turned out such a disaster. I can't remember what happened to the rest of the meal, but I remember thinking, 'I can't even heat soup.' I felt useless. Michael and his mother had a tendency then to have their soup so hot that it shredded the roof of the mouth; it was actually very unhealthy. My mum was only thirty or so miles away, but even that was a long way away when you didn't have a car.

Okay, so after the trial what happened next?

Following the end of the trial the group was split. Terry and I as old lags were taken to Wandsworth, and Helen to Holloway. Wormwood Scrubs was only for first offenders. However, you could be what they called re-starred, and that's what happened to Terry and me, so we spent only one night in Wandsworth. By the time we arrived at the Scrubs the others in the group had already been processed.

What do you mean by 'processed'?

When you go into the prison you step onto a mat in front of the Prison Governor – in our case the Deputy Governor – , the Chief Petty Officer in full uniform, and the prison chaplain. 'Stand here' [laughs]. Then the Chief Petty Officer barks out, 'Give your name and number to the governor!'

Now, what happened in our case was that Terry and I had decided beforehand that though we'd be perfectly respectful to the governor we wouldn't call him 'Sir'. Terry was in the queue ahead of me, when I heard a shout from inside the room, and he was marched out between two screws because he hadn't called the Deputy Governor 'Sir'. And I thought, 'Jesus. I've got to go ahead with this now. I can't not do it.' So, I gave my name and number, and the Chief Petty Officer, who was standing behind the Deputy Governor shouted, 'Say Sir!' Well, I didn't. Then the Deputy Governor leaned forward and said, 'Now then, Randle. Why won't you call me Sir?' I said, 'I want to talk to you man to man'; that was the phrase I used. He said, 'Well, it's a matter of prison discipline. Are you going to call me Sir or not?' I said, 'No'. 'Right', he said to the screw, 'Put him down for a week of non-associated labour' Then I too was marched out.

But I was allowed to keep a small collection of books. This was something that they didn't generally allow when you were in solitary, which was what non-associated labour meant. Even when I exercised, I was with men who were on the same regime or who were 'in patches', which were sewn into their uniforms to make them more conspicuous because they were thought likely to attempt to escape. Special watch, they called it. Actually, for me it wasn't too bad really as I had time to study. They used to bring this rough material to your cell, and you sewed it into mail bags, which was a pretty dispiriting task. But I was unsupervised. They didn't give you any rewards for the number of mail bags you sewed. There were no incentives [laughs].

The main governor, by the way, Thomas Hayes, was quite a progressive figure, but the Deputy Governor, Colonel Higham, was of the old school; he had no real understanding of rebel types like us, and no sympathy either. He'd been an officer in India and he'd kept his military title.

Anyway, after the week of non-associated labour, they put me in a shared cell with Trevor Hatton.

And then what? They found you another job?

That's right. For the first few months or so, I worked in the bakehouse, so I had to get up earlier than the rest of the prisoners and work weekends. It wasn't a bad job though. I worked together with other men and there was quite a reasonable atmosphere. Then, after a while, I applied to work in the tailors' shop, so I'd have my evenings and weekends free for study.

And then you all came up on appeal.

After four months or so we came up on appeal and the other members of the group, including Trevor, were sent to open prisons. But because I'd had a couple of other run-ins with the authorities by that time, Hayes, who had me up before him, said, 'We don't like exporting our troubles to other prisons,' so I stayed at the Scrubs. But, for me, that was all good news in a way because I'd started correspondence courses in English, history, French and Latin with a view to going on to university after I'd served my sentence, and it was much easier to study in a prison cell than in the dormitory of an open prison.

Do you remember much about the men you shared a cell with after Trevor Hatton?

Yes. One chap was from Northern Ireland. I got on alright with him. Then there was another man there for a while who drew up an escape plan on the first night he was there. I didn't take him seriously, and quite rightly too. But, in general, I got on well with most of the prisoners. And, at a certain point, they gave me a single cell.

These other 'run-ins' with the authorities that you've just mentioned. Can you give me some examples?

One of them concerned a guy with diarrhoea. It was just like at Norwich! And I thought, bloody hell, I'm not going through that again. So, I kept on ringing the bell to try and get someone to help the poor guy. But the screw kept on saying, 'Use yer pot!' Eventually, he opened the door. If you don't let this man out to use the toilet', I said, 'I'm going to put you on report.' 'Ha! You're putting me on report, are you? You're on report!'

Then there was an occasion when someone put some posters up including one about nuclear power with the idea of making the wing a bit less grim and I complained about that as well. Finally, I said, fine, keep it, but I'd like a poster as well, one that is against nuclear power. In the end, though, they decided that the simplest solution was to remove their poster.

Then another time, I was watching television in the association area when a news report came on about Macmillan meeting the Americans at Nassau to sign up for the deal for Britain to have the Polaris missile for deployment on British submarines. I wrote a letter to Anne in which I said that the Prime Minister looked drunk. Well, of course, the Deputy-Governor was having none of that; he refused to send it on the grounds that it was disrespectful to the 'authorities'. So, I put in a complaint to the visiting magistrates. I remember going into the wing and seeing this very friendly PO with a moustache, an ex-RAF man, and saying, 'I want to raise an objection.' And he grinned and said, 'Yes, we thought you would.' [laughs]

Eventually, I went before the magistrates, who rejected my complaint, but on the feeblest of grounds. They said they couldn't decide in this case who the authorities were. I said, 'It's got nothing to do with the prison. I can say what I like about politicians. What's that got to do with the authorities here?' He told me to write another letter, but I simply refused to do that.

Anne, presumably you visited Michael in prison.

Anne: Oh, yes. In the London prisons of that time, you got half an hour every twenty-eight days. That's one person every twenty-eight days, so if another person, say his mum or Terry, wanted to visit him then that was it for me. He didn't see our first son, Seán, until he was four weeks old. Apparently, I could have applied for an extra visit under a special prison rule or something. But if you're not told about these things how do you know about them?

Seeing Seán for the first time must have been very moving for you, Michael.

Michael: Oh, it was. I met them both in the garden.

What, the Scrubs had a garden?

Anne: Oh, yes. There was a lawned area. Lewes Prison, that's another prison that Michael was in, even had an aviary! The kids loved that. But at Wormwood Scrubs, the conditions were very harsh. I used to come down from Luton where, following the honeymoon, I'd gone back to living with my mum, dad and sisters, and we used to sit together at a table and hold hands. I remember that there used to be a lot of snogging going on; people would pass stuff, drugs and the like, from mouth to mouth.

Michael, can you tell me something about some of the more extraordinary prisoners you came across? For starters, there was an Austrian chap called Kurt and another man who wrote under the pen name of 'Zeno'. Both won Koestler Awards for their writing.

'Zeno' was in the English class with me. He was a 'trusty', which meant that he wore a blue band and was allowed to escort people around the prison, even though he was doing life for murder. His real name was Gerald Lemarque and in a previous life he'd been an army officer. Apparently, he'd murdered a man who was having an affair with his girlfriend. He was a very strange character and very aristocratic in his ideas; he certainly had no time for the left, for the working class or for what we nowadays call political correctness. But he struck up a very close relationship with the George Blake I previously mentioned. He wrote a book called *Life* which has quite a bit on Blake's escape. He tells of the great elation in the prison when the escape became known; a carnival atmosphere. Obviously, I wasn't inside at that point, but apparently there was a Christmas feel about the place. Blake had beaten the system.

Before we get onto Blake and the escape, there were also a couple of American chaps that you struck up friendships with.

Oh, yes. Dan Persyko and Bob Bayless. They were on the same lines as me politically. I remember during the Cuban Missile Crisis we went around the yard together saying how disgraceful it was that these politicians should threaten world peace. I kept in touch with them afterwards. Both of them were great prosyletisers for cannabis. Dan was another one on the English course with me.

That was taught by Pat Sloan, wasn't it?

No, Pat was in overall charge of education in the prison. The English tutor was Peter Bowering, who had a particular interest in the writings of Aldous Huxley. When he learnt that I was studying for A-level English, he took the class through several of the set books. He also smuggled some diaries of mine out of prison, passed them on to friends at *Peace News,* who in turn passed them on to Anne. I kept in touch with him for a time after I left prison. He attended at least one meeting of a *Peace News* discussion group about the future of the paper.

Among those who attended Peter's classes were Seán Bourke, George Blake, Kurt and 'Zeno'.

Your diaries?

They were my way of venting some of the pressures of prison life. Like the occasion when I was sent to the dentist to have a tooth extracted and he took out the wrong one; he was that incompetent. I was absolutely raging. I wrote an account of the experience in phonetics and Peter smuggled it out. Anyway, as you can imagine, we had some very interesting conversations during the classes, particularly after I joined a diploma course in English Literature run by the University of London.

Was that the one organised by John Morris?

No. Generally the classes were organised by Pat Sloan, the Irishman I've just mentioned, though I can't say for sure that it was he who negotiated the arrangement with UCL to run the English Diploma course. However, John did arrange for a postgraduate student from UCL to come into the prison once a week to coach me through Latin O-level, as that qualification was a minimum requirement for entry into University College London at that time, at least in the English Department. John worked at UCL in the Classics Department and later put in a good word for me when I applied for a place in that department.

John was active and influential in the Committee of 100 and a member of the Communist Party, though on its more open-minded wing. It was John who introduced me to the poetry of Catallus and encouraged me to choose him as one of the set books for the course. He said that Catallus was by far the most readable of the ancient poets and quite modern in his attitudes.

I'm surprised you didn't take Latin at school.

Oh, I did. But I wasn't very good at it in those days and it wasn't one of the subjects I took for my School Certificate.

Anne: Thinking back, it's amazing what Michael achieved in that year. Not only was he working, scrubbing the floors and whatever. But he also managed to pass A-levels in English literature and economic history and O-levels in Latin and French. I think that was pretty damn good.

Perhaps schools should be more like prisons …

Anne: It's interesting you say that because in one of Michael's letters of that time, he actually said to me, 'Don't worry about me because boarding school is a very good preparation.'

One other figure that you might have come across: the fascist, Colin Jordan. He was also in the Scrubs at this time.

I came across Colin Jordan once. We were in a queue together in C-wing, outside the deputy governor's office. We struck up a conversation. He said that he knew what I was in for and I said that I knew what he was in for.

Did you feel any sympathy for him? After all, you were both dissidents, though from opposite ends of the political spectrum.

Michael: I can't say that I felt for him as a fellow dissident. But as a fellow prisoner, yes, I did feel something. There was a solidarity in that.

Finally, what about John Vassall, the civil servant, who was, I believe, quite friendly with Jordan?

Michael: I got to know Vassall well. When I was in the tailors' shop, he sat at the desk behind me.

Was it in the tailors' shop that you first met Blake?

No, I'd spoken to him already. He was on the music appreciation class, but it was during the English diploma class that I really got to know him. If you were on that you had one Monday morning study session of about three hours, which was unsupervised except for the 'trusty', the blue band, in our case 'Zeno'. With George, I discovered quite a lot in common, though we had lots of disagreements too, in particular on espionage. It was Seán Bourke who worked in the tailors' shop who told me about the English diploma class. Seán was one of the people who dealt out material in the tailors' shop and made tea for the Principal Officer (PO) in charge of it. I had another tiff with authority there. They started us on making uniforms for the navy, to which I naturally objected. I was then sent before the Governor, Hayes, who was actually quite sympathetic and excused me from working on uniforms. My job after that was to scrub the floors, which was a lot less boring than sitting at a machine for hours on end. At least I could move around and meet people. And I was in that coterie who were working around the PO and making the tea and so on that I got to know Seán Bourke. There was one occasion when we were getting the kettle ready and I thought that he said, 'Should we do it?', meaning should we help George to escape? But, in fact, he was only referring to the fact that I hadn't put the water in the kettle. It heated up and started to melt! You can imagine that the PO was not best pleased.

Was it Bourke who first broached the possibility of Blake's escape with you or was it Blake himself?

Bourke didn't say anything at that point. I first learned about the escape plan from Pat Pottle. Pat was in the mailbag shop with Blake sewing mail bags. They were at the urinals together on one occasion, where plots are hatched as it were. Pat said to him, 'Have you ever thought of escaping?' And George said, 'I never think about anything else.' And they mapped out a rough plan, which wasn't followed up. But one of the ideas was that it would involve the Russian embassy, which as far as Pat was concerned was anathema. Pat did mention it to me. My reaction at the time was, well, this could bring CND into disrepute. Anyway, there was no real follow-up to that.

I was very friendly with Pat and worked with him on various matters after the time in prison, but the subject of George's escape didn't come up between us again until Seán paid Anne and me a visit. I had sent Christmas cards to both Seán and George and on one occasion I'd sent Seán a letter, so we'd kept up some form of contact. And then when Seán was on the hostel scheme he got in touch. The prisoners on the hostel scheme worked outside in a normal civilian job during the day but returned to prison in the evening. They'd also have weekends off and usually be released under licence towards the end of their sentence. The idea was to get them used to the outside world again. Seán came to see Anne and myself sometime in early 1966. At one point I said to him, 'How's George?' And he said, 'Well, actually that's what I've come to talk about. We're going to spring him.'

He then told us about the plans he had made to carry it out. He assured us he was not asking us to be involved. He just needed some cash to get a car and some equipment. I said, 'Well, I'm on a student grant and Anne hasn't got a paid job at the moment. But I know some people who might be able to raise some money.' And, in fact, we did manage to raise a couple of hundred pounds.

Can I ask you who you raised the money from?

Anne: Some friends [laughs].

Michael: Their names shouldn't be mentioned.

How many people are we talking about?

Michael: Two or three; I can't remember the exact number. But it was very small. We had to be very careful. We could not be certain how people would react.

So, you didn't have any conversation with Blake about the escape during the time that you were in prison then?

No. As I've just said, he discussed it with Pat. But, in my case, such opportunities as were available were never taken.

Now, Michael, shortly before your release from prison in February 1963, Helen Allegranza committed suicide.

I was sitting my A-levels and O-levels for the University entrance exam at the time, so I was usually locked up in a cell. I would be collected and then taken to the examination room. On this occasion, I met Pat Sloan and another prisoner. And the prisoner said, 'Have you heard? Your friend Helen Allegranza is dead. She's killed herself.' I was absolutely shocked. Pat Sloan made some sort of trite remark about how in the midst of life we were in death. But, really it was a huge shock to me. I really couldn't believe it because I'd had a telegram from her just before she was released saying that she'd only two weeks to go or something like that and then she'd written me again shortly after her release.

Fig 15: Helen Allegranza, following her release from Holloway Prison on 28 September 1962. She committed suicide about four months later. Photographer unknown. University of Bradford, Special Collections, PN 11/53.

Anne: All in all, 62-63 was a very dark period. It wasn't just that Helen committed suicide. I remember sitting up late at night during the Cuban Missile Crisis, holding Seán, and thinking of Michael in his cold cell. I kept on thinking that Michael would get blown up and there'd be nothing I could do about it

Of course, unlike other couples you couldn't make an arrangement to meet somewhere out of the immediate danger zone ...

Michael: Pat Arrowsmith and Wendy Butlin went off to the west coast of Ireland and my sister, Terry, came down from Leeds to be with Alan in Hampstead.

7. Greece, Vietnam, and George Blake

Michael, before we move on to talking about your life following your release from prison, I wonder if you came across Lord Longford? He had a particular interest in penal reform.

Not during my imprisonment. But he arranged to see me after I got out. We had lunch together in a canteen somewhere in the Palace of Westminster. We chatted about prison reform and he asked me about my experiences. I also joined the Howard League for Penal Reform and another group made up of people who'd been imprisoned for anti-nuclear demonstrations. Finally, I published a flurry of articles on prison conditions and prison reform in *Peace News*.

Did you return to an official position in the Committee of 100?

By the time I came out of prison I'd taken my O- and A-levels and the university entrance exam, so I was due to go to university the following September. But, in the meantime, I worked at *Peace News*, so no I didn't. But, in any case, I'm not sure the Committee was doing a great deal at that point. But Anne and I did go on the demonstration against the state visit of the Greek royals, in July 1963. The police were incredibly rough. I'd never before seen them behave like that. They were riding their horses right onto the pavements. It was really scary.

This was a Committee demonstration?

Not quite. It was a joint effort by the Committee of 100 and the Save Greece Now Committee. The *Peace News* cartoonist, Donald Rooum, was among the people arrested, which, incidentally, was one of the factors which led to the famous Challenor Case. There was a play at the Aldwych Theatre and Queen Frederika and King Constantine and some of the British royals went along. Anyway, the crowd booed them as they went in, and that incensed the police.

The royal visit was preceded by the murder of the Greek Socialist Grigoris Lambrakis. Can you explain why Lambrakis was so important to the left in England?

In April Lambrakis took part in a peace march from Marathon to Athens with Pat Pottle and many other people with Committee of 100 links. It was attacked by the police and the only person who was able to complete the march was Lambrakis because he had immunity as an MP. But shortly afterwards he was run down by a couple of people on a motorcycle. Most of us were sure that it was a government-inspired assassination, as indeed it turned out to have been. It was just a couple of months after that the Greek royals visited England, so Lambrakis was still very much on people's minds. And then the other thing was that the movement for greater democracy in Greece looked very much to the kind of demonstrations that were happening in Britain. In fact, one of the main opposition groups involved in direct action in Greece called themselves the Bertrand Russell Committee. They even adopted Holtom's symbol. There was, in other words, a very close connection between the Committee of 100 and the Greek democratic opposition, who were calling for the release of political prisoners and the introduction of political freedoms.

You just mentioned Donald Rooum and the Challenor Case. What was the Challenor Case about?

The Challenor case involved a bent policeman called Harold Challoner who got into the habit of planting evidence on suspects and who was charged with corruption at the Old Bailey. Donald Rooum was one of his victims. If he wanted to get a conviction, Challenor would line people up and say something like, 'We found this brick in your pocket'; that sort of thing. Anyway, he went through this procedure with Donald, who was working at the time for the National Council for Civil Liberties, now Liberty. He realised that Challoner had made a mistake: he hadn't actually put a brick in his pocket, so there would be no forensic evidence to support the case against him. So immediately he was released he took his coat to a laboratory and had it forensically examined. This showed no sign of brick dust. The charge against Donald was dropped, and subsequently so were the convictions of a number of other people whom Challoner had framed.

Although, I don't think I wrote about the Challenor Case for *Peace News* I did write a couple of articles about one of the other *causes célèbres* of the period, a case involving a spy named John Vassall, who I'd met in prison.

Can you tell me something about Vassall?

It so happened that when I was working in the tailors' shop in Wormwood Scrubs, he was on a machine directly behind me. He had seen the governor and told him something in confidence and the governor had let it be known what it was. But I can't remember at the moment the details of it; I'll have to look it up.

Was it something to do with the case of Brendan Mullholland and Reginald Foster, two of Fleet Street's finest? They were jailed in February 1963 for refusing to reveal some of the sources behind their reporting of the Vassall spy case.

Yes, that was it. Again, I'll have to look it up. I can't remember the details. But then there was a report into it all, the Radcliffe Report. But Radcliffe just dismissed what I'd said in a few lines. It got a lot of coverage in the newspapers at the time, but it turned out not to be particularly significant.

Why was the Vassall case so important at that time? It was pre-Profumo, of course.

Well, it was another spy scandal. There'd been the Blake case and another case involving some Admiralty people down at Portsmouth. In fact, there'd been a number of scandals to do with espionage, so there was heightened anxiety. But Vassall had no ideological commitment to the Soviets. He was blackmailed into spying because he was a homosexual. They held that over him. I don't know how important the secrets were that he divulged, but they gave him several years. He was actually quite a gentle figure. He was very much a victim. He was really out of his depth in the world of espionage.

I believe that he became a Catholic during his time in the Scrubs.

He did become a Catholic. But I don't remember whether it was while I was there or not.

Maybe it was Lord Longford's doing ...

Maybe [laughs].

Thinking about some of the other Committee-related events of 1963, were you involved with the 'Spies for Peace' campaign?

No, but I was one of the people who was sent the material and I found out afterwards the names of a few of the people who were involved with it. The 'spies' broke into a nuclear bunker near Reading, gave away the location, and exposed the government's plans for the period following a nuclear war for what they were, a hodgepodge of self-delusion and lunacy. I was working at *Peace News* at the time. In fact, I was the one who wrote the editorial and the headline, 'The Spies were Right'. The editorial caused a scandal. Even *The Guardian* was a bit sniffy about it. But we supported what the 'spies' had done in exposing the government's plans.

Two of the 'spies' were Nicolas and Ruth Walter. Were you friends?

I knew them very well. Ruth died quite recently. Unfortunately, we didn't manage to get to her funeral. In fact, we kept in touch more with her than with Nicolas. She was probably less of an ideological anarchist than Nicolas, but certainly very much on the same lines in her general orientation.

Nicolas, by the way, was one of a small number of people who worked out that Pat Pottle and myself had been involved in the Blake escape. In fact, he dropped hints about it in something he wrote. They were so strong that Pat went to see him about them.

That seems extraordinary. After all, he was very protective of his own anonymity.

Well, perhaps I'd better describe them as a nod to the wise.

Ken Weller was another person involved with the 'Spies for Peace' campaign. You were yourself involved with him later on in the Greek Embassy demonstration. What do you remember about him?

Ken was one of the leaders of the Solidarity group along with Dr Chris Pallis. He had a line that was critical of Marxism but decidedly anti-Trotskyist. The group published something on the Kronstadt Mutiny, which was very critical of Trotsky's role. I don't think that Chris Pallis was working class at all, but Ken certainly was.

April 1963. The sixth Aldermaston march. Did you take part in that?

Yes. That was when the whole 'Spies for Peace' thing happened. A part of the march broke off and went to one of the RSGs, which is to say Regional Seats of Government, near Reading. As I said earlier, before the march I was sent the document which identified the locations of some of these RSGs. You've mentioned Nicolas and Ruth Walter and Ken Weller, but I'm pretty certain that Pat Pottle was involved with the 'Spies' as well.

Let's turn to one or two others matters now. Around the time of the Greek Royals visit, you attended the Non-Governmental Aid to Algeria conference. What was that about?

That took place during the summer of 1963, just a few months before Ben Bella became president. The conference brought together at a conference in Algiers some of the people who had supported Algerian independence. Some who went were from the New Left; indeed, it was quite a strong contingent. I went there for *Peace News* and wrote two or three articles about it. It was an impressive event. But there were already tensions between Ben Bella and his defence minister, Houari Boumédiène. Subsequently, Boumédiène took over from him.

Do you remember who those New Left people were?

Some of them were connected to the *New Left Review*. Tom Nairn was one of them and Perry Anderson and Juliet Mitchell two others.

Juliet and my sister, Terry, by the way, got to know each other very well and became close friends when Terry was studying in Leeds. In fact, we all got to know her well. She used to come to the house a lot. The first car that Anne and I ever owned was given to us by Juliet. Juliet's mother told her she wasn't to drive it anymore because it was a death trap! But it wasn't that bad. It did us for a couple of years, anyway.

What about some of the other New Left people of the period? Robin Blackburn? Raphael Samuel? Stuart Hall? Did you see anything of them? [Anne who had been in the room a while, entered the conversation at this point]

Anne: Oh, yes. On one occasion, Robin got me to type up an article for him, for the *New Left Review*. It was quite a long article, but he paid peanuts!

Michael: We got to know Stuart through Terry and Alan. Stuart was an Oxford friend of Alan, one of a large group that included Mario Lippa and a bunch of other people on the left.

Anne: We were introduced to the Lippas when they lived in Barnet, North London. Terry and Alan said you should meet Tessa and Mario because they had two boys who were more or less the same age as Seán. Mario and Tessa had been at the School of Art, in Oxford. He was an Italian-American from Philly. Later on, they moved to Hertfordshire, to a very colourful house, where they had this amazing spread of friends and interests. I mentioned to you earlier that before meeting Michael I worked in an advertising agency in London. Well, later on, I discovered that Mario had also worked there. I think he may have been one of the directors; he was a big cheese, anyway. And there I was working in the market research department! [laughs].

Michael: The other person that Alan lived with for a time was Lindsay Anderson. That was before he met Terry. Lindsay Anderson was also on the Committee of 100 and I remember going on a delegation with him, just the two of us. I can't remember who we were going to meet, but we were lobbying them. Lindsay, as I've probably mentioned, directed a film about the first Aldermaston march. Somewhere I have a note that he wrote to Eileen Brock about it.

Michael, you've mentioned that you returned to Peace News *following your imprisonment. Can you give me an idea of the atmosphere at the publication during this period? This would be about a year or so before Ted Roszak took over.*

Well, Hugh Brock was still there as editor, but he was taking much more of a back seat by this point, letting the younger people have their say. Adam Roberts started at about this time and Michael Freeman was there too, I think as features editor. It was still the period when we were trying to broaden the scope of the paper, bringing in people like Alan and Albert Hunt. Alan wrote about film and Albert about theatre. Richard Boston and Rod Prince were also there. Richard was a very witty man and for a while he became quite a media figure. He used to go on the radio and do one of those jokey shows, which he later gave up on the grounds that it was all a bit flaky. I remember Rod Prince very well. He was part of the group which used to have regular meetings to review the week's news and to decide on the line we'd take. I think that he married a woman who was working on the paper. John Arden used to contribute a regular column. In fact, Hugh was disturbed, on one occasion, when John Arden used the word 'fuck' in one of his articles. Hugh said, 'Maybe there are some contexts which would justify the use of that word, but why here?' I don't think that Hugh himself went public with his views, but there was a bit of a row in the paper about it. I remember we published a series of letters discussing the issue.

Tell me about John Arden. He's most famous today for Serjeant Musgrave's Dance, *his play about colonialism.*

We used to socialise together. Anne and I and John and John's wife, Margaretta D'Arcy, who was also a playwright and who collaborated with John on a few of his plays. We went to their house in London several times and on one occasion to their house in Kirby Moorside in Yorkshire. Sometimes they'd put on shows for the children. By coincidence, I'd been at the same convent school in Dublin as Margaretta, where, of course, there was strict segregation of the sexes except during family visits, when we would all gather together. My sister, Margaret, got to know her very well there. Then, later, Terry got to know both John and Margaretta.

During the Autumn of 1963, you went back into full-time education. You started a degree in English at University College, London. What do you remember about that experience?

Well, before the term started one of the lecturers invited me to come and have a chat with him. I can't remember his name though.

Was it Randolph Quirk?

No, it wasn't Quirk. But I did study under Randolph Quirk. He taught linguistics. Students had to choose two specialist areas and I went for the classical background to English literature and linguistics. This was at a time when linguistics was very much an up-and-coming topic. I remember the occasion when Quirk announced that Chomsky was coming to deliver a lecture. He said, 'Don't miss this man.' So, I ploughed through his *Aspects of the Theory of Syntax*, which was incredibly difficult. I went along to his lecture, which was probably the most stimulating one I attended during my time at UCL. In it, Chomsky branched out from linguistics to cover broader philosophical issues. I came away thinking that this is absolutely amazing stuff. Of course, later on, Chomsky became much more of a political figure.

Any other memories of Chomsky?

At one point, sometime after being arrested for the Greek embassy event in 1967 and before going to prison, I worked at the International Confederation for Disarmament and Peace, typing up background papers for a conference on Vietnam. One day this lady, whose name I've forgotten now, but who was working very closely with Peggy Duff, came into the office and said, 'Does anyone know who Chomsky is?' And I said, 'I do.' But, really, his name in that context came as a surprise. I hadn't realised until then that he was politically engaged

I also wrote a piece called 'Towards Liberation' for War Resisters' International (WRI), which contained a reference to Chomsky and in which I developed some ideas about non-violent revolution. Anyway, someone forwarded me a letter by Chomsky in which he praised it. As you can probably imagine, that was enormously pleasing.

Were you politically engaged in new ways at UCL or did you stick with your usual networks?

I joined the Socialist Society at UCL. But because I was married and had a young child I didn't get very much involved with politics at the university. Generally, I did my stint and went home. However, there were a couple of students that I did spend some time with. One of them was Margaret Marchmont. She was about twenty-two, so nearer my age than most of the other students. Both of us were very interested in linguistics. I remember we went very carefully through Professor Quirk's textbook, the one we used on the course, and came across a passage that didn't seem right. I think it was something to do with a linguistic form that fitted into two categories. So, we arranged to meet Professor Quirk to talk about it. He said, 'You've picked up on a mistake. I'll have to correct it in the next edition.' He was a very strict teacher, the sort of man who would never put up with any nonsense. Some people didn't like him. But he was also fair. Certainly, I got on very well with him.

Who else taught you at UCL?

Geoffrey Leach. He also worked on the linguistics side. Another lecturer I greatly appreciated was Winifred Nowottny, an eminent Shakespeare scholar, whose husband was Polish.

How did you do in your exams?

In the end I only got a 2.2. But then I started an MPhil in linguistics and poetry. I was particularly interested in the poetry of Adrian Mitchell, you know, the author of 'To Whom it May Concern' and 'Hit Suddenly Hit'. Later on, when I taught at Bradford Art College, I became very good friends with Adrian. I was such a huge fan of his work! He also had a regular column in *Peace News*, so there was that connection as well. I have a number of his books in my shelves. Some of them are inscribed to me.

Did you go to the still-famous poetry event at the Royal Albert Hall during the summer of 1965, the one with Ginsberg, Harry Fainlight and Ferlinghetti? Adrian Mitchell read 'To Whom it May Concern'.

I didn't. I wanted to go and most of the people in our circle at the university went. But Anne and I had two children by then, Seán and our second son, Gavin. And then I had the studying to do. But it's one of my big regrets that I missed that event.

Anne, do you have any thoughts about Michael's time at UCL?

Well, actually, it was a bit of a blow, I mean the fact that so soon after serving a prison sentence he went into full-time education. Not only did I have one child to look after, but I'd got another on the way. It was a very difficult time, living in London and trying to cope on virtually no money. The children used up all of my energy. There were no disposable nappies in those days. They were cloth ones you had to boil up in a bucket. And I was always tired. I remember Bayard Rustin took us to see a production of *King Lear* in the West End, with Paul Scofield as Lear. And I fell asleep. I was just so tired. The other thing that I remember about the play was that Bayard had a hip flask filled with whisky. There was something strangely shocking about that [laughs].

Michael, while you were at UCL you helped found an anti-racist organisation, a precursor of the Campaign against Racial Discrimination (CARD).

That was with Alan Lovell, Ted Roszak and Marion Glean from the West Indies. The idea was to challenge racism, the sort of attitude that manifested itself in notices in shop windows for lodgers which read, 'No Irish, No blacks, No dogs'. In 1964, we set up a group to campaign on the issue. I think we called it Multi-Racial Britain. There was one other black member of the group besides Marion—Barry Reckord, a well-known playwright. Marion too was a writer as well as an activist. She ran a Quaker centre in London and was married to an ex-Catholic priest from Cork. I got to know them both well when I worked for six months for UNESCO in a division Marion headed. I remember one occasion we were chatting about the modernisation of the Catholic church, and he remarked, 'The blessed virgin now is out altogether and you'd hardly hear a Benediction.' [laughs]
    Incidentally, until that time I'd only known people who accepted Catholic teaching *in toto*. But Marion seemed to be able to pick and choose to some extent what she believed. She'd say things

like, 'I don't believe in that bit, but I do believe in that bit.' And she
was very good company. Anyway, ours was one of the groups that
came together to form CARD in 1964. It was launched publicly to
coincide with Martin Luther King's passing through London on his
way to Oslo to receive the Nobel Peace Prize. I didn't actually join
CARD. We'd discussed it amongst ourselves and decided that it
might harm the cause if I did so because of my reputation for civil
disobedience and direct action. We thought I should stay in the
background. But I was there at some of the meetings that led up to
its formation and met up with Bayard Rustin before the public
meeting at which Martin Luther King spoke. Bayard was part of
Luther King's entourage in the Dorchester Hotel.

*A year or so after the foundation of Multi-Racial Britain, you became
involved with an organisation called Volunteers for Peace in Vietnam.
Can you tell me about that organisation?*

April Carter was probably the main figure in that. The idea
was to send a group of well-known people to North Vietnam to
draw attention to the indiscriminate US bombing campaign. One of
them was A.J. Muste, who was in his early eighties by that stage.
Another was Bishop Ambrose Reeves, the Bishop of Lewes. Martin
Niemöller and Rabbi Feinberg were the other two members of the
team. The idea was that they would go to Vietnam and run the same
risk of falling victim to an American bomb as the people who were
living there. We had the support, I remember, of Claude Bourdet,
who'd been in the French resistance movement and was later editor
of *France Observateur*. Though not a pacifist, he had huge respect for
A.J. Muste and a great friendship for Peggy Duff. I mentioned
earlier the International Confederation for Disarmament and Peace.
Well, Bourdet was its vice-chairman.

So, Muste came over to Paris as did Ambrose Reeves. We had
a public meeting and Claude Bourdet put me up with some of the
others. I remember Muste saying from the platform of the meeting
that he would go to go to Vietnam even if it was the last thing that
he ever did. And there was a moment of silence in the hall. I

suppose that people thought, as I did, that maybe it will be. He was younger than I am now [laughs]. But, nevertheless, he was an old man. It struck me as a really poignant moment. And indeed not long after his return from Vietnam, he died. His death even made the main BBC news on the radio. The announcer said that 'the well-known American pacifist, Abraham Johannes Muste has died.' It took me a second to realise that he was referring to 'A.J.', as we all knew him by those letters.

We had endless negotiations getting the team into North Vietnam, not just with the North Vietnamese, but with the Chinese as well. But eventually the visas came through and we were able to go ahead. We were helped a lot with the background material by the writer and journalist Malcolm Caldwell. He was an academic who did a lot of work for *Peace News* and who was very knowledgeable. Indeed, we got him to write a regular column for the paper because he was so well informed about the situation in Vietnam.

How did you fund the project?

That's a good question. I can't remember exactly. I think we probably just appealed for funds. We went to people we knew who had a bit of money, that sort of thing.

Was one of them Vanessa Redgrave?

I don't remember whether or not Vanessa contributed. But I did get to know her very well around that time. She contributed to another group that I was involved with: The Vietnam Action Group. Ken Weller was very much involved in setting that up, as was Pat Pottle.

At the risk of sounding naive, why was Vietnam such a big issue for the left in 1965? It practically eclipsed the nuclear issue.

It had caused so many casualties and it was clearly an unjust war. I certainly wasn't exceptional in focusing on the issue at the time. *Peace News* had made it a major issue. I remember, in particular, an article quite early on called 'Kennedy's Secret War'. It was during Kennedy's presidency that the Americans became deeply involved.

Did you attend the WRI's triennial conference in Rome in 1966? That was very much dominated by Vietnam.

Yes. In fact, I had just become chair of the WRI. Joan Baez came to the conference, though I missed her contribution. I was late because I had just started a part-time typing job with Dictaphone in West London. There was a big drive by the United States section of the WRI, the War Resisters League, to make Vietnam a major issue in its campaigning. One of the people who really impressed me on that occasion was Dave McReynolds. Indeed, Dave was the moving force behind the entire conference. He became chair sometime after me, following Devi Prasad and Myrtle Solomon. He was very much involved with the War Resisters League. After the conference, the WRI produced a leaflet, which urged American men facing the draft to register as conscientious objectors or to refuse to fight on if they were already soldiers. That was another one of Dave's achievements. By the way, on one occasion when we held a WRI Council or Executive meeting in England he had trouble obtaining a visa. I likewise had trouble getting a visa to go the US on the occasion of the Haverford WRI Triennial conference in 1969.

Were lots of Americans leaving the army at that point?

Well, certainly some were, though there wasn't anything like a mass exodus. There were even a number of safe houses for draft refusers and deserters in London. You may have come across the journalist and writer Clancy Sigal. Well, he ran one.

Didn't you leaflet the NATO airbase at Wethersfield at about this time? Perhaps that was that part of the same campaign.

It was. We produced a leaflet with the innocuous-sounding title 'Some Information for US Soldiers', which informed GIs of their right to conscientious objection. The cartoonist Vicky produced a couple of cartoons to include in it. Around this time there was a small group conference in Paris which brought together various people and organisations opposed to the Vietnam war. This was in 1966. Anne and myself went along to it. There were many people at the conference including a Dutchman who saw our War Resisters' leaflet and paid to have several thousand of them printed. Then there was a Vietnamese council member of the WRI, Vo Van Ai, who arranged through his contacts to get the leaflets into Vietnam and into the hands of the American servicemen.

Fig 16:   Anne Randle, in Paris in 1966. Photograph by Michael Randle. Private Collection.

166 Ban the Bomb!

So, this all took place after the Wethersfield leafleting, which I understand was a Committee of 100 undertaking in August 1966?

I don't know whether the Wethersfield leafleting took place under the aegis of the Committee of 100, but certainly the same sort of people were involved in all these undertakings. Pat Arrowsmith was involved in the Wethersfield action as was another Committee of 100 woman. We all drove to the base together.

There were three or four of you, one of whom may well have been Pat. I believe that you leafleted the married quarters and a number of the barracks.

Yes. Pat was definitely in the group. We drove up to Wethersfield and then just drove into the base without being challenged. Some of the servicemen invited us into their barracks. They were friendly and happy to chat to us. It was surprising. But then some of the higher-ups realised what was going on and ordered us to leave. We were met by two British policemen as we came out. We weren't charged, but they took our names and gave us a lecture about how the Americans could easily have taken us for saboteurs and shot us.

Going back to your time at UCL, do you remember the teach-in you attended about Vietnam? You wrote an account of it for Peace News.

I don't remember much about it. But I know that there were some very good people there.

You had Fenner Brockway, Eric Hobsbawn, Isaac Deutscher and Ralph Miliband. Miliband was totally in favour of the Viet Cong; no nuances in his case!

Yes, I remember his contribution. I wrote the event up with a woman called Joyce Rosser, who was a fellow member of the Committee of 100.

For the opposition, there was John Gummer and Peregrine Worsthorne, a rather interesting right-wing journalist.

Oh, yes. I remember John Selwyn Gummer. Later on, he had something to do with beef burgers and the BSE crisis.

Interestingly, you described Deutscher as looking like Lenin and telling the students in the audience to take to the streets and talk to working people about Vietnam.

I think in Deutscher's case ideology overtook reality. But I suppose it did for many of us to some extent. We still had this idea of a popular uprising that would change everything. But things never got to the stage of ferment where that could have happened.

Finally, on the subject of Vietnam: you earlier mentioned Malcolm Caldwell. Caldwell, I think I'm right in saying this, was also very pro-Viet Cong. I wonder how your take on Vietnam differed from Caldwell's and indeed from others on the left? What made your take special?

Well, I still took a pacifist position. So, I didn't support the idea of guerrilla warfare. Like most of the other people at *Peace News* I also put less emphasis on the economic factor than they did. We saw it as a less determining factor.

You said in an article responding to something that Caldwell had written that the New Left was overly cynical about the phrase 'free world'. In your view the West was free in a way the Soviet Union was not.

Yes, that's right. That was something that went right back to the invasion of Hungary. I and many people on the left, particularly pacifists, were highly critical of the Soviet Union's brand of authoritarian communism.

Then you mentioned Ralph Schoenman and Bertrand Russell in the same context. Both of them had described American policy in Vietnam as 'Hitlerite'.

Yes. I remember the article. One of the tutors at University College came up to me after the article was published and said, 'I've read your article in *Peace News* and I very much agree with you.' That was the article where I was distancing myself from those very ideological stances.

We spoke briefly about Vanessa Redgrave earlier on. Were you seeing much of her at this point?

I don't know on how many occasions, but I was certainly still in touch with her. She actually financed our leafleting of Wethersfield and the printing of the leaflets on my offset litho.

So, she was someone who the left would turn to finance their projects. Who were the other people that you'd turn to?

Howard Cheney was one. I don't remember any other names. But, generally, they were wealthier people with Direct Action Committee or Committee of 100 connections.

Did you meet Vanessa's brother, Corin Redgrave?

Yes, certainly. He wasn't just an actor, of course; he was also a stalwart of the Workers Revolutionary Party. But I never took to that. Just as I never took to its leader Gerry Healy. There was something quite sinister about him. I remember that one of Healy's group wrote to ours. But we didn't really engage with them. Corin was married to one of the Markham sisters, Kika, daughter of the actor, David Markham. He had been a conscientious objector and did lots of good work and I think set up the Sussex Committee of 100. Our good friend, Ernest Rodker, who was active in the New Left, the DAC and the Committee of 100, married another of the Markham sisters, Sonia Markham. Kika and Sonia had another, younger, sister, Jehane, who lived quite close to us when we were living in North London. She was, and is, a talented poet. In 1967, I tutored her for her A-level English literature exam before being sent down for the Greek Embassy demonstration. I then continued to tutor her by post from Pentonville prison, and she came several times to see me for discussions at Pentonville prison.

So. you socialised with the Rodkers as well.

Haven't I told you about my first meeting with Ernest Rodker? Okay, it was at the public launch of CND in February 1958. We'd printed up some leaflets about the Aldermaston March, which we spread on the seats at Central Hall in order to get some publicity. Anyway, at a certain point, Canon Collins announced that a group of people were going to take a message to Downing Street. So, a lot of people went down and crowded into Downing Street. The police, for their part, were completely taken by surprise. They panicked and threw people out of Downing Street with brute force. When I got down there, I saw this tall young man being beaten up by the police. Somebody next to me photographed the assault. Then, as he walked off, a policeman chased after him, took his camera and ripped out the film. The tall young man being beaten up was Ernest Rodker. After that, I got to know him through the co-ordinating committee that CND set up. Then he became a member of the Direct Action Committee as well, in fact one of its most active members. I remember saying to one of the policemen during the Downing Street demonstration, taking a middle-class view of what the police were there for, 'I think that was unreasonable.' 'Shut up', he retorted, 'Or I'll smash yer face.' So, I got a new insight into how the police could behave.

Were you ever frightened by the police?

No. I, and the movement as a whole, had quite a good relationship with them. Why? Because we followed the Gandhian principle of keeping them informed about what we were up to. I remember on one of the Committee of 100 demonstrations, something came up about the police, and I said, 'Their job isn't to suppress demonstrations.' But, I wasn't attacking them. And Hugh Brock said to me, 'You've said the right thing.' We had some run-ins with them, of course, but we really weren't into provoking them. We tried to stick to our non-violent principles and to foster some sort of relationship with them. It was an approach that worked. Many years later when we had a demonstration up at Faslane, again we let them know we were coming. Although they did arrest people, there was one young woman from Holland, who was studying Peace Studies at Bradford. People were queuing up to give the police their names and she got chatting to this policeman. At one point, he said, 'If I let you go will you rejoin them?' And she said, 'No, I wouldn't.' And he just let her go.

I suppose that some policemen were sympathetic to what you were doing.

Yes, Especially in Scotland. We had some very good Scots in the movement, like Hugh MacDiarmid. I remember him coming on one of the Polaris demonstrations at Holy Loch. He was involved in the Committee of 100's first major sit-down in London. You can see him in one of the press photographs of the demo.

Let's return our attention to George Blake now and try and pick up on some of the other things that were happening in your life post your imprisonment for Wethersfield. Can you begin by telling me why you were drawn to him?

I wasn't sympathetic to his espionage activities, but I was shocked by the unprecedented length of his sentence: forty-two years. I thought that it was vicious. It wasn't only left-wing people who thought this; the opinion was actually a lot more general. We'd had the Klaus Fuchs case back in the early fifties. He'd got fourteen years. That was the statutory penalty. Then there were the people involved in the Portland spy ring; they were exchanged after several years' imprisonment. But what they did with Blake was to charge him with five separate offences. And then they gave him the maximum sentence of fourteen years for each of them, though two were to run concurrently.

Was there any other significance in the forty-two years?

Well, there was some speculation by Chapman Pincher, the well-known right-wing journalist. The trial was in secret, *in camera* as it's called, so not much came out. But, anyway, Pincher had a front-page piece in the *Daily Mail* saying that Blake had confessed to betraying forty-two British agents, who were executed by the Soviets. This piece appeared, I think, the day before Blake's appeal was heard. But it was a figure plucked out of the air.

Nonetheless, it made very good copy.

It did. Forty-two years. One for every life. I think that figure, wherever it originally came from, was simply an attempt to sway the appeal judges.

You did understand though that Blake had damaged British interests?

Of course. But we had a pretty strong line against espionage by either side. When Pat and I wrote our book about the Blake case we said that we disagreed with Blake's activities, both when he was working for British intelligence and for the Russians.

When I was in Wormwood Scrubbs *Peace News* published a scathing article on the whole espionage business, which I very much agreed with. I gave a copy of it to George Blake, wondering whether he'd ever speak to me again [laughs]. He gave the issue back to me a week or so later, and said, 'I agree with what it says. But as long as there are nations states there will be spying.' And he was probably correct.

Do you think your actions would have been different had Blake been given a much shorter sentence?

I can't swear to it. But I doubt if we would have got involved. We weren't going out saying, 'Free all spies!'

You said in the article I just mentioned that there was no moral equivalence between the Soviet Union and the West. But surely your action in helping to free Blake suggested otherwise.

There were certainly moral differences in the causes to which they were attached. But, spying is different. It's worth pointing out that some of the special operations carried out by the West were just as heinous as those carried out by the Soviets. Some of the American actions in South America were appalling. The American CIA and the British MI6 jointly masterminded the coup in Iran that overthrew Mosaddegh. That did exercise us. Even at the time, I thought it was straightforward imperialism. Quite often the West has acted out of pure self-interest. The so-called Red threat was often exaggerated in order to further actions that were taken for quite other reasons.

To make countries safe for American capitalism?

Yes, exactly.

Okay, general point here: in the context of the work you'd done for the DAC, the Committee of 100 and other movements, your involvement in the Blake case meant that you were in new territory. What you took part in was a conspiracy.

Yes, it had to be [laughs]. We couldn't have sprung the man otherwise. I suppose we *could* have followed the Gandhian method, told the police that we were planning [laughs]. But, nonetheless, that's what it was.

On a related matter, did you make plans for the care of your children had both Anne and you been arrested?

We made plans for the children to go to my sister, Margaret. However, we didn't tell her what it was we were doing.

Do you really think that Blake was worth running that sort of risk, in spite of the great length of his sentence?

A few years back, I was interviewed by Gordon Corera, the BBC's security correspondent, and he brought up that very question. At the time, he seemed sympathetic. But then the BBC broadcast an episode of that chat programme, *The One Show*, and he went on that, taking this line that it was all terribly shocking and shameful, whereas, as I've just said, when he spoke to me he'd been very friendly, posing for a photograph with me and all that sort of thing. He said how scandalous it all was that this couple had two young children, who did not know that there was a Russian spy in the camper van in which they were travelling. But, of course, that was total nonsense. How would the children have even grasped the notion? Seán was just four and a half, Gavin was just two and a half. But the tone of it was how disgraceful it all was, putting young children in such a context. He was making judgments on that programme to which I would have liked to have responded and ought to have been given the opportunity to do so. Anne and I should have been invited. Anyway, I had a huge row with the BBC about it,

So, in retrospect, you still think that you made the right call?

Oh, undoubtedly. I think we did. Our sons who are now grown up have always been thoroughly supportive.

Now, by the time you planned the Blake escape you were living in Torriano Cottages.

Anne: That's right. After living with Terry and Alan near Clissold Park for a while, we moved into Ted Rozsak's old house, Torriano Cottages, in Kentish Town. We moved in when he went back to the States, which would have been in 1965. Actually, we lived in two houses there; the Roszak house was the first one. The house was part of a housing co-operative. We were in 25 first, then we moved into 23, when our friends, the Archers, moved out.

Were there lots of co-ops of this sort in London at the time?

Anne: Not that we knew of. The one that we lived in was very small. There were just three houses and two flats. There was a family that didn't pay their rent for months. We were the treasurers at the time; and, I suppose, that in a way we let that happen. We certainly got it in the neck for that—which was a bit ironic, because, of course, you're supposed to be nice to people in a co-op. But we really didn't know how to deal with it. The husband, Tom, was working away and his wife, Caroline, kept saying, 'Oh, we'll pay the money next month.' It was £7 a week, which was a very reasonable rent. Camden Council provided the money for the mortgages and we all paid the rent, which was supposed to stay the same forever. They're privately owned now. Anyway, getting back to Tom and Caroline, we believed them. But the other members of the co-op were quite angry with us, because they thought that we hadn't been entirely open with them. Heaven knows how we resolved it!

I suppose that being a co-op you were in an out of each other's houses.

Anne: Initially. Most of us had children. The front gardens were all open, so the kids could play freely. That was why we wanted to move there; there was that aspect to it.

[Anne left the room for a few minutes at this point]
*Can you describe the visits that Seán Bourke made to you in Torriano
Cottages?*

The first time was when he was still in prison, but on a scheme
whereby prisoners were freed on licence for weekends, or
sometimes for longer periods to work in order to accustom them to
life outside prison. After that we mainly met him at Pat Pottle's
place where we did most of the planning. Pat used to make us a fish
pie. I think that it was about the only recipe not containing meat
that he was good at! I can't remember whether Seán came very
much or at all to Torriano Cottages after that, except, of course, after
the escape happened and, to our shock, we saw him the next day
walking down the path towards us.

*I believe that Anne contributed to the escape in a particular way. Can you
tell me about that?*

Well, the children had a rope ladder for the bunkbed and
Anne realised that if we were going to use a rope ladder to free
Blake then the rungs would have to be strengthened in some way.
Unless there was some kind of strengthening, the sides would
simply pull in when George put a foot on it. So, she came up with
the idea of strengthening the rope with knitting needles. She even
told Bourke what size of needle was needed. He certainly wouldn't
have known. He then went to a shop and bought the entire stock of
them [laughs].

*How would you describe Bourke's personality? He seems to have been a
bit of a maverick.*

He was a bit of a maverick. You never knew what he was
going to do next. Perhaps even he didn't know. After the escape, he
parked the car that we'd used in the escape just a few streets away
from the prison in Harvist Road, but told us that he'd driven it a

long way off so there was no risk of the police discovering it. Pat was particularly worried about that because he couldn't be sure if his or George's fingerprints were on it. I kept on asking him for the keys, and he'd say things like, Oh, I've thrown them away or I can't find them. But then finally he came clean. Yes, the car was in Harvist Road and, yes, the keys were in his pocket! And then here's another example of Seán's unpredictability. In the book he wrote about the case, *The Springing of George Blake*, he says that a day or two after the escape, he actually rang the police and *told* them where the car was. He was entirely unpredictable [laughs].

Fig 17:   The Artillery Road side of Wormwood Scrubbs Prison. Blake escaped over this wall in October 1966. Photograph by Michael Randle. 1989. Private Collection.

What do you think Bourke's motive for getting involved with Blake was? I've read somewhere that he had a grudge against the British state.

I think that he was a bit of an anarchist as well as a maverick. He had no respect for the law or for the state. He was actually a complete non-conformist. He says in his book that he wanted to focus all the attention on himself, to take it away from us; that was why he told the police about the car. But what was totally, utterly, irresponsible was that when I pressed him about it, saying that we needed to move it, to get rid of it, he said that he'd thrown the key away, thrown it down a drain or something.

Eventually, as I've said, I did get Seán to give me the key, and we got Hugh Brock to drive me to Harvist Road, by which time, of course, there was no sign of the vehicle. Already *The Evening Standard* had this headline, 'Escape car found'. So, Seán, bloody hell, he knew that he'd told the police. He did his utmost to dissuade us from collecting the car, saying things like, 'It's too risky; the police may be watching, you don't know. If you go there you're liable to be arrested.' So, we did take a risk, we knew that we were taking a risk. I went there with Hugh and drove up and down and, as I say, the car wasn't there. Then we found out that the police had actually got it. But it was only when he wrote that bloody book that we realised what he had done. He had this sort of happy-go-lucky attitude.

The police didn't pick up the prints then?

Seán said that it was thoroughly wiped. You can believe that or not.

I don't want to brush too hard against the veil of anonymity that still covers some of the actors in the case. But now you've mentioned Hugh – for the first time in this context I think –, can you tell me a little bit more about his involvement?

Right from the beginning he was dead against it. He thought that it was a stupid thing to do; we should never have got involved with it. But he understood our motivations. Then seeing that we were in a tight spot, he helped us out. That if you like was Hugh all over. He was a very good friend and entirely honourable.

You also drew on some medical connections as well. Was it one doctor or two?

One.

It wasn't Alex Comfort, was it?

No. I did approach him about raising some money to help with the expenses of freeing Blake, but he said, 'I don't even want to hear that name again.' He absolutely blocked the idea; he said that he would have nothing to do with it.

Why the concern?

First of all, he was an anarchist in the best sense of the word, and thus in no way sympathetic to Russia. Then, secondly, he wouldn't have wanted to be party to anything with the potential of bringing the anti-nuclear movement into disrepute, which had also been my first reaction when Pat had raised the idea with me at Wormwood Scrubbs.

Many years later, when our involvement became public, Alex gave an interview to *The Sunday Times* about our involvement in the escape in which he said that some of these people, meaning us – I forget which phrase he used – were as wise as doves and as harmless as serpents, reversing the sense of the biblical quotation. I was really annoyed about that. I had worked with Alex Comfort. I'd been on good terms with him. I had a lot of respect for him, as he had, I think, for me. So, I challenged him on this. He said, well I didn't mean you; the person I had in mind when I made those remarks was Ralph Schoenman; Alex was another person who had no time for Schoenman. Anyway, the interview appeared in *The Sunday Times* as a follow-up, by the way, to an earlier piece in which they'd said that Alex had known about the escape. In the interview, he acknowledged that he *had* known about it, but also said that he'd had nothing to do with it.

In early November 1966, following a series of other scrapes, some of them amusing, you and Anne moved Blake from a friend's house to Pat Pottle's flat in Hampstead. In your book about the affair, Michael, you call that a turning point. Here's the quote: 'Pat, Anne and I recognized that we had to throw caution to the wind and take full responsibility for hiding George and organizing his flight from the country.' So, you, Pat and Anne were more or less on your own at that stage.

Well, it certainly wasn't going to be Bourke anymore. When he had first approached us he said that he'd look after everything. All we'd have to do would be to find some money. But then, as you know, George broke his wrist when he jumped off the prison wall and we had to deal with that. Then, when we went to the flat where Seán had chosen to hide him, far from being self-contained, as he had told us, we discovered that it was a bedsit, with a shared toilet in the corridor and with a landlady who came every week to clean. In other words, there was very little that was suitable about it. Seán, in his book, says that George was there only as a temporary measure, so he excuses himself on that basis. But, actually, that was not true. So, we first involved one group of friends, who put him and Seán up for a couple of days. Then another friend, John Papworth, took over—he, by the way, has since publicly acknowledged his role. John owned a house in London that was part-empty at the time. It's in the book what happened next. A series of events which I'll come to made us realise that we had to get George out. And Pat, bearing in mind no fingerprints had been found in the car and that there was nothing to lead the police to him, courageously agreed to put him up at his flat.

John Papworth. That name rings a bell. Oh, yes. Wasn't he the so-called 'shoplifting vicar'?

Yes, but what you're alluding to happened later on. And what John said was not that people should shoplift, but only that he could understand their motivations if they did so.

John helped us out by allowing George and Seán to stay at his house for a while, though it's important to add that he was out of London at the time and didn't meet George or Seán until his return a couple or so days later. I had only spoken to him on the phone and didn't tell him who the people were we were asking him to put up, and he didn't ask. I took it for granted that he'd guess, though he said afterwards he thought that I was probably talking about a couple of US draft resisters or deserters. John was in East Anglia with his wife at the time. The woman who let us into the house was his mother-in-law, a very elderly French lady, who was deaf and had only a limited grasp of English.

Anyway, a few days after the move I arranged to meet John's wife, Marcelle, who by then had returned to London. We met outside a tube station near Cambridge Circus. Naturally, she asked me about her two unusual house guests and I said, 'Well, one of them is George Blake.' 'George Blake!' she shouted and stopped dead in her tracks. I remember thinking, for God's sake, keep your voice down. But, fortunately, none of the passers-by reacted. Then, John arrived back and said in no uncertain terms that he didn't want George Blake living in his house. Then, a day or two later, he told us something else which decided the issue. Marcelle, he told us, was seeing a psychotherapist and for the psychotherapy to work she had to be absolutely frank and tell him everything that was worrying her. I said, 'You mean, she's told the therapist about us?' And John said, all very casually, 'Of course. Otherwise the treatment won't work. But don't worry. He thinks she's imagining it, because Blake's name has been so prominently in the news.' At that point, I remember Seán dived under the bed, grabbed his case and started stuffing things into it, while George, in his very calm, unruffled, way said, 'I think that under the circumstances we should move.' Within the hour, Seán was gone, returning to Highlever Road. And then, of course, we had to find somewhere else for them both.

Even before the escape, one of you had the strange idea of colouring Blake's skin, disguising him as an Egyptian in order to smuggle him out of England. Whose idea was that?

That was my idea. I'd read this book called *Black Like Me*, by John Howard Griffin. He was a white American who wanted to experience what it was like to be black. He described what he used, namely a drug called Methoxsalen. You took that, had several sessions under an ultraviolet heat lamp and it would change the colour of your skin. It was also used to treat a number of skin conditions. Unfortunately, you could only get the drug on prescription. But Pat had a printing press, so he was able to forge a doctor's note for me. I went to a pharmacy with Seán, one right in the centre of London, in Wigmore Street. Once we'd got the drug we also had to buy an ultraviolet lamp. After that, Seán carelessly tossed the receipt away. Well, the next day, I thought, Jesus. What if it all comes out? The police might then start looking for the shop that sold the lamp to us. So, I went back to Wigmore Street and found the receipt. It was paranoia, of course. The difference between Seán's cavalier approach and our ultra-cautious one was huge. But, anyway, Blake would have nothing to do with it. And he was quite right. After all, it was a mad idea. We were complete amateurs. What did we know about the drug?

Who came up with the idea of smuggling Blake out of the country in a van?

Well, that had always been a possibility. It just came up as part of the general discussion as to what possibilities there were. In a sense, it was an obvious thing to do, to hide the person in a vehicle of some sort and drive him over to the continent and on to Eastern Europe.

Anne: Something similar had been done before. But in the reverse direction, from East to West.

Were you always going to take him to East Germany or did you discuss other alternatives?

I think we did. But East Berlin seemed the best option because of the East-West autobahn. Any citizen of one of the four occupying powers could get a visa to go to West Berlin, and to get to West Berlin you had to drive along the autobahn in East Germany, Once in West Berlin it would be relatively straightforward to cross into East Berlin.

I won't take you through all the details of your journey to East Germany. In brief, the two of you, your two young children and George set off for Germany in a camper van during the middle of December 1966. At the border checkpoints, George hid in a secret compartment under a bed. If anyone wants to read about that part of the escape they have only to buy or borrow the book you wrote with Pat: The Blake Escape: How we freed George Blake and why. *But I do want to ask you about your parents' response to your involvement.*

They didn't know about it at the time. After dropping George off at the East German checkpoint at the end of the autobahn and returning to Britain, we spent Christmas with my mum and dad at the family farm in Sussex, which after what we'd been through was quite a different sort of experience [laughs]. Neither of them knew anything. How could they? I remember that we spent a lot of time cleaning the van because we wanted to remove all the evidence of George's presence, fingerprints and so forth. Although my mother said nothing about this at the time, later on, when she knew the full story she said, 'I did wonder why you were cleaning the van so thoroughly.'

8. The Greek Embassy 'Invasion' and Czechoslovakia

Okay, Michael, forward again to 1967. Before returning to George Blake and the escape to East Germany, we'd been talking about Vietnam and your relationship with Vanessa Redgrave and Ernest Rodker. But Vietnam wasn't the only major issue to exercise the left in 1967. For instance, there was still the matter of Greece.

That's right. By then Greece was a tyranny, in spite of what our own government was telling us. During April, a military junta seized power. Thousands were arrested. People were executed. That's why we wanted to do something, to show our support for the democratic opposition.

I was struck by something Anne said when you set off for the Greek embassy action: 'You'll get done this time.' What do you remember about your feelings?

We had a lawyer, a fellow member of the Committee of 100, who was good, but probably too close to us in a way because he was inclined to downplay the possible risks. He said, well, formally it's Greek property, so they'll probably just turf you out and that will be it. So, we went in thinking not much would happen. But it did.

You invaded sovereign property. Any particular scruples there?

Not really. We'd always been internationalist in our outlook and had carried out demonstrations in various countries, including Russia where Committee of 100 people at the World Peace Congress in Moscow in 1962 handed out leaflets criticising not only its nuclear policies but other aspects of its policies and ideology as well. So, the protest at the Greek embassy was perfectly in keeping with that.

I believe there were a couple of Greek women in the advance party with you and Pat. Can you tell me about them?

I can only think of one of them at the moment. Her name was Felitsa Matziorini. The plan was for the advance group of me, Pat Pottle and the two women to go up to the door. The women would be carrying a bunch of flowers and as soon as the door was opened a lorry would draw up with about fifty demonstrators inside. We would push passed the person opening the door – that was the only part that was not one hundred per cent non-violent, though we certainly had no intention of injuring anyone. We knew there wouldn't be many people there because it was a weekend; at most there'd be a skeleton staff. We intended to take over the embassy. We had someone with us who knew how to operate a telex machine and we had this very ambitious idea that we would telex other Greek embassies across the world, stating that the Greek embassy in the UK had declared in favour of the ousted democratically elected government and asking them to take similar action.

So, you were going to impersonate them?

That's right. Well, as soon as the door opened all the people in the back of the lorry piled out and followed us into the embassy. There is a film taken by one of our number showing people jumping out of the Post Office van and racing to the open Embassy door. It's rather like a scene in a Buster Keaton film. That part of the plan worked well, except for one thing: the janitor who opened the door panicked. He started to shout, 'No! No! No!' That gave me a really uneasy feeling. Immediately I felt sorry for him and began to wonder if we were doing the right thing.

Anyway, we got into the embassy. We knocked the wedges we'd brought with us under the doors to slow down any incoming police and give us time to operate the telex machine. But someone did manage to get out, I think from a basement door and he or she raised the alarm. I remember, we had just got into the embassy, people were rushing about onto the different floors. I said to Pat,

'We've made it.' But just at that moment the police arrived and far from being deterred by a few wedges under the door, they simply smashed their way in.

I ran upstairs and locked myself in a bathroom. Meanwhile Terry Chandler, who clung on to one of the bannisters, was roughed up by some policemen. And because they roughed him up, they then had to charge him with assault. Otherwise they would have had to explain his bruises.

As for me, I waited in the bathroom. Everyone else had been cleared out, so all was quiet. Then someone tried to open the door, found that it was locked, and demanded to be let in. So, I was taken into custody as well. I was wearing a mohair duffle coat, given to me by our friend Mario Lippa, which was rather smart. In fact, one of the funnier sides to the story is that when the police escorted me out of the embassy some of our supporters assumed that I was a member of the embassy staff and actually ran up to me and challenged me. Well, the police soon put them right about that!

I was put in a police car on my own while most of the other protestors were driven away in police vans. Anyway, Pat noticed that the rear door of the van he was in was not properly closed and when the van stopped at traffic lights, he kicked the door open and shouted, 'Everyone out!'. So, they all piled out and ran and most of them, including Pat, managed to get away.

One of the Greek women, unfortunately, was wearing a tight skirt, so she couldn't run fast enough and was soon caught. So too was Howard Cheney, who walked with a limp. But another woman went into a phone box and pretended to be making a call. She did get away as, in fact, a number of them did.

George Brown, who was Foreign Secretary at the time, made a statement that same evening calling the action an absolute disgrace. We then thought, right, they're now going to come down on us like a ton of bricks. And they did. They held us in the police cells overnight. I remember thinking, Oh, my God, what is this going to do to Anne and the kids? I really felt guilty. The thing had worked out in a way that none of us had anticipated. We were first charged with causing a riot, which is a very serious offence. We were then charged with contravening section five of the Public

Order Act, 1936. We were held overnight and on the following morning taken to a magistrate's court and bailed to await trial. Things then dragged on right through the summer, with lots of negotiations between our lawyers and the prosecution. I thought at one point that they'd come to some sort of agreement. I think the idea was that if we pleaded guilty to one offence, they would drop some of the more serious charges, including the assault charge against Terry Chandler. But we all had to agree; they wouldn't accept some of us pleading guilty and others not guilty. We did become quite disunited at one point. The LSE people were particularly worried about their careers, so they were a bit more conciliatory.

Eventually, we went on trial at the Old Bailey. This was on the 3rd and 4th of October. We all pleaded guilty. I remember that I started to make a speech justifying our actions. The judge said, 'If you carry on like that, we'll put you down as offering a not-guilty plea.'

Anyway, most of the LSE students were given a conditional discharge, while those of us who were left were sent off to spend the night in Brixton Prison. I remember the chat we had amongst ourselves. We said, 'The LSE lot have got off with a warning. They can't come down too heavily on us.' So, we felt a bit more confident in the morning and our optimism seemed justified when the first few people to be sentenced received fines. Terry Chandler, however, was sentenced to fifteen months, myself to twelve months and another man, Del Foley, to six months for no obvious reason.

We were given the opportunity of making a statement. I made a very strong statement defending what we had done and saying there were circumstances in which it was right to break the law. That didn't go down well at all with the judge. But Pat very strongly approved. He said that I'd done the right thing.

What about Pat? They'd had him in one of their vans, after all. Didn't they arrest him as well? Surely, he would have been recognised afterwards?

Of course, the police knew that Pat had been involved, but no, they didn't arrest him. Cheekily, he stood surety for our bail, prior to the hearing. He came up, bold as brass.

So, there was Terry, me and the other guy, the first two of us with form, both in the Direct Action Committee and the Committee of 100. I'm sure they looked at the evidence and said, these guys must be the ringleaders.

They were right.

They were right, but we weren't the only ones. Ken Weller had played a key role in getting the protest organised. They didn't jail him. He was a member of the Committee of 100, but he didn't have an official position. He came up before the court a bit later than most of us for some reason. His partner was one of the people fined.

Was Bob Overy involved in that action?

He was. He'd been on several demonstrations before, but this, I think, was the first time that he'd been arrested. Bob was working for *Peace News* at the time and he wrote up a report of the event.

He also, I believe, fell out with Ben Birnberg, your solicitor on the occasion.

Yes. Bob wrote something for *Peace News* in which he was critical of Ben. He felt that we'd been improperly pressured into pleading guilty to the lesser charge when a stronger, more robust, defence might have drawn some of the attention away from me and the two others. He really felt for Anne and me. However, I trusted Ben, as I do still. He was virtually a Committee of 100 person himself. He didn't actually sign on the dotted line because he had to keep some distance from the people he was defending. But he was absolutely with us and afterwards married Felitsa. We're still very good friends with both of them.

I read somewhere that there was talk of Amnesty International taking up your case. Do you recollect any discussions of that nature?

No, not really. But I do remember that my friends in the WRI put a short account of the case by Ammani Prasad, one of Devi's children, on the front cover of the WRI journal. I was very touched by that.

One woman went on a hunger strike.

That was Pat O'Connell. She was a great Irish lady, a teacher and an activist. I had a lot of time for her. She always had something sensible to contribute to the conversation. Anyway, yes, she went on hunger strike as a protest against the length of my imprisonment. Pat, by the way, was one of the people who took part in that famous demonstration at Holy Loch, the one after the 1961 Aldermaston march. A small group of them, led by Pat, walked all the way to Scotland. I took the train to Scotland and met them there.

Fig 18.   Michael, with Anne, Seán and Gavin on Parliament Hill Fields, London, shortly before standing trial for the Greek embassy 'invasion'. Photographer unknown. Private Collection.

Where were you imprisoned following the sentence?

At first, I was sent to Pentonville. In fact, I spent a few months there. It was a lot more lax than Wormwood Scrubs and a lot more run down. There was a Polish guy there, Paul Pavlovski, who was also inside for a demonstration of some sort, and who was very well known in Committee circles as an ardent Maoist. I used to chat to him during exercise. Before coming to England, he'd got up the nose of the authorities in Poland, so I imagine they were pleased to see the back of him. He went on to publish a number of pamphlets describing his experiences there, which made very amusing reading. On one occasion he lent me a copy of Mao's *Little Red Book*. I was no Maoist, but rather foolishly I mentioned the book in a letter to Anne. What happened next, I suppose, was rather typical of prisons in those days: they hauled me out of a workshop, searched my cell, and the *Little Red Book* was confiscated [laughs].

Weren't you allowed political literature?

There wasn't a blanket ban on political literature, but all books that were sent in had to be checked and approved by the authorities. If they were confiscated, they were returned to you when you left the prison. So, I've still got that *Little Red Book* somewhere.

You were in Pentonville when two police officers arrived to interview you. In the Blake book you wrote with Pat Pottle you say you panicked because you thought they wanted to interview you about Blake.

I remember thinking, God, I'm going to end up spending several years in prison. But, in fact, they weren't there to talk about that. They wanted to interview me about the leafleting action at Wethersfield. As soon as they mentioned Wethersfield, I breathed a sigh of relief. God, is that all! I thought. A prison officer was with me at my request. I didn't trust the police, so I wanted there to be a witness present. They may have mentioned the possibility of bringing charges, but in the end nothing came of it.

What was it like for Anne at this period? I imagine things were very tight financially.

Well, they were. But we had a lot of sympathy from various friends and the public at large. Has she told you what Vanessa Redgrave did for her? Just before Christmas, she turned up at the house with Karel Reisz and his wife, Betsy Blair, and had her and the boys driven to the prison in a limousine. Vanessa gave me a bottle of champagne and a book of poems which I still have, though the champagne, alas, was confiscated. Then Geoffrey Moorhouse interviewed Anne and wrote a sympathetic article in *The Guardian*, which brought in some donations and a lot of sympathy. The money enabled Anne to take driving lessons and to buy a second-hand Mini. Then the Committee set up a fund to help all three of us, me, Terry and Del, and that raised quite a lot. There was a strong sense of solidarity in the movement.

This may be an intrusive question, but I'll ask it anyway: was Anne angry with you for getting yourself into such a predicament?

My recollection is that she was very supportive. But ask her yourself. She might have a different take on it! But, in any case, remember, we had very good friends, like Ernest Rodker and Sonia Markham. They were a great strength.

There's a line in the Moorhouse article that struck me when I first looked at it. He quotes Anne as saying that 'Michael ought to be a single man when his conscience and his person are placed so freely at everyone's disposal.'

I forgot about that one! [laughs].

Tell me about life at Lewes Prison. You were moved there from Pentonville during the spring of 1968.

Lewes was a reform prison, which is to say that the authorities were trying to change how things were generally done there. There was a lot more emphasis on rehabilitation and rather less on punishment. The governor there — I can't remember his name — was fairly liberal and supportive of the reform project. I was put in a workshop where we assembled children's toys. I think they had a wind-up mechanism; they certainly ran on rails. It was an arrangement with an outside firm. But, anyway, I hated it; it was so bloody boring. It was production line stuff. You know the sort of thing. You stick one piece in place and the next chap puts in another piece. Jesus Christ! And it was supposed to reform you!

What about agricultural work? Did you do any of that?

Well, that's the interesting thing. There were at least two 'work parties' in the prison. There was the 'garden party', which was very popular because you worked outside the prison walls growing vegetables. And then the 'coke party', which no-one wanted to be on because its task was to load up coke into sacks, put them on a trolley and take them to the various furnaces round the prison. You could be assigned to the coke party as a punishment for breaking the rules. I, however, applied to go on one because I thought that anything would be better than working on that damn production line. It took me outside, I was with a small group and I got a shower as well at the end of the day. Also, there was only one officer in charge of us. It was infinitely better than sitting in the workshop.

One of the other prisoners on the coke party was very tough and controlling; something of a bully. Well, there was a black prisoner working on one of the furnaces and the tough guy who effectively bossed our group, told us not to empty the coke in the assigned place but further off from the furnace. I certainly didn't agree with that, so I told him so. And then he turned against me as well and became quite hostile. But, later on, I was on the same side as him playing rugby — the Deputy Governor, quite a genial chap, had organised two teams from among the prisoners to play against each other. As I'd played rugby at school and for various clubs, including Brighton, I'd volunteered for it. I was a demon tackler, that was always my forte, and during one of our internal matches, this same guy who had become very hostile to me was highly impressed. 'Look at him', he said to the others, 'He weighs nothing and seems so mild, but he is knocking people down several times his size!' That was a turning point. After that he was friendly to me. It was all 'Hi Mike', whenever our paths crossed.

I worked on the coke parties for a while. Then an opportunity turned up to join the garden party, which I eagerly signed up for. The screw in charge was a Scotsman, ex-army, but friendly and quite the radical in his politics. I remember him telling me that he'd made a disparaging remark about royalty on the occasion of the abdication of Edward VIII and was severely reprimanded and punished for it. He said to me, 'Would you mind telling me what you're in for?' Because, you see, the screws weren't supposed to know. I told him about the embassy occupation. 'Shake my hand', he said, 'There should be more people like you!'

Did you keep in touch with political events outside the prison? 1968, after all, was a particularly interesting year for leftists.

Of course, just before I left Lewes the student uprising took place in Paris. Obviously, I was very encouraged by that. You know, in a strange way I ended up in a very good place in Lewes Prison. By the time I got back into civvies I was very fit. I even came out with a tan.

What did you do when you left prison? This would have been at the end of May 1968.

Well, I didn't have a job to go to. I had, however, done some teaching of English as a foreign language for the Inner London Education Authority (ILEA). I suppose that I could have gone back to doing that. But I'd fallen out with the man running it. I used to go in quite respectably dressed, at least I thought so; sort of smart-casual. But the person who ran the college, an Australian, who I supposed not to stand on ceremony, insisted that I wore a collar and tie. 'We've got to differentiate', he said, 'between the staff and the students.' Sometimes I did wear a collar and tie. I certainly wasn't doctrinaire about it. So, I wore a collar and tie a couple of times after the warning, but then came in one day wearing a polo-neck sweater. He hauled me off to his office and said, 'If you don't wear a collar and tie, you're sacked.' Which is precisely what happened.

Funnily enough—I can't remember how—, the papers got interested in the case and *The Sunday Telegraph* ran the story with a photo of me wearing the sweater.

Before getting on to your time in Bradford where, of course, you did get a job, you travelled to Vienna for a meeting of the WRI Council in August 1968. During the course of that meeting you were part of a WRI delegation who met with members of the World Peace Council at its international HQ in the city. Do you remember anything about that latter experience?

I do, yes. This was the time of the Dubcek reforms in Czechoslovakia aimed at building 'communism with a human face'. Dave McReynolds played a key role, along with Devi Prasad, in setting up both meetings. Dave, as I've said, was a leading member of the War Resisters League, the US branch of WRI, which was keen to keep open the lines of communication with the WCP and the various national Peace Committees.

The meeting with the WCP was formal and correct. We paid each other compliments and discussed issues on which we were in agreement. But at a certain point, I thought, 'This is good as far as it goes, but we still have concerns and disagreements and should express them.' I said something along the lines of, 'Well, this is all very positive, but we are worried about the Warsaw Pact manoeuvres on the borders of Czechoslovakia. Can you say something about that?' This genial Russian—I can't at present remember his name—responded: 'Manoeuvres is manoeuvres. We have manoeuvres. You have manoeuvres. Everyone has manoeuvres.' In other words, there was nothing to worry about [laughs]. Then just days later, Soviet and Warsaw Pact forces invaded.

Meanwhile, we accepted an invitation from the Slovak Peace Committee to visit them in Bratislava which proved to be fantastically interesting. I don't know whether it was my imagination, but I felt there was a sense of freedom and optimism in the air. The Slovak Peace Committee members too when we met them spoke frankly about their fears that the Warsaw Pact manoeuvres might be the prelude to an invasion. For a Peace Committee, affiliated to the WPC, to express to us such fears of Soviet intentions, or criticism of Soviet policy, was in my experience unprecedented. I'll have to check on the dates, but I think that it was only a matter of weeks later that the Slovak Peace Committee accepted an invitation to visit us in London. Not long after that, however, most of them were ousted.

Another thing that sticks in my mind from that meeting in Vienna is that when we were at the border on our way back into Austria, we saw a young man with his hands in the air being frogmarched at gunpoint by Czechoslovak border guards in the other direction. Clearly, he was someone attempting to escape to the West. That we all found truly shocking.

A few days after the WRI meeting ended, Soviet and Warsaw Pact forces moved into Czechoslovakia. Dave McReynolds had gone to Prague after the WRI meeting ended and was actually there when the Warsaw pact forces moved in. John Hyatt, of the Peace Pledge Union had also stayed behind at the end of the WRI meeting and he took part in a sit-down in front of the invading tanks in Bratislava.

Following the invasion, Michael, you coordinated an international protest. How did that come about?

When the news came through that the Soviet and Warsaw Pact forces had invaded Czechoslovakia, April Carter phoned me and suggested that War Resisters' International should organise an international protest against the invasion. After some telephone consultations, the WRI Executive agreed, and April and I, with help and support from the WRI secretary Devi Prasad, spent a frantic few weeks helping to organise it. I flew at one point to Copenhagen to speak to the leader of the Danish branch of WRI, Aldrig Mere Krig, and April and I met Marco Panella of the Italian affiliate, Partito Radicale.

The protest which we called 'Support Czechoslovakia' took the form of teams from WRI sections taking part in simultaneous demonstrations on Tuesday the 24th September in Moscow, Warsaw, Budapest and Sofia. The participants handed out leaflets expressing support for the people of Czechoslovakia and displayed banners with the slogans in English and the appropriate national language; 'End NATO', 'End the US War in Vietnam', and 'End the Occupation of Czechoslovakia.'

Participants in the protest came from several countries including Britain, the US, the Netherlands, Italy, Denmark and India, and among the supporting organisations were the International Confederation for Disarmament and Peace and an American Quaker Action Group. Bertrand Russell made a public statement in support of the action.

April Carter took part in the demonstration in Hungary. I, as I had only recently been released from prison for my part in the occupation of the Greek Embassy, decided against participating directly, but played a co-ordinating role in London, including dealing with the press.

Two people took part in the action in Moscow: Vicki Rovere, of the War Resisters League, and Andrew Papworth, formerly of the DAC and the Committee of 100. Five in that in Budapest, including Bob Eaton, who had captained the Quaker peace ship, *Phoenix,* which sailed medical supplies to Haiphong in North Vietnam in 1967, and two Indian activists, Satish Kumar and E.P. Menon, who had completed an 8,000 mile peace walk from Delhi to the capitals of the nuclear weapon states: Moscow, Paris, London and Washington.

Altogether, we were able to assemble a good team. There were even some people from the German Federal Republic.

They demonstrated and then what happened? They contacted you with their accounts?

We arranged with the different groups to phone through and tell us how the protests had gone on. Pat Pottle and Sue Pottle were involved in that side of things.

It hit the news over here in quite a big way. Some were able to give out their leaflets, urging people to condemn what had happened in Czechoslovakia, and some were not. Of course, most of them were simply arrested and sent home on the next available flight. But those who demonstrated in Budapest, including April, were detained in prison until Saturday. In London we spent an anxious few days wondering how long they might be held for.

According to an article in The Guardian, *ordinary Moscovites were actively hostile to Vicki Rovere and Andrew Papworth. The paper quoted a report from Izvestia denouncing the demonstrators as 'unknowing pawns on the chessboard of the imperialist intelligence services'!*

We don't know, of course, how 'ordinary' these hostile Moscovites were. The Warsaw demonstration was probably most successful in as much as it got the warmest response from people. In fact, some of the students from Warsaw University with the agreement of the demonstrators, ran off with the banner before the police had a chance to seize it, and kept it.

No demonstration in East Germany?

No, after intensive discussion we decided that nut was too hard to crack, given the hard-line, repressive character of Ulbricht's communist government. Also, we didn't want to jeopardize our West German socialist and peace movement friends' long-term relationship with groups and individuals critical of the regime in East Berlin and the rest of the GDR.

I mentioned earlier that you did get a job eventually. You found a job teaching in Bradford.

Yes. That was in October 1968 at the Bradford Regional College of Art, whose most famous alumnus is David Hockney. In fact, some of lecturers there had taught Hockney. I was taken on to teach complementary studies, the department run by Albert Hunt. And thank goodness I was. Following the prison sentence for the Greek embassy action and the trouble at ILEA, I was pretty much unemployable in a conventional setting.

You've mentioned Albert once or twice already. Wasn't he at the 1958 North Pickenham demo?

I don't think he had a part in obstructing the lorry drivers building the base, but he was a key contact and support during the whole of the campaign against the base. Albert had been living in Swaffham, near North Pickenham, when the Direct Action Committee had its demonstrations there. He and his wife Dorothy were some of the people who supported us by coming along to the demonstrations and providing help of various sorts. Then, later on, when we were trying to liven up *Peace News*, I put his name forward as a potential contributor. I'm glad I did. He did some fantastic work. He covered theatre and Alan Lovell covered film. They sort of worked in tandem.

Were they friends as well as co-workers?

Yes, they were. I don't know when they first met each other. But they certainly went back a bit. I remember Terry telling me that Albert 'drove like a madman!' She used to be frightened of going in his car [laughs].

One of the great things about Albert was that he had these fantastic connections. He knew Adrian Henri and several of the Liverpool poets. Adrian Mitchell was a personal friend of his and he knew lots of others in the literary and theatrical world including Peter Brook. In fact, Albert worked with Peter Brook and Adrian

Mitchell on a show about Vietnam with the Royal Shakespeare Company called *US*. This was in 1966, at the same time as Pat and I were thinking of ways of getting George Blake out of Britain, assuming the escape plan succeeded.

I remember one day, I walked into the rehearsal rooms at the National Theatre. They were rehearsing *US* at that point and there were notices everywhere: 'No Entry Beyond This Point'. Anyway, I walked in and there was Albert, very surprised to see me. I had a talk with him about the sort of disguises that we could use, and he said, 'If you're going to use black up, make sure that it isn't too amateurish.' Then when the Blake escape happened, I got a postcard from him with just one word on it: 'Congratulations'. He'd just stopped off somewhere while out driving with his family and posted it.

So, anyway, when Albert came to Bradford to take up the running of complementary studies, he brought lots of interesting people with him. Before that, it had been run in a very traditional way.

How so?

Well, there'd be a certain number of lectures that the students had to attend and if they didn't attend, they'd be disciplined. Albert said no, let's do it differently. We'll take students away from all their other work and do fortnightly blocks with writers, artists, theatre people and other interesting people coming in and running them. We'll put together a number of projects and allow students to sign up just for the ones they're interested in.

So, you moved to Bradford?

That's right. We moved from London to Yorkshire. To begin with I worked part-time on a couple of teaching projects for Albert: first at Shrewsbury Art College and then at Bradford. After that I was appointed to work at the art college and Anne and I took the plunge and moved to Bradford properly. The principal of the college at the time was a man called Fred Coleclough who had a lot of confidence in Albert and was prepared to give him his head.

My first project at Bradford involved taking the students through Orwell's *Nineteen Eighty-Four*. Some of them brought in tape recorders and recorded passers-by and then I got them to make images. This was a way of working initiated by Albert. The second project was called 'The Other Veterans', during which students interviewed people who'd been conscientious objectors in the First World War, many of whom by then were already in their seventies or eighties. Hence the title, 'The Other Veterans'. That one was probably the better of the two. I remember Alan Lovell saying that 'This one has really worked', which was high praise indeed. In fact, I'm still proud of it.

One of the other projects I was involved with was 'Living in Wartime', which was run by Albert. Students went out into the community and interviewed people in their homes. Other people came into the college and talked about the period. Then, Albert put together a show which showed how Britain itself had moved in a more authoritarian direction during the course of the war. He called it 'The God Show'. The show traced the transition of an evangelical movement from having a very open-minded approach to a tight disciplinarian one.

One of my responsibilities after I was appointed was to arrange a weekly lecture. With Albert's help and guidance, I got a lot of interesting people to come along, including the poets Michael Horovitz, Adrian Henri, Adrian Mitchell and Roger McGough and the architect Ted Cullinan.

While we're on the subject of poetry, were you also interested in the American Beats? Ginsberg, Ferlinghetti, Corso, those sorts of people? You did say earlier that you would have liked to have attended the 1965 International Poetry Incarnation, at which these poets read.

Peace News published some of Ginsberg's stuff. I really enjoyed 'Howl'.

Did you enjoy teaching?

Oh, very much so. But then after a couple of years they started to make some changes. They brought in a new principal as part of the move to merge the art school and the technical college and to create what is now Bradford College. In the art school we were resistant to the merger because we wanted to keep our autonomy and this new principal marked me down as an obvious dissident.

I saw him again a few years ago at an event to celebrate the college's history and we had a friendly exchange. I introduced myself as one of his old sparring partners and it turned out that he, like me, had been a conscientious objector! It was such a relief. I had half expected him to give me the cold shoulder. In other circumstances, I'm sure that we would have got on all right. Anyway, I was one of the people on the front line as, so to speak, was Albert. Then I also got into a bit of a fracas with one of the other staff members, who I think may have taken over the leadership role from Albert at that point. I had a confrontation with him one day. I was so incensed that I actually took him by his lapels and shook him, which was technically an assault. It was very stupid of me to have done this. He reported it to the new principal and of course I was disciplined. Eventually I resigned. It just wasn't what I wanted to do any longer.

[Anne came in at this point]
Anne, we've just been talking about Michael's stint at Bradford Regional College of Art. How did you take to Bradford?

Anne: Oh, gosh. Not willingly! Initially Michael came up on his own and stayed with a lecturer named Bill Gainham and also with Jeff Nuttall, who had a place in the centre of town near the old police station. Then we all came up and stayed for a while in Albert Hunt's house while he and his family were away. The house was so cold that we woke up one morning to find the water in the glasses at the side of the bed had a layer of ice on them. I thought, well, if this is the North, I really don't want to make this move at all. It really was foreign territory. You have to remember that a) I didn't want to come. b) I had two young children. And c) I had to find a job because Michael wasn't earning much money in those days. Eventually, we got a mortgage on a house in Paradise Road, Heaton. The cost of the house was £1,900 and we couldn't afford it. It was a terraced house that needed a lot doing to it. It hadn't been lived in for a while. I'd left London and my friends for somewhere I didn't want to be. Having to start again was very difficult. In retrospect I probably blurred it out a bit. I certainly don't remember talking to the boys about it. The first time Michael went up, I was in a really bad way. I'd got mumps off the kids and he was up in the north. I got it on both sides. The kids were five and seven. It was very very difficult. I was just a housewife, so practically voiceless. I'd done a bit of temping, but I was a nothing really [laughs].

Michael: One of the people who eased the move was Donald Rooum. I already knew Donald, as I've said, through *Peace News* and the business with Detective Sergeant Challoner. Prior to moving up to Bradford, he and his partner Irene invited us to a meal at their home in London, to where he had moved from Bradford. I remember a quip of Donald's was that Bradford was 'a good place to have cum from'.

He also told an anecdote about the experience of young Asian pupils learning English. At the start of the class the teacher would read out the names on the register, and if the child wasn't there the white pupils would respond, 'Sh'int here, Miss' or 'Sh'ant cum.' And Donald remarked that if you didn't know 'Sh'int here' or 'Sh'ant cum', you didn't understand English.

Anne: The house we ended up buying in Bradford wasn't far from Donald's sisters, Shirley and Denise. Shirley and her husband, Gordon, lived virtually around the corner. They rescued us on our first night. We arrived too late to get the electricity and the gas turned on. The removal firm we used to bring our stuff up from London were very cheap. They were Cockney lads who were very rude about where we were going. 'Gor, talk about *Coronation Street'*, one of them said, remarking on the cobbled street. We only had candles for lighting. But Shirley arrived at just the right moment. We were thinking, 'God! We've got no light, what are we going to do?' Thank goodness, it wasn't cold; it was July, the day before the Moon landing. Shirley whisked us off to her place for a big fry-up; a proper Yorkshire welcome. Then the next day we watched the moon landing as by then the electricity was turned back on.

What was Bradford like in those days?

Michael: Its reputation was that of a northern industrial town, with a very lively art college: Bradford Regional Art College. I remember, sometime in 1967, reading an article in *New Society* about one of Albert's projects called 'The Russian Revolution in Bradford', in which he got people from the community to take some of the major roles and to re-enact scenes from the Russian Revolution.

Of course, economically, Bradford was going downhill. I remember doing a project at one of the mills, interviewing people about the decline and where things stood.

Anne: It was at this time that many of the buildings were being sandblasted, so the city was starting to look rather blonde again.

What about the politics of the period? I should imagine that they were pretty lively too.

Michael: There were demonstrations by the National Front and counter-demonstrations, though I can't remember exactly which year that was.

I went on a counter-demonstration on the piece of waste ground at the end of Lumb Lane, opposite the Beehive pub. We all took down the number of a good radical lawyer, Chris Vincenzi, so if we were arrested we would have his number to ring. Chris was also a member of Bradford Nuclear Disarmament group and he and his wife Ruth became close friends.

Anne: I was too nervous to go on that one. I had an intimation that something bad was going to happen.

Would you say that the political climate was more brutal in Bradford than London?

Michael: No, I don't think that struck me particularly. However, in London the confrontations had been mainly with the police and I hadn't taken part in any counter-demonstrations against the far right.

Anne, were you involved with the college at all, at social events for instance?

Anne: Yes. I got to know several people. Ian Taylor, one of the students, subsequently a lecturer, there, became our lodger. He did up our basement and then lived in it. He's retired now, but he's a talented painter and sculptor and still exhibits regularly at Dean Clough Gallery in Halifax. He's part of a nucleus of people from that period who we still see regularly. You know, the usual suspects, the people who turn up at a new theatre piece or to a gallery opening.

What about Albert Hunt? Did you see much of him?

Anne: Michael stayed with him and Dorothy at their home on the outskirts of Halifax when he was running projects at the art college but before he was appointed as a lecturer. The two of us also stayed at the house once when they were away and we were house hunting. But, generally, Albert kept his family life pretty separate from the college activities.

Michael: Dorothy always made us very welcome.

Anne: Yes. But it was Albert who was the party animal. Dorothy only rarely accompanied him. Albert, by the way, had a deformed hand, with vestigial fingers. But, wow, he could really play the piano. There's a story he told us about his birth: he said that the midwife tried to persuade his mother to have him put into a home. He also used to have this trick with a coin. Whenever he was speaking. he'd roll coins through the stubs. He never dropped them. Our kids used to be fascinated.

Anne, you mentioned Jeff Nuttall earlier on. Any memories of him?

Anne: Not really. I knew his long-suffering wife better. She was a very gentle soul named Jane. I used to meet up every so often with her and other women, including Bob Overy's wife, Ruth. We were members of a women's group based in Wyke.

Michael: Jeff Nuttall taught at the art college as did John Fox, Tony Earnshaw and Bruce Lacey. Jeff was a larger than life character, an artist in the surrealist tradition who taught on the Foundation Course and did some occasional acting. I remember he played a character in a TV television drama. Something of an anarchist in his disposition and convictions, he also came with me on one occasion to distribute leaflets at the US base at Menwith Hill.

Tony was based at Leeds, but he did regular sessions at the art college. When the college put on a show at the Serpentine in London, Tony was one of the main people involved in it.

Anne: Bruce ended up living in Norfolk and by coincidence my youngest sister and her partner got to know him through the Norwich art and music scene. He used to come out to annual events they held at their house there. They'd set up tents for the musicians to use and the music and dancing would go on well into the night. Bruce was a great storyteller. That said, towards the end of his life — I have to say this — he did get a bit arrogant. It was like he was holding court almost. I really went off him at that point. There was always a very young woman hanging around him.

By the way, Michael, did you get Bayard Rustin or any of your other American friends, for that matter to lecture at the art college?

No. Bayard lived in the US and came only occasionally to the UK. However, some years later, in 1986, I did persuade him to come to an international consultation at Bradford University run by the Alternative Defence Commission.

Anne: Michael mainly saw Bayard at conferences. We did, however, stay with him once in Manhattan. That was during the summer of 1969, which was just after we moved up to Yorkshire. Michael was at the WRI triennial in Haverford, Pennsylvania. I remember taking a call from him at about three o'clock in the morning while I was house-sitting at a friend's house in London. He said that he was with Bayard who had offered to pay my fare to travel there. So, I hastened up to Yorkshire and dropped the children off at Guisborough with Michael's sister, Mary, and then dashed back to London.

I'd never flown at this point, so my first plane journey was taken alone across the Atlantic. It was exciting, of course, but landing at the end of August in New York was another thing entirely. For starters, the heat was overwhelming.

After the conference, Bayard insisted on us using his room in the apartment while he took the other room. It was a very grand apartment, full of antiques, and the bed was a four-poster, with a carving hanging down from the top canopy. I asked Bayard what it was, and he said, 'I call that the bishop's dick.' [laughs]. Why? Because apparently the bed had belonged to a bishop in the seventeenth century.

Bayard was so generous. He even gave us his credit card to use as we wanted, to get presents for the boys. He also gave us a phone card, so we could make transatlantic calls. I'd never met anyone like him. His appearance alone was astonishing. He was six-foot something and extremely handsome.

Fig 19:   Michael greeting Bayard Rustin at the War Resisters' International triennial conference, in 1985. Photographer unknown. Private Collection.

Michael: Bayard was always buying antiques. When he came to London, he went around the antique shops. He had a vast range of knowledge.

Anne: I remember once he visited Michael's parents' home in Fletching and was intrigued by his dad's collection of jade. He knew exactly how valuable they were. There seemed to be nothing he didn't know something about.

Bayard, of course, was gay. Did you discuss the issue of gay rights with him?

Michael: No. Bayard was simply not in the forefront of the campaign on the issue at that time. However, later, when he was interviewed for the film *Brother Outsider,* he remarked that whereas for his generation the touchstone issue was race, now it was homosexual rights. It wasn't until a later period that he took a public stand on the issue. Previously, he was rather discreet.

I did wonder, looking back to the DAC, that you might have been uncomfortable with the issue. Of course, if so, there may have been good political reasons for that: you might not have wanted the movement to be seen as cranky or odd.

Well, as a Catholic I was taught that it was a mortal sin to have sex with someone of the same gender or indeed to have sex at all except in the context of marriage. But homosexual intercourse was still illegal in Britain and there was a stigma attached to it. I really came to admire those people who came out and said they were gay and proud of it. That called for exceptional moral courage, more so, indeed, than taking a stance against war, at least in peacetime. In the peace movement you had a community of people supporting you and there was a tradition of pacifism which was quite widely accepted. Things would have been different in wartime, especially during the First World War.

Did you have other gay friends besides Bayard?

Anne: Not in London, but up in Bradford certainly. One friend, Don Milligan, who was openly gay, was badly beaten up on the steps of Cartwright Hall. This was during the seventies at the opening of an exhibition. I don't think I'd ever seen an actual fight. It was absolutely horrible. Don was a slightly built man, tall and thin. I remember him coming for a meal at our house and his asking beforehand, 'Can I bring a friend?' He turned up with a man in full drag. The boys were at primary school at the time and they were like, golly we've never seen anything like this before! In fact, even I was taken aback. But Don was like that; he was naughty. I'm sure he and his partner did the drag thing knowing it could be tricky for some people. Eventually, he had to move away from Bradford because of threats made against him.

9. Peace Studies and the Alternative Defence Commission

Before we return to Czechoslovakia, Michael, can you tell me something about your contribution to the so-called Pacifist Manifesto *or, as it is perhaps better known,* A Manifesto for Nonviolent Revolution? *I noticed when I went through your notes for the project that you were influenced by Barrington Moore's once-famous* Social Origins of Dictatorship and Democracy.

I wrote a long analysis cum review of Moore's book, which was published in a shortened form in *Peace News*. I took some of his ideas and related them to non-violence.

As for the *Manifesto for Nonviolent Revolution* itself, that was a WRI initiative. The idea was not necessarily to be *The Communist Manifesto* of pacifism, but to set out a fairly considered position in favour of pacifism and non-violence. A few people, George Lakey among them, worked on versions of it. Eventually the WRI published the whole of it in their journal.

So, it was more academically robust than the norm for this sort of publication?

It was an attempt to look at the arguments for non-violence systematically, while at the same time remaining accessible to the ordinary, non-academic, reader. In fact, the emphasis was actually rather more on action than on intellectual argument. After all, the whole rationale of the WRI was — and is — practical action.

Nonetheless, did you feel any tension between your activism and this more scholarly, reflective, side of your practise?

No, I can't say that I did. I suppose I felt that this was attempting to provide a tougher basis for my non-violent activism. I didn't feel there was any contradiction.

Why George Lakey and what was your relationship with him like?

I've always had a very good relationship with George. I'm not sure when I first met him, but he was certainly at the War Resisters' triennial conference at Haverford College in 1969. After the conference I went to his house and worked with him and a group of people on ideas for action. He was involved with a Quaker action group at the time, who sailed a boat with medical supplies to North Vietnam in defiance of a US embargo. I had come out of prison the year before the conference, having served nine months of a year's sentence for my involvement in the occupation of the Greek embassy. There were some very interesting radical people at the conference, including Daniel Ellsberg. It was at that conference that Ellsberg decided that the *Pentagon Papers* showing the machinations behind US involvement in Vietnam should be made public. So, that conference had a very big impact.

What was your role at the conference?

I was chair. I had become chair in 1966, the year that Joan Baez was one of the speakers at the Triennial conference in Rome. Not that my responsibilities were in any way onerous. It was the General Secretary, Devi Prasad, who really had his nose to the grindstone. But, yes, I was involved and I did contribute to the WRI journal and to the discussions of the time.

How was the WRI funded in those days?

By voluntary subscription. As is still the case, there were branches in different countries. I don't know what the situation is like now, but certainly in those days it operated on a shoestring. The headquarters for many years was in Enfield, North London. Then it moved to Brussels for a few years, before moving first to East London, then to Caledonian Road above the *Peace News* and Housmans bookshop in North London.

I don't want to push the distinction between activism and scholarship too far, but do you think the peace movement lost something when so many of you moved into academia as seems to have been the case at this period?

It's hard to say. There was a peak period of activism with CND and the wider peace movement in the late 1950s with the Aldermaston marches, the missile base demonstrations and so on. Then by the early 1970s activity did die down to some extent. I don't think that was to do with people moving into academia, though it did partially coincide with it. A great deal of people's energy on the left and in the peace movement went into opposing the war in Vietnam and similar projects like opposing the colonels' coup in Greece and the apartheid regime in South Africa. All these things were seen to be related. We weren't just for peace; we were for freedom as well. The firmly non-aligned majority in the peace movement were entirely sympathetic to the moves towards liberalisation and opposition to the regimes in Eastern Europe as well as to right-wing dictatorships.

Why do you think the nuclear issue ran out of steam?

It appeared to do so in the sixties when the war in Vietnam became a central focus of campaigning. But then in the eighties it came back in a bigger and more international form with the creation of European Nuclear Disarmament (END) by Mary Kaldor and Edward Thompson, both of whom had been involved in CND in the sixties. There was a huge rebirth of interest, of life, and activism.

Let's return to Czechoslovakia now. During the early 1970s you worked with Jan Kavan, one of the leading Czech dissidents of the period.

That's right. His mother was called Rosemary. She's dead now, but she was a very courageous woman. Her husband, Pavel, was one of the victims of the trials centred on Slánský in 1952. Pavel, unlike Slánský and ten other defendants, wasn't executed, but the treatment he received in prison affected his health and shortened his life. Anyway, sometime after the WRI's demonstrations in Moscow and the three other Warsaw Pact countries, April attended a conference in London where she got talking to Jan and shortly afterwards she introduced me to him. He wanted to set up a link with the democratic opposition inside Czechoslovakia and supply them with equipment and information in the form of books, pamphlets and leaflets that would not have been available to them in Czechoslovakia.

In November 1970, I went to Prague by boat and train and stayed with Rosemary, and also made contact with other Czech dissidents. I brought them messages, though, essentially, I was just making contact at that stage. Thanks to the Support Czechoslovakia campaign, the WRI was regarded as genuine and reliable by the dissident communities in Eastern Europe. It also had many friends in these countries, so that was also a help.

On my next trip, this time in a camper van adapted by Ian Taylor, a fellow lecturer at the art college, I smuggled in a consignment of materials to Jan's contacts. Anne didn't come on that occasion. I went with another young woman, who was part of an leftist group that supported what we were doing, plus Seán and Gavin, so it was something of a repetition of smuggling George Blake out of Britain. In fact, Seán once said to me years later when I told him what had happened, 'You did make use of us, didn't you!' But it wasn't said in the spirit of you shouldn't have done that. He was simply stating a fact, and I know he was proud of what we had done.

Anyway, on this second trip to Czechoslovakia I took the consignment to Brno and met up with someone who later became quite a prominent figure in the first Post-Communist government, the foreign minister, in fact. Subsequently, other people from our circle of friends and another group with Trotskyist leanings carried on the smuggling operation. But what the Czechoslovak opposition really needed was a duplicating machine because at that time Czechoslovak citizens weren't allowed to have one, without official approval. So, the trip I made in 1971 was also a practice run for that. The duplicator was taken in on the next trip.

You mentioned 'materials'. What do you mean? Literature?

Yes. It was mainly political journals and pamphlets. You have to remember that the censorship was very rigorous in Czechoslovakia in those days.

Who funded the organisation?

You'd do better asking Jan about that. But it came from various voluntary sources. Jan also set up Palach Press and was involved in producing a journal called *Labour Focus on Eastern Europe*, with a somewhat Trotskyist emphasis. I think that Tariq Ali contributed to it.

Were you approached by any 'non-state actors' at that time?

No, never.

What about on other occasions?

No. As far as I'm aware I've never been approached by anyone with secret service connections.

I wonder why?

Well, like many people who engaged in peace activism we were vehemently opposed to authoritarian governments of every complexion. We made a point of insisting that we were a non-aligned peace movement. We were highly critical of Russia and also many aspects of Western policy such as the CIA/MI5 inspired overthrow of Mosaddegh in Iran, in 1953, the US war in Vietnam and the intervention in Suez in 1956. So, we were *personae non gratae* with both sides, which was just where we wanted to be [laughs].

That said, the help you'd given to George Blake did mean that you were open to blackmail.

Well, let's say that if someone from the security services did approach me, they certainly didn't make their intentions clear. If they had done so, and we had agreed to work with them, we could have been living in a mansion somewhere on secret service pay! [laughs]

Your own position vis-a-vis the Soviet bloc had by this time moved on a bit. During the fifties and early sixties, you'd worked with the World Peace Council, which was basically part and parcel of the Soviet state, and then here you are, in the early seventies, working with dissidents.

No, not at all. To say I'd worked with the World Council of Peace/World Peace Council during the fifties and early sixties gives a totally misleading impression. I was always wary of the WCP and their affiliated national peace committees precisely because of its pro-Moscow line. This was true also of Hugh Brock, and even more so of Gene Sharp who came over to Britain and joined the *Peace News* staff around 1955. Gene supported my attempt to get a team of pacifists to walk into Hungary in 1956, which we discussed earlier.

Don't forget also that during the first Aldermaston march in 1958 I had the unenviable task of going ahead of the main body of the march making sure that the only songs sang had DAC approval. Why? Because some of the marchers at the front were in the Communist Party, which was Moscow-oriented, and we wanted to make it clear that the march was non-aligned.

So, there was no big shift in my position on the Soviet Union between the 1950s/1960s and later. But one thing we did encourage was to keep the dialogue going. We were open to talking to anyone, but at the same time we made our own position clear. During two years in the 1980s, War Resisters' International ran anti-militarist marches in Europe, East as well as West. I remember we tried to get

into Poland and had lengthy negotiations with a Mr. Tyrluk of the
Polish Peace Committee.

You interviewed a remarkable Czech woman in the early nineties for your
People Power *book. Jirina Siklova, what can you tell me about her?*

Jirina Siklova was a sociologist and one of Jan's contacts. I first
met up with her at a UNESCO 'consultation' in Prague in the 1970s.
It was one of a number of preparatory events leading up to a big
UNESCO-sponsored conference that I attended in Paris. Jan gave
me some materials to give her. So, we arranged to meet up and she
gave me some information to pass on to Jan.

Adam Roberts was also at that meeting in Prague and he too
was helping the democratic opposition in Czechoslovakia.
However, I don't know how much he knew about what I was doing
on behalf of WRI.

I set the cat among the pigeons at that Prague consultation.
The World Peace Council people were there as well as a range of
people representing various positions, and everyone was being
very polite and friendly with each other, not bringing up anything
controversial. But then I spoke about civil resistance, giving the
example of the Czech opposition to the Soviet invasion. Well, there
was a stunned silence. Then the Russian at the meeting objected in
very strong terms. Vaseky, the chairman of the meeting and himself
a Czech, rebuked me with a polite rap on the knuckles. He said
something along the lines of it being important to observe 'certain
niceties'. But, after the meeting, he had this to say to one of my
UNESCO friends at the meeting, Steven Marx, which Steve passed
on to me: 'Michael, a eu tort de parler comme ça. Mais, il a
vachement raison' ('Michael was wrong to speak like that. But he is
absolutely right.') Rarely in any country is a population so united
as the people were in Czechoslovakia opposing the Russian and
Warsaw Pact intervention.

Did your involvement in Czechoslovakia go beyond people and politics?
For instance, did you visit as an ordinary tourist?

Not much at that point, but I went again in the 1990s to a
conference in Prague linked to END and met up with Jan. On that
occasion I was able to be more of a tourist and, for instance, visited
with others the café which features in Jaroslav Hašek's comic
masterpiece, *The Good Soldier Schweik,* long a favourite of mine.

By the way, were you involved with Charter 77?

Well, Jan was involved in that. And, yes, I certainly helped
publicise and support what they were doing. In fact, Jan's contacts
were mainly Charter 77 people, including Jirina Siklova. So, yes, I
suppose I was involved. But Jan was the only one of the signatories
that I knew really well.

Let's talk about Peace Studies at Bradford University now. Following your
resignation from Bradford Regional College of Art, you joined the
university in 1974. What was your role there?

I began part-time, as a research assistant. I worked and shared
an office with another researcher, Tom Woodhouse, who went on
to teach full-time in the department. In addition to the research I
did some lecturing on the undergraduate course. I used to travel up
once a week from the place to which we'd moved to, Gib Torr, on
the Staffordshire moorlands, near Buxton. I tried to make the
lectures as accessible as possible.

Why Bradford University and why the research job?

I applied for a lectureship after I left the art college. I wasn't
appointed, but I did get the research post, which involved some
lecturing. I remember a very friendly interview with Adam Curle,
who was then head of the department. It was unorthodox in as
much as he opened his drinks cupboard when I came in and we
both had a sherry [laughs]. At the time I had been working on a

study of militarism and repression which became the basis of an MPhil.

Did you know anything about Adam Curle before meeting him on that occasion?

No, I'd never heard of him. But I got to know him fairly quickly and liked him immensely. His approach was very inclusive, so he appointed people with very different outlooks and disciplines, which became quite a problem at the time.

So, they weren't all of the left?

I'd say they were left or centre-left. There certainly weren't any diehard conservatives.

What was Curle's background?

He was a Quaker and the Quakers were very important in setting up Peace Studies at Bradford. I'm not sure how far he engaged in activism. He did spend time in Ghana at the same time as I was there during and after the international protest against French nuclear tests in the Sahara. He was actually at the university in Accra at the time, though I didn't find that out till later. We happened to be chatting on one occasion in Bradford and it just came out.

I get the sense that Curle wasn't overly impressed by academic qualifications.

No, he did set a lot of store on sound academic procedure. He wanted people to be properly qualified and rigorous in their research and teaching. But, he was open to various approaches to teaching. I wasn't particularly well qualified academically. I had an undergraduate degree in English and my approach was somewhat unorthodox in as much as I was probably a bit more open than some of the other lecturers to new approaches. I had, after all, worked at the art college with Albert Hunt, a pioneer of new approaches to teaching. Then I'd also worked in the community and been an activist. I tried to bring these sorts of experiences into my work at the university.

How so?

One day we decided in one of the classes in the 'Peace and Change' course that we would all bring in knitting. The point was to challenge the distinction between so-called men's work and so-called women's work. I was relating it also to Gandhi's constructive programme exemplified by his encouragement of domestic spinning to make India more self-reliant. I also ran some projects, as Albert had done, in the city, including one called 'Mother Claus' or 'Mother Christmas', in reference to Father Christmas. We set up a stand in the street and ran a raffle, but because we didn't believe in competitiveness, we arranged things so that everyone won a prize at the same moment [laughs]. We had lots of fun.

An activity that would have been seen by many as 'barmy'.

Yes, I suppose that's true. But then some of the projects we did at the art college were a bit like that as well [laughs].

I've heard that the first cohort of undergraduates didn't sit examinations. Is that true?

I've got a feeling it might be, but I'm not very clear because I was very much on the edge of it. I wasn't working full-time, after all. During this period, I operated an off-set lithographic printer. Initially I kept it in the basement of the house in Bradford, then I moved it into the garage. Then, when we moved to Gib Torr, I installed it in an annex at the side of the house which had been used as a cowshed. I printed a lot of gay and radical literature for local people. In Bradford, one of the magazines I printed was called *Bradford Banner*. It covered the alternative scene in the city. I still have one or two copies of it.

Can you say something more about your colleagues at Bradford? You mentioned Tom Woodhouse briefly. I wonder who else was there.

One figure I remember very well was Tom Stonier. He was an American academic, who taught a course called 'Science and Society'. He brought some interesting ideas with him. I remember he put together a show at the university called 'A Multi-Media Treatise on Nuclear War and Peace', in which he related psychedelic and avant-garde ideas to peace.

Then there was another major figure who I'm still in touch with today: Nigel Young. Nigel had lectured in the States and contributed to *Peace News* while he was out there. He was in the first batch of appointments to Peace Studies. He held strong views and was very definite in his opinions.

Another controversial and very interesting figure was Uri Davis, an Israeli who was a very well-known activist on the Palestinian side. He and Nigel were at daggers drawn as far as one can be in a peace setting and one certainly can! They quarrelled violently.

Andrew Rigby was another lecturer and we became and still are close friends. In fact, he was my co-teacher on the undergraduate 'Peace and Change' course. Even before meeting him, I'd read some of his articles in *Peace News* and been impressed by them. His big interest then was the communes movement and alternative living. Then, when he left the university, Jenny Pearce took over the 'Peace and Change' course. She too is someone I greatly admire and get on with.

As an aside, were you attracted to communal living yourself at this period?

Oh, yes. Both Anne and I were. But we never actually did it unless you count the housing co-op in London. But I did run a project while at the art college looking at community living, in the course of which I and the students visited a couple of alternative communities, one in Belgium and one at Formby in Lancashire.

Afterwards one of the students wrote it up and I printed it on my printing press.

Another person at Peace Studies who has caught my attention is Aleksandras Shtromas. Any memories of him? He looks rather dour in his photograph.

I don't remember very much about him except that he was in the first batch of Adam's appointments and that he'd held some sort of official position in the Soviet Union. In fact, he was a very good example of the range of people that Adam brought together in the department. Though in his case I don't think it really worked. Alex Shtromas and Uri Davis were not a good mix [laughs].

And then what about Vithal Rajan?

Oh, he was a lovely, very open man. He had worked in Northern Ireland, but had to leave because of threats from the IRA over some misunderstanding. I don't know why they picked on him, but for some reason he became *persona non grata* as far as the IRA were concerned.

Was he in the Gandhi camp?

Yes. But he was also a Marxist. I suppose he was at the meeting point of Marx and Gandhi.

During the summer of 1975, a Peace Studies student named Andrew Lloyd was charged under the Incitement to Disaffection Act. This was a big deal in the department.

Yes, he was part of the British Withdrawal from Ireland Campaign, which I had helped set up. But I wasn't ever arrested or charged. However, the police did interview me at Gib Torr, because I had a hand in the drafting and distributing of one of the leaflets. There was quite a big trial, but fortunately Andrew Lloyd and the others were acquitted.

I believe that some members of the department at Bradford mounted their own protest. They distributed leaflets outside the Army Careers Service building in Bradford. Professor Curle was there, Professor Corbett, a Quaker called Laura Fletcher, a lecturer Colin Flood-Page, a Methodist minister called David Page and Bruce Kent.

Oh, yes. I can't say for certain, but I may have been the one who organised it.

Now, Michael, you've mentioned a few times that you lived at a place called Gib Torr at the same time as you worked part-time at the university. It's taken a while for the penny to drop, but you were farming there, weren't you?

On a small scale, yes. We had a couple of milking goats and two geese, and we grew vegetables and some soft fruit. I also continued to do some printing on my off-set litho machine. Gib Torr was owned by a very well-known architect, Edward 'Ted' Cullinan, who had won a lot of prizes for his work. I think that for him the farm was initially a sort of weekend retreat. He'd go up there from London and work on the barn or refurbish the house or work on the garden.

Anne and I had known both Ted and his wife, Roz, down in London. They were on the left, like I suppose most of our friends. Anne met up with them through the children; our kids and theirs went to the same school in London. Ted and Roz read about me going to prison for the Greek embassy action and then we became very good friends with them. At the beginning, we used to go up just for occasional weekends to help with the work there. Most of the land was then rented out to a local farmer, who ran sheep on it and we helped with them also. I suppose you could say that we were trying to live the 'Good Life'!

And then you made the farm your main residence for a while?

Yes. After my first spell at Bradford, it just seemed like the right thing to do. I continued also to print a lot of subversive and gay literature.

And anything else?

Yes. I also printed some material for Ted's wife, Roz, who was active in the campaign for state education. She edited a journal and I printed it.

Were you interested in the aesthetic side of printing?

Not really, not at the time anyway. I'm more interested in that side of it today. We have a friend, Dennis Gould, who's set up a printing press in Stroud, close to Painswick where Seán now lives. Dennis worked for some years on *Peace News*. He's very much into letterpress and publishing poems, his own and others, on hand-made paper.

Was your father still alive? If he was, he must have been pleased to hear about the farming side of your activities.

He was pleased. He must have thought that it might get me back to Fletching. But, of course, that didn't happen. Eventually, my younger brother, John, took over the farm.

Am I right in saying that you hid some British servicemen at Gib Torr?

Yes, we put up a couple of deserters for a while. They were people from the Menwith Hill base who had decided to leave the forces. We helped to get them to Sweden. But they absolutely freaked out living in an isolated farmhouse in the Staffordshire moorlands. After they'd left, the police raided the farm. Anne and I weren't there at the time. The Cullinans were.

I see from my notes that from July to September 1976 you worked for UNESCO on research into training for non-violent action. So, you'd left the university at that point?

That's right. It was a sort of interim period before I moved back to Bradford again. An American activist with War Resisters League, Beverly Woodward, set up an institute for the study of training for non-violent action (ISTNA) with support from the peace division of UNESCO and I spent six months in Paris working there as a supernumerary, in other words as a short-term employee of the organisation. It was a project about training for non-violent action. I ended up publishing a bibliography for them, I think at the beginning of 1978. Beverly was also for some years on the council of War Resisters' International.

By the way, the person in charge of the peace division at that point was a very lively and dynamic women from the West Indies: Marion Glean, whom I mentioned earlier in the context of the Campaign Against Racial Discrimination. She had by then married a former Irish priest and was Marion Glean O'Callaghan.

Was that your first bibliography?

Yes. I wrote it with the help and the cooperation of Beverly. I wrote a first draft and then she edited and added to it.

This might sound like a slightly daft question, but why is bibliography important?

People need to be informed of what's out there. If you're getting involved in something, you need to know what's already been done and the ideas that need to be considered.

Let's talk a little more about Bradford now. Adam Curle retired in 1978 and James O'Connell took over. I've got a quotation from Robert McKinlay's history of the university, which I'd like to read you, if I may. McKinlay writes, 'Many students never came to accept O'Connell's position that Peace Studies was not a peace movement organisation, but a

standard university department, whose main activism was scholarship.'
What do you make of that?

Well, the idea was to make sure that it was intellectually sound and for the activism to be based on well-informed judgments. But the department did attract people who had been and continued to be very active. Certainly, part of my association with it was going out into the streets. Obviously, we had seminars and lectures and so on. But Adam Curle was probably more interested in the activism side than O'Connell.

In 1980, you left Gib Torr and returned to Bradford. Was that related to your work with the Alternative Defence Commission?

Yes, it was. The initiative to set it up came from April Carter, with support from Professor Adam Roberts. Adam had been on the editorial staff of *Peace News* and was by then a professor at Balliol College, Oxford. James O'Connell welcomed the setting up of the commission and offered Peace Studies in Bradford as a base. This was agreed. O'Connell took on the role of Chair for the first three years of its existence, a role subsequently taken on by Paul Rogers. I was the coordinator. It was a demanding job, so it made a lot of sense to be on site, at the university. I also continued to do a certain amount of teaching.

Can you tell me a little about the Commission?

As I've just said, it was April Carter's idea. We wanted to look at how practically and politically one could move from a position of protest, if you like, to implementing the policies, to make nuclear disarmament actually happen. Two other people who worked with me were Howard Clark, a former joint editor of *Peace News*, and a young American woman, Lisa Foley.

The Commission met regularly and also held a number of wider consultations, many in Bradford but others elsewhere, especially after the first report was published.

The first report being Defence without the Bomb.

Yes. It appeared during the spring of 1983.

You took evidence from all sorts of people, I imagine.

That's right. We wanted the make-up of the commission to be as broad as possible. The members included academic experts, trade unionists, one or two clerics and a number of people with political interests. We had Viv Bingham from the Liberal Party and Daffyd Ellis Thomas and then Daffyd Wigley from Plaid Cymru. The person from the Scottish National Party was Isobel Lindsay, a very good woman, who had helped set up the Scottish Committee of 100 and who is still in Scottish CND. She made a particularly important contribution to the work. We also had someone to represent the Labour Party. Mary Kaldor first then Dan Smith. I should emphasise, however, that none of these people were official representatives of their parties. Indeed, it was very important to us that we weren't tied to any political party. But, of course, we sent material to their key people. We also gave talks at party conferences. I remember making one at The Ecology Party's conference. That was before it became the Green Party.

Did the university fund the Commission?

No, beyond providing us with premises, which was an important contribution. The funding came chiefly from the Joseph Rowntree Charitable Trust and the Cadbury Trust.

One of the trade unionist members of the commission was Ron Todd. Did he have much to say?

He didn't come often, if indeed at all [laughs]. But I remember visiting him at his offices in London and discussing issues with him. He did also correspond with us and remained a supporter of the project.

What about Joseph Rotblat, who was also a member?

Yes. Joseph Rotblat played a key role in the Commission. He had been one of the people behind the famous Russell-Einstein Manifesto of 1955, calling upon the world's leaders to renounce nuclear war, and one of the founders of the Pugwash Conferences, which take their name from the place it first met in Pugwash, Nova.Scotia. The conferences bring together scientists from various countries, East and West. Rotblat was very active on the Commission. In fact, I don't think he missed a single meeting.

What were your impressions of him?

He was a very attractive, warm, personality. There was nothing of the bigwig about him, nothing self-important, in spite of his huge reputation. He was never as well-known as Russell; he wasn't a public figure in that sense. But in academic and peace-related circles, he was a very important figure indeed.

And Dan Smith? Any recollections of him?

Dan was a key contributor to the discussion and, particularly, to the second report, *The Politics of Alternative Defence*. He contributed drafts on particular aspects of the study and critically engaged with drafts from other members. He was able to draw on his experience of involvement in CND and other peace organisations, and his work as a freelance researcher. His book, *The Defence of the Realm in the 1980s*, was published in 1980 just as the ADC was being set up and in the same year he became a co-director of the Transnational Institute in Amsterdam. He was Secretary General of International Alert from December 2003 to August 2015, when he became Director of SIPRI, the Stockholm International Peace Research Institute.

Dan, by the way, was a good friend of Mary Kaldor, who, as I've said, was also a member of the Commission.

Yes, and you also mentioned her in the context of END.

Mary was involved with the Armament and Disarmament Information Unit (ADIU), based at Sussex University. It produced a series of valuable reports during the 1980s. Then, as you say, she was also very much at the centre of the European Nuclear Disarmament campaign (END), with Edward Thompson and, again, Dan Smith.

The other person I should mention is Walter Stein, who was a very thoughtful, philosophical, figure on the Commission. He was a strong Catholic in his convictions and an academic at Leeds.

During March 1983, Reagan made his Star Wars speech. Then in November of that year the first Cruise missiles arrived at Greenham Common. People were getting very worried indeed.

It was a frightening period because you had all the nuclear deployments in Europe. But it was an exhilarating period as well because it saw a huge revival of CND, which had gone into a period of relative quiescence during the 1970s, when Vietnam became the centre of attention in peace movement circles and a concern grew about nuclear power as much as nuclear weapons.

Did you go to any of the demonstrations at Greenham Common?

I went there once, before it became a women-only protest.

You were still attending demonstrations then.

Oh, yes. I remember that huge rally against the Falklands War, in Trafalgar Square, in 1982. Then the one that CND organised in 1983, which had to end in Hyde Park to accommodate the numbers involved.

Did you hold an official position within CND or END?

I didn't. But obviously I knew Mary Kaldor and Edward Thompson and went to meetings. I went to the meeting where END was set up. I remember Edward Thompson, Claude Bourdet, Mary Kaldor and Dan Smith were there. That was in London in 1980.

How was the commission treated by the Tory press of the period? I imagine that you weren't very popular.

What I best remember was a very civilised discussion that Walter Stein had with another prominent Catholic intellectual, Michael Quinlan, an adviser to the Conservative government on nuclear issues and on defence policy more generally. The debate was about the morality of nuclear weapons and it appeared in the Catholic magazine, *The Tablet*.

The ADC was also invited to a conference at the Institute of Strategic Studies, attended by a government minister and several other bigwigs.

Did you have submissions from military people?

I can't remember any submission from military people, but I went to see Michael Howard, of the Institute of Strategic Studies. He was, and still is, a very eminent military historian. We had an interesting discussion, during which one of the points made was that civilian-based defence or defence by civil resistance would lack credibility as a deterrent.

I also remember discussing the ADC and its work with Ronald Gaskell. He was a poet and an academic and very active in CND, as was his wife, Alice. Ronald died some years ago, but Alice is still active in the movement. I went down to Bristol to give a talk at the university, where he was a lecturer in English, and later to their home in Cornwall.

The Commission's first report was published just a month or so before the 1983 general election. Do you think it had much of an impact on Labour Party thinking after that?

I think it did though how much I don't know. Certainly, the Labour Party were looking at the whole nuclear issue. They wouldn't have gone as far as us in denuclearising NATO. Although I think that we were quite balanced on that issue. We accepted that any change would be gradual.

I would imagine that someone like Denis Healey would have had no time for the Commission at all.

Well, funnily enough, Denis Healey came to an END public meeting in Leeds, which brought people together from different perspectives. He was certainly open to debating the issue.

You don't remember a young Jeremy Corbyn, do you?

I remember him coming up to Bradford to address a CND meeting during the first Gulf War. I also spoke at that one.

I've mentioned the two reports that came out of the ADC, but there were other publications, weren't there.

In fact, there were three books, or four if you count *Without the Bomb*, which was mostly an abridgement. The two reports, plus *Without the Bomb* and *Alternatives in European Security*. The last was edited by Paul Rogers and myself and comprised contributions to a gathering at Bradford University, which the ADC organised. We brought together researchers, campaigners, and leading scholars from a number of countries in Western Europe. We also produced a small number of supplementary papers.

You've said you were the coordinator of the ADC, but did you also write the reports?

As regards the two reports, usually we worked like this: someone would produce a draft of a particular chapter, perhaps looking at a possible strategy and weighing up the pros and cons for it. That would be sent to all the members of the Commission and amended or commented on. Finally, there would be an agreed version for publication, if necessary indicating contrary opinions on particular points by some members. The chapters were very much joint efforts.

I contributed most to the first report, *Defence without the Bomb*, in particular to the chapters on civil resistance, the area in which I had a particular interest, and guerrilla warfare. The last was an option that we didn't particularly go for. We did, however, devote a great deal of attention to defence by civil resistance, which was Adam Roberts' speciality. He was a key figure then as he still is in strategic studies on the peace front. I had known him from the period in the early 1960s when he was a member of the *Peace News* editorial team.

Reading the defence by civil resistance chapter I found myself thinking of Stephen King-Hall's intriguing book Defence in the Nuclear Age. *There was a lot about that in* Peace News *during the late 1950s. King-Hall also advocated a non-nuclear defence policy.*

Yes, he did, though, of course, he was far more of an establishment figure than I was [laughs]. He had been a commentator on the radio during the war. But he had seen the possibilities of non-violent resistance. In fact, I'm pretty sure that Gene Sharp went to see him. He was someone who saw nuclear disarmament as happening constitutionally, through parliament. In other words, it would be an official decision not to have nuclear weapons and to move towards a defence based on non-violent resistance.

In the chapter on civil resistance you discuss when the method is most likely to succeed against an occupier and when it's least likely and describe 1980s Britain as lacking cohesion, as being riven by class and nationality. How do you think your ideas would stand up today when we're even more riven?

Well, it's certainly a great help when you have a solidly united country, but I don't think it's an absolutely necessary condition for defence by civil resistance. After all, there were big divisions in France and Norway during the Second World War, where was civil as well as military resistance. One of the great things about Czechoslovakia in 1968 was that people came together. Of course, they still had differences, but they united in a common cause; they said, we've got to oppose this occupation. There were big divisions in Europe before the Second World War too, but it didn't stop people coming together on the central issue.

So, you would advise the country to rely on civil resistance nowadays?

I think so. But the more united you are, the better. But, of course, we are a long way from accepting that policy, I mean the centrality of civil resistance. But what we were suggesting in the book was that it could be a component. Now, I'm very keen on civil resistance, as you know. But if I ask myself, 'What is the likelihood, politically, of this method being accepted as a viable option?' I would have to say not very. But we can still hold it out as something to be aimed for. You'd need training and a lot of investigation. Individuals could say, well, I'm not going to be involved in military action, but I'm going to use the best of my ability to promote a non-violent alternative. But, as I say, politically, we're a long way from all this. But maybe that will change if we get a Labour government.

10. The Blake Trial

Let's begin today by talking about the publication of Montgomery Hyde's book George Blake, Superspy *in 1987.*

It was a disgraceful book in that large parts of it were plagiarised portions of Seán Bourke's book *The Springing of George Blake*. Hyde did add a couple of things though: he added that the two men who helped Bourke with the escape were members of the Committee of 100, who had served eighteen-month prison sentences for their involvement in the Wethersfield demonstration. That was something that positively identified Pat and myself. Of course, Seán had dropped a lot of hints in his book. He'd mentioned the age of our children and whereabouts in London we lived, that we were socialists not communists. Then he'd given us these silly pseudonyms: Pat Porter and Michael Reynolds [laughs]. I remember Richard Boston saying to me before we were publicly named that a boy scout reading the book could have worked out our identities. And indeed, we discovered later during the trial when we were given a number of police files that a Special Branch officer named Rollo Watts had tipped off the security services about who he believed Seán's helpers were, and his reasons for reaching that conclusion. Watts named both Pat and myself and a third person who in fact had nothing to do with the escape. The police files show not only that the police knew, or at least strongly suspected Pat's and my involvement from the time they got an advance copy of Seán's book but that they had decided not to take action against us. As one police memo put it, 'The big fish had got away, and to go after the little fish would look like persecution'. But, anyway after Seán's book was published we'd been waiting for the knock on the door, which never came. So, we thought, Okay. They're not going to do anything. But then a reporter for *The Sunday Times*, Barry Penrose, who had seen a copy of Hyde's book, realised it was Pat and myself who were being referred to and then there we were on the front page of *The Sunday Times*. Penrose himself, by the way had been what he called a 'foot soldier' in the Committee of 100.

Were you at home in Bradford when Penrose's article came out?

No. Anne and I were camping up in the Yorkshire Dales at the time with a group of friends, including Andrew Rigby. We knew that the article was coming out though, so on the Sunday we went to the local shop and bought the paper. And bang there it was, on the front page. Then the local paper picked up on it.

That was The Telegraph and Argus, *wasn't it? They put you and Anne on the front page with the headline: 'We are Couple in Red Spy Mystery', which, to say the least, must have been very interesting for the neighbours.*

Well, that had a greater impact on Anne than on me. Anne was working as a nurse at the time and the last thing she wanted was to have her career ended. Fortunately, that didn't happen. As for the neighbours, the reaction was probably mixed. But I do remember people coming up to me in the streets and saying things like, 'Good on you.' So, there was certainly sympathy for what we'd done as well as condemnation.

Anne: When we got home from the Dales, the phone was ringing off the hook. Someone from the *T&A* asked me, 'Are you the couple referred to in *The Sunday Times*?' All I said was, 'Yes.' But, out of that, they made a front-page article. As Michael says, I was working as a nurse at the time. I was working the late shift at the Bradford Royal Infirmary. On the day I returned to work, the ward sister said she needed a word with me in the office. I went in and said, 'I know what you're going to say to me. But I have to tell you I've taken legal advice and I can't discuss the matter.' Which wasn't true, actually. She just smiled and said, 'I thought that's what you'd say.'

Of course, people were reading the *T&A* all over the hospital [laughs], but not a single other person said anything to me.

I felt I just had to hold my breath. Neither of us had any idea where things would go at that point.

Wasn't there a campaign, linked to Norris McWhirter's Freedom Party, to prosecute you, Michael?

Michael: There was. And one of the interesting things about that was that Norris had been a personal friend of Pat's wife's father, the athlete, Harold Abrahams. But, anyway, yes. After *The Sunday Times* article came out there was a build-up of Tory MPs calling for our prosecution.

Anne: They even demanded the closure of Peace Studies at Bradford.

Michael: Before Penrose's article came out, Pat and I had written a review of Hyde's book for *The Guardian* in which while we didn't explicitly admit our involvement in the Blake escape, we didn't deny it either. But then we'd decided not to publish it. Following Penrose's article we changed our minds again, and the review appeared in *The Guardian*.

That said, it wasn't just a review was it?

Michael: Well, we also sent the paper a statement, in which we made some of the same points. I can still remember one of the final lines: 'If we were not involved [in the escape] we would not regard it as a slur to be named as having been so.' Basically, we wanted to make it clear that, yes, we did help Blake to escape, but not to make an explicit admission that would be certain to land us in court. So, we said, that whoever did the thing was fully justified. We thought that was sufficient.

What was the reaction of family members to these pieces in The Guardian? *I would imagine that some of them were horrified.*

Michael: Several members of the family thought we'd made a bad mistake. But my brother, Arthur, said, 'Oh, I don't know. It was the most famous escape of the century, after all'.

I wonder if Arthur had his suspicions before the affair blew up?

Michael: No, that would have been very unlikely. Some of our friends had twigged it, of course — Richard Boston because he'd seen something I'd written for *Peace News,* which mentioned in passing that I'd met Blake in prison. He read that and thought, Hmm. Maybe. But then he was also very discreet. He had his suspicions, but he didn't broadcast them.

Subsequently, Michael, both you and Pat were interviewed at Holborn Police Station. Ben Birnberg was with you. Why him?

Ben Birnberg was one of the lawyers who had helped us way back during our Committee of 100 days, so we knew and trusted him from that period. Not that I knew him very well personally at that time. But, later on, when I went on trial for the Greek embassy demonstration, he was my solicitor and I did get to know him well. Earlier on, I mentioned that one of the people who took part in the demonstration was called Felitsa, which I think is an abbreviation of her Greek name, Triandafili. She became Ben's wife. Anyway, Ben was simply the obvious choice. Not only was he a friend but a very good lawyer with a particular interest in civil liberties.

And then, in February 1988, you started work on your own book about Blake, the one with Pat Pottle.

After the review and our statement in *The Guardian,* I suppose that we could just have shut up and nothing more would have happened. But rumours started that Vanessa Redgrave was involved. Now, Vanessa was a good friend and had been a member of the Committee of 100. She'd even financed the printing of the leaflets which I and others had distributed at Wethersfield. But she'd had nothing to do with the Blake case. Then other rumours arose saying that we'd been involved with the KGB. So, we thought, look, we've never had any time for the Soviet form of communism or indeed for any kind of totalitarianism or authoritarianism. So, we thought the only way to scotch these rumours was to write our own account. We'd say what happened and why we did it. And then if they wanted to prosecute us after that they could. In fact, we did indeed expect to be prosecuted. But that seemed a better alternative than to have these suspicions hanging over us and other people.

But then before the book appeared, a 100 or so Tory MPs demanded our prosecution. And, I suppose, it was open season. There was a right-wing MP, fairly local to us, and he was particularly aggressive.

You've mentioned briefly that The Telegraph and Argus *people got onto you after the Penrose article, I wonder, what were the repercussions for you at the university?*

The department was very concerned about it. Though all in all I think that they did very well under the circumstances. James O'Connell was worried about the implications for the department, but he didn't sack me or ask me to leave. But I thought it would be better for Peace Studies if I resigned. And I did.

Just to spell things out, the repercussions for Peace Studies being what?

Oh, that it was a disgrace, the fact that here was a lecturer in Peace Studies in Bradford, employed by the university who had helped free a convicted spy.

What was O'Connell's response when you told him that you were writing a book about the case?

He was very dubious about the wisdom of it.

On the grounds that you would be profiting from your activities?

I don't remember him making that objection. It was raised by some of the Tory MPs though. I think that he was more concerned about what it might mean for Anne and me and for the department. I didn't have any beef with him about the position he took. In fact, I felt he handled the situation rather well. It can't have been easy having so many mavericks in his department [laughs].

During November 1988, you did at last unambiguously admit your involvement ...

Yes, we did an interview with *The Observer,* where Pat remarked that we were actually quite proud of what we had done. In our book, I called that moment a 'great relief'. And indeed it was. At last we'd acknowledged publicly our involvement.

Okay, The Blake Escape *appeared during the Spring of 1989. It's clear to me that you contributed to it, Anne. I wonder why you're not listed as one of the authors?*

Anne: the reason why I'm not described as one of the book's authors is that it seemed likely that there would be legal action at some point. And if I was convicted of anything other than a motoring offence, I would have lost my registration as a nurse. I wasn't prepared to risk that. Of course, in the event, Michael and Pat weren't convicted, so I wouldn't have lost my registration [laughs]. But at the time I couldn't have known that!

But your involvement is all over the book. Surely, you could have been prosecuted in any case?

Anne: Detective Inspector Eileen Eggington, who was in charge of the investigation, questioned me as well as the other two at length. This was all on the same day. I replied to all her questions with 'No comment'. That's what our legal team had advised. At a certain point, she said, 'Well, there are a lot of questions that I'd have liked to ask you, but I will leave them for now.' It was the 'for now' bit that worried me. Anyway, Michael and Pat were arrested. But I wasn't. Michael and I had a quick whispered word. He asked me to go and find the tapes. These were tapes of telephone conversations with people who knew about our involvement in the escape but were not in any way involved in it. We didn't want suspicion to fall on them.

So, someone made a decision not to prosecute you, Anne.

Anne: Well, the prosecution of Pat and Michael was based on the book. That was the evidence.

Michael: The only evidence they had against Anne was circumstantial because though she was named by us, she hadn't directly admitted her involvement. Then they might also have had strategic reasons for not prosecuting her. There would have been no point in increasing public sympathy. Of course, had we not written the book, they wouldn't have prosecuted us either, even though we know they knew that we'd done it.

The book was published during April 1989. Leaving the legal ramifications to one side for the moment, how would you characterise the response?

Michael: Well, first of all there was the whole business of launching it. The publisher, Harrap, was worried that Pat and I would be arrested before publication day, so the details of the press conference were kept under wraps right until the last minute. They were very keen on my keeping a low profile for a while. They didn't want me to do anything that the authorities could interpret as provocation.

You had an agent presumably and they gave you support.

We didn't have a literary agent. We actually negotiated directly with Harrap ourselves.

That sounds very Michael. Was Harrap supportive?

Oh, I think so. Not that their interest wasn't primarily commercial; it was. But the people that we met there were entirely sympathetic and friendly. There was a young woman there — I can't remember her name — who came over with us to Ireland. You see, after the press conference in London we immediately flew to Dublin, where, of course, I had lots of friends and family members, and we had another press conference there in Easons', one of the big Dublin bookshops. She was very nice and thoroughly professional.

What kind of publisher was Harrap? I don't think they're still in business.

They were mainly known for dictionaries. I can't remember why we ended up going with them. We tried a number of places, and Harrap said they'd do it.

And the reviews?

They were pretty good on the whole though I remember far better the response from *The Sun* after Pat's and my acquittal. They left it a day and then made us the subject of an editorial, using some such words as the following: 'These people should crawl back to whatever stone they emerged from'. They were utterly contemptuous too of the jury. The editorial ended: 'Ladies and Gentlemen of the jury you stink.' [laughs]

Okay, so following the publication of the book you were charged?

Michael: Yes, during the July of 1989 both Pat and I were charged with three counts: helping Blake escape from Wormwood Scrubs, conspiracy with Seán Bourke to harbour him, in other words to hide him away, and conspiracy to interfere with his recapture.

In spite of everything, these charges must still have come as a shock. The die was cast, so to speak.

Michael. It was. But it was also a relief.

But then the case didn't go to trial until the summer of 1991. Which was almost two years. Why did it take so long?

Michael: That was to do with the length of time that had elapsed since they'd first known about us. They could charge us, fine. But first they had to explain why they hadn't charged us back in 1970, when Seán Bourke's book, *The Springing of George Blake,* appeared. I've already mentioned that Seán had dropped several hints that Pat and myself were involved with Blake's escape. But then we found out during the appeal process that we'd actually been under suspicion as early as 1966! And that, in 1970, someone at the Home Office had reviewed the case, but decided not to prosecute us. We felt that they hadn't charged us then out of embarrassment. In other words, due to the fact that they'd been beaten by a couple of amateurs. We also felt that the reason we were being charged in 1989 was simply to placate Norris McWhirter and some very angry Conservatives!

Before the trial, you and Pat went to Russia to interview Blake. I would have thought that Blake was the last person you'd want to drag into your situation at that point.

That was Geoffrey Robertson's idea. We were represented throughout the abuse of process hearings by some very good lawyers. Geoffrey Robertson was one. Another was Anthony Scrivener. Geoffrey thought that a statement from Blake would ensure that if the case did go to trial that a large dose of publicity would work in our favour. So did I, for that matter

So, you met Blake. Where? In Moscow?

That's right. He came to see us at our hotel. There was a group of us waiting for him: Pat, Sue Pottle, Anne and myself and two of the other lawyers involved in the case: Ben Birnberg and John Wadham. Sue spotted him first. He turned up in this huge chauffeur-driven Volga. Afterwards, we all went to visit him at his residence. I remember his wife was there. She was a lovely, friendly, woman, who prepared a meal for us. Of course, we spent much of our time with George talking about politics. At a certain point his wife said, 'Too much talking. Too much talking.' Then she started to sing and encouraged us to join her [laughs].

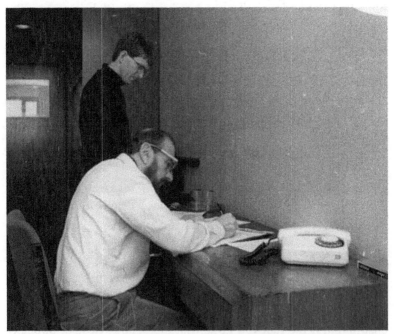

Fig 20:   John Wadham watching George Blake writing the statement read out at Michael and Pat Pottle's trial. Photograph by Michael Randle. Private Collection.

The trial began, following the final attempt to halt the prosecution, on 17 June 1991. Can you talk me through some of the main events?

The first thing to say is that was very good natured and therefore quite a contrast with the Wethersfield trial in 1962. Even the relationship with the prosecution team was quite cordial. Why? Well, partly, I suppose, because of the passage of time — there wasn't the heat that there would have been had we been tried in the late 60s or early 70s — and partly, I think, because they understood us. They obviously had to stand by the law. But, on the other hand, they didn't set out to be vindictive like Manningham-Buller. As for the judge he was very tolerant. He could have shut us up at an early stage, but he allowed us to confront the prosecution witnesses with some very difficult questions.

The second thing to say is that we ended up defending ourselves.

Why so?

Because the argument we eventually used was that of necessity, which wasn't one that the judge was willing to allow our lawyers to use — or, as it turned out, us for that matter! But, nonetheless, we persevered in spite of him! We used the defence that we were forced to act on George behalf, that the sentence he'd received was inhumane.

It was one of the lawyers who first suggested that particular defence. He went off and did some work on it, then I did some work myself. I remember reading somewhere that the defence of necessity does exist in English law, but that it can only be used in exceptional circumstances, which is precisely what the judge said. He didn't think that it applied in our case. But we pressed on with it, anyway, and finally the jury accepted it.

Anne, what were your feelings during the trial?

I felt that it was good that the story was finally going to be aired, but then I also felt that the jury were bound to find them guilty. So, in a sense, the first day marked the beginning of a waiting game: how long were they going to get?

You were there for the pre-trial hearings as well as the trial?

Yes, that's right. One of Michael's legal advisers, Edward Fitzgerald, was lovely. He wore the scruffiest gown. I remember walking behind him into the high court and noticing all the rips. It was actually hanging off him! I suppose he was too posh to care about such things [laughs]. I think he'd just got married to Antonia Fraser's daughters, Rebecca.

We were in the pub across the road from the Old Bailey while the jury was out. I remember Pat and Michael handing over most of their stuff to me and Pat's wife, Sue, just keeping back what they would need when, as we all thought, they would be sent down: toothbrushes and books for both of them, glasses for Michael and a packet of tobacco for Pat.

Then when it was time to hear the verdict, everyone streamed back in from outside including lots of people from the other courts. I remember talking to Eileen Eggington, who led the case for the Crown Prosecution Service, outside the court. The boys were with me and she said, 'Oh, are these your sons? Well, it's not as if he hasn't been inside before.'

Michael: I remember Pat saying that if we could get just one member of the jury to say, 'Not Guilty', that would be a victory, a moral victory.

But then when they came back to answer the first count and it was Not Guilty, I thought, hold on, hold on, something's happening here. But there are two other counts. But then when they answered Not Guilty to the other two counts, I felt overwhelmed: it was quite extraordinary.

Anne: Following the first count, the court sort of erupted and Seán, our eldest son, who was sitting next to me, burst into tears. I said, 'Hold on. There are two more verdicts to come.'

Where did you stay during the trial? In a hotel or with friends?

Michael: Anne and I stayed with Richard Norton-Taylor. He was security correspondent for *The Guardian* and by then a close friend. These days, whenever we go down to London, we stay with him and his family.

Richard told me a lovely story. When he returned to *The Guardian* offices on the day after our acquittal, everyone clapped and cheered.

Would you say that the case was a landmark case?

Anne: It was certainly a noticeably perverse verdict.

Michael: I call it a rebel verdict. I've written a four-hundred-page account of the case, going through it stage by stage, from the High Court hearings to the trial itself.

Anne: You've likened it to Penn and Mead in your summing up, Michael.

Penn and Mead being?

Michael: That was the trial in the seventeenth century of the Quakers William Penn (he of Pennsylvania fame) and William Mead for causing a 'tumultuous assembly', but which was really for nothing more than preaching in Gracechurch Street in the City of London. In their case, the jury too went against the judge's wishes. In fact, he had them locked up, 'without so much as a chamber pot, though desired', as a contemporary account puts it. The trial established a precedent, which is still occasionally referred to today, that a jury must reach an independent decision; the judge cannot direct them to reach a particular verdict. There's actually a plaque commemorating the case in the Old Bailey. When I cited the case at the trial. I said, 'Now, members of the jury, I'm not suggesting that his lordship is going to lock you up if you find us Not Guilty ...'. And for the first time they all laughed at something one of us had said. I remember thinking, maybe we've made a breakthrough here.

During the trial, we noticed that sometimes members of the jury smiled and nodded at some of the judge's comments, but that they didn't respond at all to any of our quips. However, we found out later from one jury member we were able to interview after our acquittal that right at the beginning of the case, when the jury members first met, they'd decided that they didn't want to give us false hope by their reactions to what we said.

Anne: They were all first-time jurors, for whatever reason.

Michael: I think it just happened that way, but they were a model jury.

You didn't object to any, as was your right?

No, but Pat did put to them, 'Are you now or have you ever been a member of the CIA or MI5 [laughs]?'

Which must have gone down like a lead balloon with some of the people present.

It was a witty question, echoing as it did the interrogation of people in the US suspected of having communist sympathies during the McCarthyite era.

What did you do after receiving the verdict?

Michael: One of the first things I did was ring my mother who, like everyone else, was convinced that we'd go to prison. She was in her eighties, so I guess she must have been thinking that if I got a long sentence she wouldn't be seeing me again.

Anne: During Michael's trial in 1962, Michael's mother and her sister Nan had 'stormed the heavens', as they called it, praying to the saints. But, on this occasion, they prayed to the Blessed Oliver Plunkett.

Michael: Oliver Plunkett was an Irish martyr. I think their reasoning was that, in 1962, they'd prayed without success to the saints, maybe because as they'd already been canonised they didn't try so hard [laughs]. But a Blessed had a greater incentive to intervene in order to achieve sainthood. Perhaps they hadn't realised that Oliver Plunkett had already been canonised in 1975, the first new Irish saint for around 700 years.

I wonder if your thoughts about Blake have changed since the trial? In your book of 1989 you wrote a lot about his idealism?

I don't know what he thinks about Putin, but I would be surprised if he was enthusiastic. But then he would have to keep his thoughts under wraps. That's the great handicap that people face when they go into exile in a dictatorial state; they have to keep their mouths shut. It's a position that I would never want to be in.

When Pat and I went to Russia to visit Blake in 1990 he told us that the Soviet authorities would be willing to give us political asylum. But neither of us had any interest at all in that. It wasn't attractive in any way.

Let's imagine that you had been sent down for a long stretch. You would have served it then? You wouldn't have tried to run away?

Assuming I had any choice in the matter, I personally would have served it and I think Pat would have done so too. The probability in any case is that we would have had no choice in the matter. It's not that easy to escape from prison!

There's a romantic idea of going on the run, but you can't go on the run for all of your life. It's a practical impossibility. My feeling too is that if you do decide to break the law, then you serve the penalty.

In good conscience?

Yes, exactly. Not that we followed the principle of complete openness with the police and the authorities in the case of the Blake escape. I mean we didn't immediately speak up and say, 'We did, this. Now what are you going to do about it?' Nor obviously did we inform the police in advance what we were planning. That would have been entirely self-defeating. But, when it all came out, we didn't hide away and pretend we weren't responsible.

The maximum sentence we could have got was nine years. The judge tried to persuade us to change our plea to guilty, pointing out that there were three charges. One: helping a prisoner escape. We could have got five years for that. Two: aiding an escaped prisoner. We could have got two years for that. And then three: for helping an escaped prisoner to get out of the jurisdiction; that also carried a maximum penalty of two years. The judge rehearsed all of that, saying that's what you're facing. But then he also said that if we pleaded guilty, he would be prepared to listen 'for days if necessary to pleas in mitigation'.

11. Bradford University and Final Thoughts

For this final interview, Michael, let's begin by returning to Bradford University and talking about The Social Defence Project, which, again, you coordinated.

Yes. That followed on from the Alternative Defence Commission, in 1987. One of the recommendations of the first ADC report was non-violent defence, or as we termed it 'defence by civil resistance', so we followed up the ADC with a smaller group focussing particularly on that option.

Can you define social defence? When I first came across the term, it struck me as slightly odd.

It's more or less synonymous with non-violent civil resistance. People came up with different terms: non-violent defence, social defence. Gene Sharp's preferred choice was 'civilian-based defence'. In the first ADC report, we opted for 'defence by civil resistance' as being the most precise description of the approach we were considering.

You just mentioned the project involved a smaller group than the one that worked on the ADC. Who was on the project?

There was a core group of eleven people, three of whom — Howard Clark, Walter Stein and myself — had been members of the ADC. The others were Tricia Allen, Christine Arber, John Brierley, Annie Harrison, Bob Overy, Lindis Percy, Carol Rank and Andrew Rigby.

Howard Clark, with whom I shared an office, played a key organising role. Towards the end of the ADC, he was one of the people with whom I discussed a successor project.

Did he teach at Bradford?

He did some lecturing and research. He had also co-edited *Peace News*. He was a very good friend and a close colleague since the early 1970s. When he died, Andrew Rigby and myself wrote an obituary of him for *The Guardian*. He had a great sense of humour and could laugh at himself and others. He once said of the Alternative Defence Commission, which was part-funded by Rowntree and Cadbury, that the alternative we should have opted for was defence by chocolate soldiers!

Fig 21:   Michael, with Howard Clark and Andrew Rigby in the Yorkshire Dales. Photographer unknown. Private Collection.

You mentioned earlier the Catholic perspective that Walter Stein brought to the Alternative Defence Commission. Which leads me to wonder if there was any residual Catholicism in your thinking at this period.

I think there was. In fact, there still is. After all, the just war approach to international conflict was a very important part of my education. Did that also make me more receptive to Walter's position? I think it did. Also, I've always appreciated the discussion of values, how you should relate to people and so on, and Walter brought a lot to that side of things as well.

Of course, your period co-ordinating the project coincided with the brouhaha over the Blake affair and your resignation from Peace Studies. How did your resignation affect your role? Presumably you weren't supposed to even be at Bradford!

I don't remember that as a big problem. People, like James O'Connell were, as I've probably already said, sympathetic, at least to my motivation. To save the university in general and Peace Studies in particular unnecessary embarrassment, I took the decision to resign from Peace Studies when Pat and I were formally indicted over the Blake escape. James, I think, appreciated that. When Pat and I were found not guilty, I was welcomed back. There was no longer any need for caution.

Did any publications arise out of the Social Defence Project?

Nothing quite as major as *Defence without the Bomb*, but yes, there were a number. Indeed, my own book *People Power* was itself very much a product of our discussions.

People power is yet another term for non-violent civil resistance. Why use that and not one of the former ones?

Again, it's really a matter of emphasis. I like the term 'people power' because it places the emphasis on the way change comes about. If enough people co-operate to achieve change or, on the other hand, refuse to co-operate with the authorities attempting to impose unjust policies, that can be efficacious politically.

The subtitle of your book is The Building of a New European Home. *You were clearly very excited by the changes brought about by the fall of the Soviet Union.*

Oh, absolutely. It was precisely what we'd been working for. The Berlin Wall had come down at last. You'd had the 'Velvet Revolution' in Czechoslovakia, the Helsinki Citizens Assembly had been founded. It was a very exciting period.

Just out of interest, did George Blake comment on the book? It came out in 1991, in fact in the same month as your trial at the Old Bailey.

If he did, I don't remember it. But, of course, he was in Moscow at that point. I'm not sure if I sent him a copy, though I might well have done.

The preface to the book is by John Berger.

That came out of an article I wrote in *The Guardian*. Berger wrote to me saying how much he agreed with it. When I started on the book, I wrote to him and asked him if he'd write the preface. You see, I had a great admiration for him. I really liked his stuff, particularly his art criticism, which always seemed very balanced and perceptive. And then he wrote about his life in a peasant community. I felt he was a kindred spirit.

Since you wrote the book, the pendulum in the East has swung away from democracy. Russia, Poland, Hungary, Armenia, Belarus ... . All have highly authoritarian governments.

You're right. Most of these regimes have swung far to the right. But at least there are still alternative political groups and movements within these countries, and the potential for peaceful change.

Following the Social Defence Project, you coordinated another project at Bradford, the Nonviolent Action Research Project.

That's right. That was another outcrop of the Alternative Defence Commission and, again, it involved some of the same people.

Did it issue any publications?

There was certainly one publication, *Challenge to Nonviolence*, which as a matter of fact I edited. That was published by Peace Studies in 2002. A number of people had made presentations in meetings of the project which were included in the book as well as summaries I wrote of the ensuing discussions.

When I looked through the list of contributors to that volume, I was surprised to see the name of Richard Norton-Taylor.

Richard was, as I've said, the security correspondent for *The Guardian* and had covered the Blake escape trial for the paper. He had become and remains a good friend and I invited him to talk about the intelligence and security services.

There are also chapters on Ploughshares, Gandhi, the Naxalite Movement in Bihar and several other subjects, so it's quite an heterogenous mix!

And on Yugoslavia.

Yes, there's an interesting discussion about that near the front of the book. Lynne Jones contributed a piece entitled 'The Moral Failure of the Peace Movement' and I responded with a piece called 'Bosnian Dilemmas'. And then the whole group had a discussion afterwards. Naturally, the situation in Bosnia was on all of our minds at that point. Lynne felt that the peace movement wasn't doing enough. After all, terrible things had happened and indeed continued to happen in Bosnia-Hercegovina. In fact, she argued for some form of military intervention. I argued against that and in favour of supporting a campaign of civil resistance.

I also, by the way, opposed both the Gulf Wars. The aim of the first was just in so far as it was limited to expelling Saddam Hussein's forces from Kuwait. The second had no such justification and its consequences have been disastrous.

Are you a pacifist now?

Pretty much. But I see the arguments on both sides more clearly than I used to, even perhaps in the 1990s. When I first became a pacifist, I scarcely had any doubts. Now, I see the counter arguments — and the counter moral arguments — as more compelling.

I am no longer an absolute pacifist in the sense of rejecting at a personal and group level *any* use of even minimum force or violence in all circumstances. There are occasions in which a refusal to use force would be a dereliction of responsibility. For example, in defence of vulnerable people in one's care, such as children. I also now think there is a right to use minimum force in self-defence, even perhaps a duty to do so, where others are dependent on your survival for their protection.

In the 1990s, I argued that you could protect vulnerable minorities by non-violent forms of action. Now, I'm not convinced this is always possible or likely to be efficacious. At any rate, it is important not to overstate what it can achieve. There are certainly situations in which it will not be effective. But at least if one rejects the use of military force, there is a responsibility to explore and develop non-violent alternatives. The international NGO, Nonviolent Peace Force, established in 2003 has intervened in a number of conflict zones and shown there are possibilities to be explored.

As to the indiscriminate use of force, the use of nuclear weapons or other weapons of mass destruction, I hold the same objections I held in the 1950s.

What are your current views on democracy?

Democracy can't just mean rule by the majority. You have to take into account the rights of minorities and individuals even. Put another way, you can't simply count heads. You also have to look at the actual policies. I remember arguing this point when I first became a pacifist: there are certain policies that are in themselves, of their nature, incompatible with democracy. These would include policies that could lead a country into a nuclear war or which trampled upon the rights of individuals and minorities.

Of course, opinions as to what qualify as minority rights are very different to what they were, say, forty or fifty years ago.

That is true. For example, it took the women's movement to wake us up to certain gender inequalities. It takes individuals, people who are at the suffering ends of things, to get up and demand change. It's important we don't ever become complacent.

That suggests to me that you hold a rather Whiggish view of democracy: Things are getting better and better. But are there also areas in which we are perhaps becoming less democratic?

Well, I hope not [laughs]. But then we must never assume that progress is inevitable; it is not. It depends upon people standing up and saying, this is not acceptable or insisting that some radical changes are both right and possible.

It's often said that a successful democracy depends on an informed electorate. How informed is today's British electorate?

Certainly not as well informed as it should be. But that applies to me as much as to everyone else [laughs]. One is always learning.

I know you're a life-long Guardian *reader. But do you read any other newspapers?*

Not systematically. I see the local paper, *The Telegraph and Argus*, from time to time. I also look occasionally at *The Daily Telegraph* to reinforce my prejudices [laughs]. However, I don't agree with *The Guardian* on every issue. But I do like its analyses of political issues. It has people like Fintan O'Toole and Martin Kettle writing about Europe. I also like Polly Toynbee, and George Monbiot on environmental issues.

It's interesting that these are veteran journalists, whereas younger readers seem to be energised by younger writers, people like Owen Jones and Afua Hirsch. Take the issue of identity.

I too like both of them and always make a point of reading their pieces. Afua Hirsch is particularly good on issues of race and class. But as regards identity politics, I remember Bayard Rustin being very critical of it during the 1960s. He much preferred to deal with what he called objective issues like poverty and inequality. For example, he didn't have any time for what used to be called negritude. However, I read an interesting article by Gary Younge in *The Guardian* recently, defending identity politics, but of a particular sort. I think he sees identity politics as a contributory stream to the wider movement. It certainly shouldn't be dismissed in the way the right has a habit of doing. Take the feminist issue which, as I've suggested, I see as absolutely crucial. But it can't be discussed on its own. I think that many feminists understand that.

Let's talk about Gandhi now. Is he still relevant to world politics?

The civil resistance side of his legacy remains of crucial relevance. He was, of course, a great advocate and practitioner of that. Gandhi understood better than most people, even the framers of the United States constitution, that governments depend on the will of the people. If a sufficient number of people are sufficiently engaged in opposing an evil government, it will fall. I remember seeing a TV interview with him. The interviewer asked him what people should do about a particular evil, and he kept on saying, 'Non-cooperation, non-cooperation, non-cooperation'. Thanks to Gandhi's writings and example, people have been able to see that the power lies with them and not with their governments. Colonised peoples in particular, saw Gandhi's approach as an important way forward. I also think that today's green movement owes a lot to him

It's clear you're still on the left, Michael, but where exactly?

I'm still somewhere on the anarcho-syndicalist left, that tradition of people organising from below instead of looking to leadership at the governmental or semi-governmental level.

So, you don't vote?

Well, for a time I didn't. Certainly not during my more strongly anarchist days. But then during my time at Bradford Art College, someone rounded on me and said, 'But you're letting the Tories in!' So, just on the grounds of preventing something bad rather than doing anything good, I decided that in future I would vote. And I think I've voted ever since.

Can I ask you who you voted for at the last general election?

I was torn between the Greens and Labour, but, in the end, I voted Labour on the basis, again, that they were most likely to keep the Tories out. Not that it made any difference. In fact, the Tory candidate in my constituency got in with an increased majority! But my vote was largely tactical. My heart was with the Greens.

Would you like to see the Greens and Labour working closely together?

I would, if not forming an outright coalition. That, hopefully, is where progressive politics is headed. I think Labour needs the pressure of the Green Party to make sure that it doesn't go down the road of technology without taking sufficient account of the threats to the environment.

Perhaps Gandhi's example could also be useful?

Yes, I think it could. His approach to economics was very green, de-centralised and semi-anarchistic.

Have we learned to live with the bomb?

Not very comfortably, thank goodness. The danger is perhaps not as acute as it was during the time of the Cuban Missile Crisis. That and our other narrow escapes were fortunately sobering. Don't forget that people of my generation experienced the Cuban Missile Crisis in our whole being. People left London in order to be in the countryside when the bombs fell. Not that that would have helped them much if that had happened. Others made the decision to be with the people they loved. It was as real as that.

You were in the Scrubs at the time.

Yes, I remember walking round the exercise yard with some kindred spirits, feeling how utterly irresponsible both sides were being.

The danger nowadays is that we've become complacent. We've forgotten how easy it is to edge towards disaster. Every day you might be getting closer and closer. But it won't be till later on you'll realise quite how close.

Fortunately, there are young people in the forefront of the peace movement who do realise the risk. They're saying to older people: look what you've done; look where you've landed us. Then they're tying the issue up with global warming and the whole ecological crisis. Take Extinction Rebellion. The nuclear threat is one of the concerns of its supporters. But is the issue resonating with young people to the extent it should? Well, maybe not. In which case, there is an even greater need for a vigorous peace movement.

Martin Amis in the introduction to his book of short stories, Einstein's Monsters, *has these sentences: 'As yet undetonated, the world's arsenals are already waging psychological warfare; ... . The airbursts, the preemptive strikes, the massive retaliations, the uncontrollable escalations; it is already happening in our heads.' It's an interesting and disturbing question: What are the psychological effects of nuclear weapons?*

I suppose the advocates of nuclear deterrence would read these remarks in a good way. They would say they prove that the weapons are working; that they're doing their job, which is to deter a nuclear attack and to stop us from rushing into war, which we might have done in earlier times, when the consequences of war would not have been quite so catastrophic. Maybe there's something in deterrence, after all. But it's still taking one hell of a risk and it is morally totally unacceptable. If you're prepared to use these weapons, then you're prepared to kill thousands, possibly millions, of innocent people.

Are you still a nuclear unilateralist?

Yes, in the sense that Britain, and all nuclear powers for that matter, should unconditionally renounce nuclear weapons and dispose of its stockpile. We should not be saying that we will retain nuclear weapons and be ready to use them unless and until other nuclear armed states are willing to renounce them. However, this unconditional renunciation needs to be accompanied by a renewed drive to ban nuclear weapons altogether. In that sense, I am also a multilateralist.

How good are the prospects for nuclear disarmament?

Not enough people are sufficiently afraid and, more importantly, sufficiently outraged. So, I don't think the immediate prospects are that good, certainly not with Trump as President. The prospects for a New Strategic Arms Reduction Treaty are not good either. In a few years it will expire. After that, who knows?

On the other hand, the growing support for a UN treaty to ban nuclear weapons is encouraging and another reason for the peace movement not to lose heart. The treaty would prohibit nations from developing, testing or threatening to use nuclear weapons or allowing nuclear weapons to be stationed on their territory. The treaty was negotiated at the UN headquarters in New York in March, June and July 2017. It will come into effect once fifty countries have ratified or acceded to it. At present, forty-four have done so.

It is true, of course, that the situation is more complicated than it was during the early 1960s. China and France have had the bomb for over fifty years. Pakistan, India, Israel and North Korea all have it. If we're going to get rid of it, we'll have to apply maximum pressure, both at the grass roots and at the government and inter-governmental level. We need people exploring what can be done jointly with others to move us towards total nuclear disarmament, to make our thinking saner, because it really is insane as well as totally immoral to contemplate wiping out hundreds of thousands or millions of people.

You said that people are insufficiently afraid and insufficiently outraged. Have we lost our sense of moral outrage where nuclear weapons are concerned?

No, I think it's still there, as the fact of Extinction Rebellion demonstrates. In fact, the moral dimension is key. Nuclear weapons are simply incompatible with any kind of decent human relationship.

That sort of language resonates with me. But I wonder if it resonates with other people. Which, in a rather roundabout way, brings us back to

Reginald Reynolds and 'The Map of Mrs. Brown' again. How do you go about convincing so-called ordinary people?

I really don't know for sure, But I feel militant non-violent action is in part at least the answer. The vast majority of people do have a moral conscience. And the task is to appeal to that rather than to scare the hell out of them.

As long ago as the 1950s, you were calling upon the UK to leave NATO. Is that still your position?

Yes, it is. But I don't see that as something that's likely to happen. We're a long way from that. Better to focus on nuclear and wider disarmament and to develop the understanding and practice of nonviolent action.

The UK has already voted to leave the EU. If we left NATO as well, wouldn't that lessen the UK's influence further?

That would depend on the alternative polices we came up with. We might have a stronger voice. Some years ago, someone had the very interesting idea of the EU offering a non-military alternative to NATO.

What makes you happy, Michael?

Making music. Exercise. Sport; I'm still active in the local rowing club. In general, I like doing things with other people. When Howard Clark was alive, he, Andrew Rigby and myself used to go on cycle rides up in the Yorkshire Dales. Anne and I still link up with Andrew and go walking, cycling and camping. Much of my writing has been collaborative. I haven't written many books on my own. I've always been happy to be part of a collective effort. I'm stimulated by the input of other people and the collective discussion that goes with that.

Fig 22:   Michael and Anne in their garden in Shipley, in October 2020.
Photograph by Gavin Randle. Private Collection.

Are you collaborating on anything at the moment?

I'm still one of the trustees of the Commonweal Collection of books and archives which, as you know, is housed in Bradford University. I value the meetings we have and the discussions of how to manage the collection and to broaden its outreach. I'm also working with Paul Rogers and others on updating and expanding the *Guide to Civil Resistance*, a bibliography of nonviolent action. April Carter is a key member of that group, someone I have worked with since the time of the first Aldermaston march and the Direct Action Committee in the 1950s. My contribution to the updated bibliography is small compared to April's. She's done a fantastic job. Not only having set the project up in the first place, but keeping it going.

Who are your heroes?

There are the obvious ones like Gandhi, Martin Luther King, Michael Scott and Bayard Rustin, who was a close friend. Then there are other people who are not well-known, but who persevered and who made an important contribution, people like Hugh Brock and Howard Clark. I admire and have been influenced by the writing of April Carter, Paul Rogers, Adam Roberts, and other colleagues on the Alternative Defence Commission, including Owen Greene and the late Joseph Rotblat. They're not, for the most part, in the public eye, but they've made an invaluable contribution and have certainly contributed to shaping my thinking.

April is an activist as well as an intellectual, and certainly more of a bona fide academic than I am. She has a huge range of interests and is very good at articulating different viewpoints. Even though I don't see much of her nowadays as she's down near Stevenage and we're up near Bradford, we remain close friends and continue to collaborate. I feel very fortunate to have worked with her and to be doing so still. Then there are other colleagues, such as Andrew Rigby and Carol Rank, both of whom were on the Nonviolent Action Research Project. But now I'm starting to worry about all the people that have influenced me, but whom I haven't mentioned!

I have a sense of a man who keeps his friendships in very good repair.

I try to. I have fallen out with people, but usually not for very long. The important thing is to keep going and to remain optimistic. Whether the issue is nuclear weapons or climate change, don't ever give up.

Chronology

1933: (21 Dec.) Birth of Michael Joseph Randle, second son of Arthur and Ellen Randle, near Worcester Park in Surrey.

1939: (3 Sep.) World War II begins.

1940: (Sep.) MR evacuated to his maternal grandparent's house in Dublin. (1940–1945) Educated at St. Dominic's College, Cabra, West Dublin.

1941: (31 May) German bombing of the North Strand district of Dublin.

1945: (8 May) VE Day. (16 Jul.) The United States explodes the first atomic bomb. (6 & 9 Aug.) Atomic bombs dropped on Hiroshima and Nagasaki. (15 Aug.) VJ Day marks the end of the Second World War. (1945–1950) MR attends Douai School, in Woolhampton, Berkshire.

1948: (30 Jan.) Gandhi assassinated. (26 Jun.– 30 Sep. 1949) Western allies airlift supplies to West Berlin, in response to Soviet blockade, aka the first Berlin Crisis. (10 Dec.) United Nations adopts Universal Declaration of Human Rights.

1949: (4 Apr.) NATO founded. (29 Aug.) The Russians explode their first atomic bomb. (23 Sep.) President Truman reveals the Russian bomb to the American public.

1950: (15 Mar.) The World Peace Council, in session in Stockholm, calls for a ban on nuclear weapons. (Jun.–Jul. 1953) The Korean War. (30 Nov.) President Truman announces that he is prepared to authorise the use of atomic bombs in Korea.

1951: (Dec.) MR registers as a conscientious objector.

1952: (11 Jan.) Operation Gandhi (OP) demonstrates outside the War Office, London. (7 Mar.) MR appears before the Fulham Appeal Tribunal and is released from national service. (Early Spring) MR joins OP. (19 Apr.) OP demonstrates at the Atomic Weapons Research Establishment at Aldermaston. (28 June) OP demonstrates at RAF Mildenhall. (3 Oct.) UK tests its first atomic bomb. (1 Nov.) The United States explodes the first hydrogen bomb.

1953: (c. Feb.) OP renamed the Non-Violent Resistance Group (NVRG). (5 Mar.) Stalin dies. (14 Mar.) NVRG demonstrates

at the Chemical Defence Experimental Establishment at
Porton Down. (18 Apr.) NVRG demonstrates at the Atomic
Energy Research Establishment at Harwell. (10 Jul.) MR
publishes open letter on 'The Use of Civil Disobedience in a
Democracy' in the NVRG newsletter. (Aug.–Nov.) MR
publishes 'Farmer's Log Book' articles in *Peace News*. (26
Sep.) NVRG holds second demonstration at Aldermaston.

1954: MR joins the Pacifist Youth Action Group (PYAG). (1 Mar.)
Fallout from US Castle Bravo test at Bikini Atoll prompts
protests around the world.

1955: (10 Mar.) Sir Richard Acland MP resigns his Gravesend seat
in an attempt to force a by-election on the issue of Britain's
possession of the H-Bomb. (18–24 Apr.) Bandung
Conference. (14 May) Warsaw Pact founded. (9 Jul.) Russell-
Einstein Manifesto issued, calling on governments to
renounce the use of nuclear weapons. (22 Nov.) The Russians
explode their first 'true' hydrogen bomb.

1956: (26 Jul.) Nasser nationalises the Suez Canal. (29 Oct.) Israel
invades the Egyptian Sinai. (23 Oct.) The Hungarian
Uprising begins. (Oct.) MR's article, 'Who are the realists?'
published in the magazine of the PYAG. (4 Nov.) Aneurin
Bevan speaks at an anti-war rally in Trafalgar Square. Soviet
forces invade Hungary. (Nov.) British and French troops
land in Egypt. (Dec.) MR walks from Vienna to the border
crossing at Nickelsdorf in support of non-violent responses
to the Soviet invasion.

1957: (Feb.) National Committee for the Abolition of Nuclear
Weapons Tests (NCANWT) formed. (c. early Apr.) First
meeting of the Emergency Committee for Direct Action
Against Nuclear War. (4 Apr.) Defence Minister Duncan
Sandys publishes white paper, committing the UK to nuclear
deterrence. (23 Apr.) Albert Schweitzer makes 'Declaration
of Conscience' speech, calling for the abolition of nuclear
weapons. (May) Harold Steele arrives in Japan en route for
Christmas Island to disrupt British nuclear tests. (Jun.) War
Resisters' International triennial conference takes place in
Roehampton, London. (Jul.) First Pugwash Conference:
'Appraisal of Dangers of Atomic Weapons' takes place in

Pugwash, Canada. (4 Oct.) Aneurin Bevan renounces nuclear unilateralism at the Labour Party Conference. The Soviet Union launches Sputnik, causing alarm in the West. (2 Nov.) J.B. Priestley publishes 'Britain and the Nuclear Bombs' article in *New Statesman*. (23 Nov.) First meeting of the Group or Committee for Direct Action Against Nuclear War, henceforth known as The Direct Action Committee Against Nuclear War (DAC).

1958: (10 Feb.) The *Golden Rule,* captained by Arthur Bigelow, begins voyage into US Eniwetok Atoll nuclear test area. (17 Feb.) The Campaign for Nuclear Disarmament (CND) launched at Central Hall, Westminster. (c. end of Feb.) DAC adopts the 'disarmament' or 'peace symbol' for the first Aldermaston march. (Mar.) Stephen King-Hall's *Defence in the Nuclear Age* published. (4–7 Apr.) First Aldermaston march, from Trafalgar Square to Aldermaston. (16 Apr.) MR appointed vice-chair of DAC. (21 Jul.) DAC begins nine-week vigil at Aldermaston. (c. Aug.) MR takes over from Hugh Brock as chairman of the DAC. (8 Aug.) Reginald Reynolds' 'The Map of Mrs Brown' published in *Peace News*. (Nov.) Second Berlin Crisis begins. (6–7 Dec.) DAC demonstrates at RAF North Pickenham rocket base (20 Dec.) MR arrested during second December protest at RAF North Pickenham and spends Christmas in Norwich Prison. (29 Dec.) MR sentenced to two weeks in Brixton Prison.

1959: (Jan.) MR leaves job at *Peace News* and begins full-time work for the DAC. (Jan.–Mar.) DAC campaigns for a 'Voters' Veto' in the South West Norfolk by-election. (late Mar.) Second Aldermaston march. (Apr.) DAC launches 'industrial campaign' aimed at workers producing nuclear weapons. (Jun.) DAC decides to oppose French nuclear tests in the Sahara. (Jul.) *Peace News* moves from Blackstock Road to Caledonian Road. (22 Aug.) DAC demonstrates at RAF Polebrook and RAF Harrington. (Oct.–Jan. 1960) MR takes part in protests against French nuclear tests in the Sahara.

1960: (2 Jan.) DAC demonstrates at RAF Harrington. (13 Feb.) The French explode an atomic bomb in the Algerian Sahara. (Apr.) MR helps organise the Positive Action Conference for Peace and Security, in Accra. Third Aldermaston march. UK cancels independent nuclear deterrent. (1 May) US U-2 spy plane shot down in Soviet air space. (17 May) Paris summit between USA and the Soviet Union convenes and collapses, following U-2 spy plane incident. (1 Jul.) US RB47 spy plane shot down over international waters. (Oct.) MR returns to England from Ghana and becomes secretary of the Committee of 100 (C100). Labour Party annual conference votes for nuclear unilateralism. (21 Oct.) Bertrand Russell resigns as president of CND. (22 Oct.) Inaugural meeting of the C100 in Friends Meeting House, Euston Road. Russell publishes *Act or Perish*. (Nov.) UK announces US Polaris submarines to be based at Holy Loch. (Dec.–Oct.1961) San Francisco to Moscow march, part-sponsored by the DAC.

1961:   (18 Feb.) C100 demonstrates outside the Ministry of Defence. (3 Mar.) USS *Proteus* arrives at Holy Loch. (10 Mar.) MR's 'Is it revolution we're after?' article in *Peace News*. (Mar.-Apr.) Fourth Aldermaston march; Ralph Schoenman leads break-off group from Trafalgar Square to the US embassy. (Apr.–May) DAC march from London to Holy Loch. (Apr.–Dec.) Adolf Eichmann trial in Jerusalem. (29 Apr.) C100 demonstrates in Westminster. (3 May) George Blake trial at the Old Bailey. (21 May) DAC demonstrators try to board USS *Proteus* at Holy Loch. (4 Jun.–9 Nov.) Third Berlin Crisis, including closure of border between East Germany and West Berlin. (6 Aug.) C100 holds silent vigil at the Cenotaph. MR begins relationship with future wife, Anne Parr. (31 Aug.) C100 demonstrates outside Russian Embassy, following Russian announcement that nuclear tests will be resumed. (6 Sept.) US announces resumption of nuclear tests. (12 Sept.) MR, Ralph Schoenman, George Clark, Bertrand Russell and many other C100 members imprisoned for refusing to keep the peace. (16–17 Sept.) C100 demonstrates at Holy Loch, then at Trafalgar Square. (early Oct.) Labour Party conference overturns commitment to nuclear unilateralism. (30 Oct.) Russians detonate 'Tsar Bomba' over Novaya Zemblya, leading to sit-downs outside the Russian embassy in London and elsewhere. (6 Dec.) Police search C100's offices plus home of MR and others. (8 Dec.) MR et al charged under the Official Secrets Act. (9 Dec.) C100 demonstrates at 3 NATO air bases, including

Wethersfield, and four UK cities. (Late Dec.) MR resigns as secretary of the C100. (28 Dec.–1 Jan.1962) MR attends World Peace Brigade conference, in Beirut.

1962: (Early Jan.) MR rejoins staff at *Peace News*. (9 Feb.) MR marries Anne Parr, in Luton. (12–20 Feb.) 'Official Secrets' trial of MR and five others at the Old Bailey. MR sentenced to 18 months imprisonment. (Spring) MR, in Wormwood Scrubs Prison, begins friendship with George Blake. (2. Apr.) MR and co's first appeal against imprisonment dismissed (Early Jun.) MR and co's second appeal dismissed. (19 Aug.) MR's first son, Seán, born. (16–28 Oct.) Cuban Missile Crisis. (16 Nov.) 'H-Bomb War: What it would be like' aka 'The Black Paper', published by *Peace News*.

1963: (21 Jan.) Suicide of Helen Allegranza, following her release from Holloway Prison. (Early Feb.) *Beyond Counting Arses* published. (11 Feb.) MR released from Wormwood Scrubbs. (14 Mar.) MR holds press conference re John Vassall and the imprisonment of journalist Brendan Mulholland. (Apr) Sixth Aldermaston march. Break off group marches to Regional Seat of Government 6. (27 May): Death of Greek politician Grigoris Lambrakis, following an attack five days earlier. (Summer) Non-Governmental Aid to Algeria Conference. (9–12 Jul.) State visit of the Greek royals. (Jul.) MR is elected a member of the international council of the War Resisters' International (WRI). (5 Aug.) Limited Test Ban Treaty signed by the US, the Soviet Union and Great Britain. (Oct.–June 1966) MR studies for a BA in English at University College, London.

1964: (12 Jan.) MR's second son, Gavin, born. (May) Hugh Brock retires as editor of *Peace News* and is briefly replaced by J. Allen Skinner. (Aug) Theodore Roszak starts work as editor of *Peace News*. (late Sep.) Martin Luther King visits the UK. (Oct.) 'Multi-Racial Britain' formed. (25 Nov.) Special issue of *Peace News* on race. (5–7 Dec.) Martin Luther King stops in the UK en route to Stockholm to receive the Nobel Peace Prize. (Dec.) Campaign against Racial Discrimination (CARD) formed.

1965: (Feb.) First public meeting of CARD at Friends House, London (24–25 Jul.) First CARD convention held. (late Jul.) MR attends annual council meeting of the WRI near Dublin.

1966: (Apr.–1972) MR chairman of the WRI. (May) MR elected onto the board of *Peace News*. Seán Bourke, shortly to be released from prison, makes contact with MR at Torriano Cottages, Kentish Town, re George Blake escape. (Autumn) MR temps at Dictaphone Ltd, West London. (Aug.) MR and co leaflet Wethersfield airbase. (Aug.–Oct.) MR, Anne Randle and Pat Pottle help Bourke with planning Blake's escape (Sep.–Apr. 1967) MR teaches English to foreign students at Princeton College, Holborn. (2 Oct.) Vietnam Action Group protestors disrupt church service addressed by Lord George Brown in Brighton. (22 Oct.) Sean Bourke 'springs' George Blake from Wormwood Scrubs. (early Nov.) George Blake in hiding at Pat Pottle's flat in Hampstead. (17–19 Dec.) MR and Anne Randle smuggle Blake to East Germany. (31 Dec.) Seán Bourke leaves the UK for exile in Moscow.

1967: (Jan.) MR and other members of Volunteers for Peace in Vietnam organise 'Hanoi Trip' of A.J. Muste and Martin Niemöller et al. (21 Apr.) Greek colonels' coup. (28 Apr.) MR and fellow members of the C100 'invade' the Greek Embassy in London. (5–10 Jun.) Six-Day War. (6–9 Jul.) MR attends Stockholm Conference on Vietnam. (4 Oct.) MR sentenced to 12 months for 'invasion' of the Greek embassy.

1968: (5 Jan.–21 Aug.) 'Prague Spring'. (30 Jan.–23 Sep.) Tet offensive. (4 Apr.) Martin Luther King assassinated. (2 May–June) Student uprising in Paris. (31 May) MR released from Lewes Prison. (17 Aug.) MR attends council meeting of the WRI in Vienna. (20 Aug.) Soviet and Warsaw Pact troops invade Czechoslovakia. (20 Aug.–Sep.) MR joint-coordinator of 'Support Czechoslovakia' protests for the WRI. (24 Sep) 'Support Czechoslovakia' protests take place in Moscow, Budapest, Sofia and Warsaw. (22 Oct.) Seán Bourke arrives in Ireland from Russia. (Nov) *Support Czechoslovakia* published, containing contributions from MR and April Carter et al.

1969: (Jul.) US begins first troop withdrawals from Vietnam. (Oct.–1974) MR lecturer in complementary studies at Bradford Regional College of Art.

1970: (5 Mar.) The Nuclear Non-Proliferation Treaty (NPT) enters into force. (Jun.) *The Springing of George Blake* by Seán Bourke published, giving strong clues to MR's and Pat Pottle's identities.

1971: MR smuggles political journals and pamphlets into Czechoslovakia.

1973: (Spring) Adam Curle appointed first Professor of Peace Studies at the University of Bradford. (6–25 Oct.) Arab-Israeli War.

1974: (Summer–1975) MR's works as research assistant in the Department of Peace Studies, University of Bradford. (Oct.) First students arrive at the Department of Peace Studies, University of Bradford.

1975: (Feb.) MR *Towards Liberation* published. (30 Apr.) Fall of Saigon concludes Vietnam War. (Jul.) United States and Soviet Union sign the Threshold Test Ban Treaty (TTBT), placing limits on underground nuclear tests. (1 Aug.) Helsinki Accords signed, leading to greater cooperation between East and West.

1976: (Jul–Dec.) MR works in Paris for UNESCO.

1977: (Oct–) MR part-time lecturer in the Department of Peace Studies, University of Bradford.

1978: (Jan.) MR's *Bibliography on Training for Non-Violent Action* published. (Sep.) James O'Connell succeeds Adam Curle as Professor of Peace Studies at the University of Bradford.

1979: (1 Apr.) Islamic Republic of Iran founded. (4 May) Margaret Thatcher becomes UK Prime Minister. (4 Nov.) Beginning of Iranian hostage crisis. (Dec.) NATO announces deployment of cruise and Pershing missiles in Western Europe in response to Soviet SS-20s. (late Dec.) Soviet forces invade Afghanistan.

1980: (Apr.) European Nuclear Disarmament (END) founded. (17 Sep.) Solidarity formed in Poland. (4 Oct.) First meeting of the Bradford-based Alternative Defence Commission (1980–1987) coordinated by MR. (10 Nov.) Michael Foot elected leader of the Labour Party.

1981: (Jan.) MR's *Militarism and Repression* published. (21. Jan.) Ronald Reagan sworn in as US president. (27 Aug.–5 Sep.) Protestors march from Cardiff to RAF Greenham Common. (24 Oct.) CND marches through London to Hyde Park. (Dec.–Jul. 1983) Martial law in Poland.

1982: (26 Jan.) Seán Bourke dies in Ireland. (2 Apr.–14 Jun.) Falklands War. (23 May) 'Stop the Falklands War' rally in Trafalgar Square. (29 Sept.) Labour Party conference votes to scrap Polaris missile system and to remove US nuclear bases from the UK. (12–13 Dec.) 'Embrace the Base' demonstration at RAF Greenham Common.

1983: (23 Mar.) Ronald Reagan makes his 'Star Wars' speech. (Apr.) *Defence without the Bomb: The Report of the Alternative Defence Commission* published. (2 Oct.) Neil Kinnock becomes leader of the Labour Party. (22 Oct.) CND marches through London to Hyde Park. (Nov.) First cruise missiles arrive at RAF Greenham Common.

1984: (Oct.) Labour Party conference adopts non-nuclear *Defence and Security for Britain* document.

1986: (Feb): 'People Power Revolution' leads to the restoration of democracy in the Philippines.

1987: (Spring) *The Politics of Alternative Defence* by the Alternative Defence Commission published. (28 Sep.) *George Blake, Superspy* by H. Montgomery Hyde published in Ireland. (4 Oct.) *The Sunday Times* names MR, Anne Randle and Pat Pottle as co-conspirators in the Blake escape. (c.7 Oct.) *George Blake, Superspy* published in England. (9 Oct.) MR and Pat Pottle review Hyde's book in *The Guardian* (30 Oct.) MR and Pat Pottle interviewed by police about the Blake escape. (early Nov.) Vanessa Redgrave publicly denies funding the Blake escape. (8 Dec.) US and Soviet Union sign the Intermediate-Range Nuclear Forces Treaty.

1988: (Feb.) MR and Pat Pottle begin work on *The Blake Escape*. (Spring) First meeting of the Bradford-based Social Defence Project (–1994), coordinated by MR. (13. Nov.) MR and Pat Pottle publicly admit their role in the Blake escape in an *Observer* article. (Dec.) Tory MPs call for MR's and Pat Pottle's prosecution. MR resigns from his position at the University of Bradford. Mikhail Gorbachev announces non-intervention policy for Eastern Europe.

1989: (14 Jan.) Salman Rushdie's *The Satanic Verses* publicly burned in Bradford. (14 Feb.) Ayatollah Khomeini issues fatwa calling for death of Rushdie. (Apr.) *The Blake Escape* published. (3 May) MR and Pat Pottle arrested by police and released on bail. (Jun.) Tiananmen Square massacre. (10 Jul.) MR and Pat Pottle charged with aiding Blake's escape plus two other charges. (9 Nov.) Demonstrators begin demolition of the Berlin Wall. (27 Nov–29 Dec.) 'Velvet Revolution' in Czechoslovakia.

1990: (Feb.) MR and Pat Pottle travel to Moscow to video statement by George Blake. Nelson Mandela released. (25 Apr.) Pre-trial hearing opens at the Old Bailey. (11 Jul.) Judicial review opens at the High Court. 'Big fish little fish' minute released, confirming that Special Branch knew about MR's and Pat Pottle's involvement in the Blake escape in 1970. (2 Aug.) Iraq invades Kuwait, leading to first Gulf War. (Oct.) Germany reunified. (15 Nov.) High Court rules that MR and Pat Pottle must face trial.

1991: (Jun.) MR's *People Power* published. (26 Jun.) Slovenia secedes from the Yugoslav federation, leading to ten years of war. (17–26 Jun.) 'Blake escape' trial of MR and Pat Pottle at the Old Bailey.

1992: (Summer–2009) MR active on the Coordinating Committee for Conflict Resolution Training in Europe (CCCRTE), later the Committee for Conflict Transformation Support (CCTS).

1994: (Mar.) First meeting of the Bradford-based Nonviolent Action Research Project (–1999), coordinated by MR. (Apr.) MR's *Civil Resistance* published. (7 Apr.–15 Jul) Rwandan genocide.

1995: (Jul.) Srebrenica massacre of over 800 Bosniaks. (Sep.) MR's *How to Defend Yourself in Court* published.

1999: (Apr.) NATO expanded to include Poland, Hungary and the Czech Republic.

2001: (11 Sep.) Islamic terrorists attack the World Trade Center and the Pentagon. (7 Oct.) US invades Afghanistan.

2002: *Challenge to Nonviolence*, edited by MR, published.

2003: (20 Mar.) US invades Iraq, leading to second Gulf War.

2004: (Mar.) NATO expands further to include Bulgaria, Estonia, Romania, Latvia, Lithuania, Slovakia and Slovenia.

2006: (Spring) *People, Power and Protest since 1945: A Bibliography of Nonviolent Action by April Carter*, MR and Howard Clark published.

2008: (Summer) US withdraws its nuclear weapons from the UK.

2010: (8 Apr.) US and Russian Federation sign new START treaty, limiting deployed nuclear warheads. (Dec.) Beginning of Arab Spring.

2013: (Dec.) Volume 1 of *A Guide to Civil Resistance* by April Carter, MR and Howard Clark published.

2015: (Aug.) Volume 2 of *A Guide to Civil Resistance* by April Carter, MR and Howard Clark published.

Acknowledgements

First thanks to Michael and Anne, without whose cooperation this book would not exist. Not only were they patient with my questions, but their humour and hospitality ensured that my visits to their house in Shipley were a pleasure. I dedicate this book to them and to all believers in the non-violent path to human and non-human felicity.

Second thanks to Alison Cullingford, my former colleague in Special Collections at Bradford University. It was thanks to Alison that my idea of interviewing Michael *in extenso* got off the ground in the first place.

Third thanks to Paul Rogers for his kind interest in the book and for his illuminating foreword.

Finally, fourth thanks to Julie Parry, the present Special Collections archivist at Bradford, and to the trustees of the Commonweal Collection for permission to reproduce certain images.

Further Reading

Readers who want to know more about Michael's life and ideas are directed to the following books.

Chester, Gail and Rigby, Andrew, *Articles of Peace: Celebrating Fifty Years of Peace News* (Bridport: Prism Press, 1986). Includes a contribution from Michael.

De Ligt, Bart, *The Conquest of Violence: An Essay on War and Revolution* (London: Pluto Press, 1989). An edition of the anarcho-syndicalist classic, with introductions by Aldous Huxley and Peter van den Dungen.

Driver, Christopher, *The Disarmers: A Study in Protest* (London: Hodder & Stoughton, 1964). A journalist's account of the anti-nuclear movement, almost contemporary with the events it describes.

Grant, Thomas, *Jeremy Hutchinson's Case Histories* (London: John Murray, 2015). Grant's book contains a chapter on *Regina v Chandler and Others*, which is to say, Michael and his co-defendants' trial at the Old Bailey for the Wethersfield demonstration.

Grant, Thomas. *Court Number One: The Old Bailey Trials that defined Modern Britain* (London: John Murray, 2019). Includes an account of Michael and Pat Pottle's Old Bailey trial for their part in the 'springing' of George Blake and in the events that followed it.

Gregg, Richard B., *The Power of Non-Violence* (London: Routledge, 1935). The classic 1930s account of Gandhi's method of satyagraha.

Hermiston, Roger, *The Greatest Traitor: The Secret Lives of Agent George Blake* (London: Aurum Press, 2013). The standard Blake biography.

Randle, Michael, *Civil Resistance* (London: Fontana, 1994). An account of people power and alternative defence. Accessible to the non-specialist.

Randle, Michael and Pottle, Pat, *The Blake Escape: How we freed George Blake and why* (London: Harrap, 1989). Michael and Pat Pottle's very readable account of their dealings with George Blake.

Scalmer, Sean, *Gandhi in the West: The Mahatma and the Rise of Radical Protest* (Cambridge University Press, 2011). Academic, but wry and enjoyable.

Taylor, Richard, *Against the Bomb: The British Peace Movement 1958-1965* (Oxford University Press, 1988). A thorough account of CND, the Direct Action Committee and the Committee of 100. Like *Gandhi in the West*, Taylor's book is based in large part on archives in the Special Collections department at Bradford University.

Index